# MAMMOTH HUNT

Other books by the same author:

# MAMMOTH HUNT

## IN SEARCH OF THE GIANT ELEPHANTS OF NEPAL

John Blashford-Snell
and Rula Lenska

HarperCollins*Publishers*

HarperCollins*Publishers*
77–85 Fulham Palace Road,
Hammersmith, London W6 8JB

Published by HarperCollins*Publishers* 1996
1 3 5 7 9 8 6 4 2

A catalogue record for this book
is available from the British Library

ISBN 0 00 255672 3

Set in Meridien by
Rowland Phototypesetting Ltd,
Bury St Edmunds, Suffolk

Printed and bound by
Caledonian International Book Manufacturing Ltd, Glasgow

*Dedicated to Dieter Plage of Survival Anglia,*
*whose outstanding films did so much to*
*promote the preservation of wildlife*

# CONTENTS

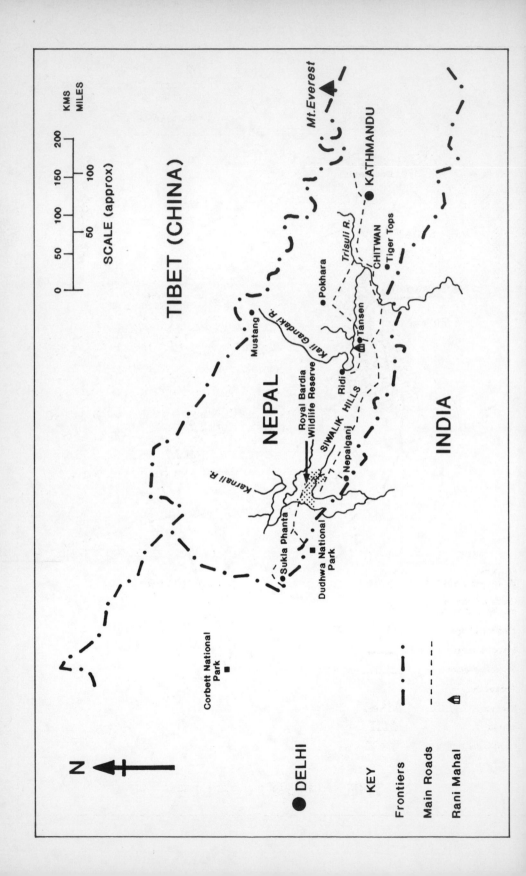

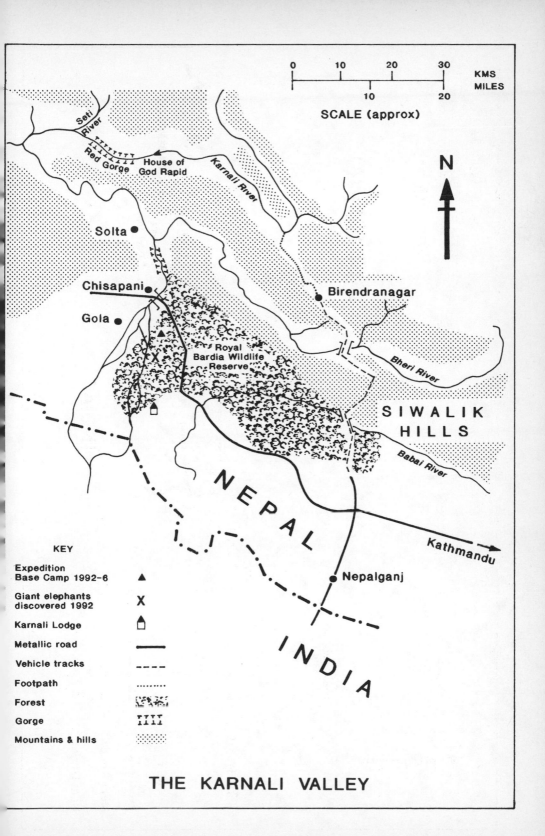

THE KARNALI VALLEY

# ACKNOWLEDGEMENTS

This is a story of exploration and discovery by a large number of dedicated people, many of whom had no expert knowledge and came together over a period of five years to investigate a mysterious creature. Although we cannot offer answers to all the questions raised, we earnestly hope that the effort put into this extraordinary venture will help to publicize the plight of wildlife in general and the Asian elephants in particular.

We are deeply grateful to all the kind and generous friends who have assisted the expeditions and helped with the preparation of this book. Without the support of Jim and John Edwards, all at Tiger Mountain, the staff of Tiger Tops Karnali Lodge, and Sara Bampfylde's chance sighting, it would never have started. The kind help of Belinda Edwards, Lisa and Tensen Choegyal, Steve Webster, Pradeep Rana and K. P. Sharma has also been most welcome. Billy Arjan Singh's wise counsel and the advice of K. K. Gurung and Chuck McDougal has been invaluable.

The success of the river journeys is largely due to Mahesh Thapa, Megh Ale Magar and Tej Rana who guided us expertly through some of the most exciting waters on earth.

Peter Knowles and Dave Allardice kindly helped with vital information on the Karnali and Kali Gandaki. Their handbook *White Water Nepal* is essential reading for anyone rafting Nepal's beautiful rivers.

In a book of this nature it has not been possible to give as much coverage as is due to the scientific studies undertaken by Dr Adrian Lister, Dr Chris Thouless, Dr Ken Reed and Mark O'Shea, but in the end it is their work that will be all important in the conservation of these massive mammals.

Our thanks are also due to Peter Byrne, who strives to protect the wildlife of Sukla Phanta, for his expert advice. In Nepal the outstanding assistance of the Department of National Parks and Wildlife Conservation has made it all possible and we are especially grateful to Mr J. B. Karki, warden at Bardia.

Almost everyone who has taken part in the project has sent in diaries and stories and thus enriched the text.

Many companies and individuals have provided equipment and we much appreciate the support of Avon Inflatables, Bausch and Lomb for binoculars supplied by J. J. Vickers & Sons Ltd, Barts Spices, Berghaus, Berkshire Hosiery, Canon cameras, Cobles, Dr Mark Thomas and Erika Hagelberg of Cambridge University for DNA testing, HarperCollins Publishers, Justerini and Brooks Ltd for helping to raise morale, Henri Lloyd for waterproof clothing, Loctite for their essential Superglue, Mariner for the loan of their robust and reliable outboards, Nikon (UK), Panasonic for video cameras and recording equipment, Philips

Dictation Systems for enabling us to write this book, Pilkington Optronics for lending us image intensifiers, Neil Rimington for allowing us to exercise candidates in his woods at Fonthill, Parker pens, Polaroid and Ranger Inc in the USA for the range finder we used in charting the rivers, the Royal Engineers for the use of the Hawley Lake training area, Reebok for shoes supplied to the anti-poaching units, Seven Seas Health Care for keeping us fit, the Sheraton Park Tower Hotel in Knightsbridge for their kind hospitality, Silva (UK) Ltd for their compasses, Stahly Foods for their delicious tinned haggis, Swaine Adeney Brigg for supporting the scientific programme, and Swiss Cutlery for their invaluable penknives that proved so useful in getting bamboo splinters out of our elephants' feet. The fishing tackle donated by Farlow's and Shakespeare provided many a good meal and Wilkinson Sword helped us to keep up appearances in the field with their shaving gear. Drugs and medical equipment for the various expeditions were supplied by Boots the Chemist, the Lister Hospital in Chelsea and several pharmaceutical suppliers in Burgess Hill, West Sussex.

The media have given us great support, especially the *Mail on Sunday*, the *Sunday Mirror*, the *Daily Telegraph*, *The Times*, the *Evening Standard*, *Hello* magazine and the BBC Natural History programme. We are also indebted to ABC TV and CNN. Through BBC Radio, Charlie Chester has been a champion at collecting equipment for the anti-poaching units.

In Great Britain we have enjoyed the support of Lord Hanson, Lord Glenarthur, Sir Tom Lethbridge and numerous members of the Scientific Exploration Society. We are also most grateful to Susan Hope of *You* magazine for her kind assistance.

Richard Snailham, Judith Blashford-Snell, Victoria Matthews, Sally Amanda Ale Magar and Carol Turner have given invaluable help, whilst Louise Woollard has struggled single-handedly to convert mounds of scribbled notes and miles of recorded tape into manuscript on the PC, kindly donated by Marks and Spencer.

We also appreciate the enthusiastic encouragement of Eddie Bell and Michael Fishwick at HarperCollins and everyone at Midas PR, as well as the photographic assistance of Nick Brown, Geoff Garratt and Jack Picone. Thank you to Nick and Jack, and to Sandy Crivello, Mark O'Shea and the *Sunday Mirror* for very kindly donating their photographs to the book.

Although the enterprise started under Operation Raleigh, it was carried on by Discovery Expeditions whose tireless Managing Director, Julian Matthews, has borne the brunt of the administration.

Like all great ventures, this was and is a team effort and there are many others who are not named here or in the text who have helped. We are deeply grateful to them all.

JOHN BLASHFORD-SNELL AND RULA LENSKA
March 1996

# FOREWORD

It seems that there is now almost nothing left in this overcrowded and over-exploited world to explore or discover; I read that literally hundreds of people have climbed Mount Everest! Is nothing left to the imagination?

I would love to think that the Yeti does exist, or that I might, when driving around Loch Ness, be confronted by a monster crossing the road. Having shared the thrill of riding out into the wilds of the Indian forest on elephant (a wonderful experience; elephants are silent and, unlike vehicles, they don't smell of diesel fumes), I can vividly imagine the nerve-tingling excitement that Blashers and his friends felt when, in the thickest of the jungle, they were suddenly confronted with Raja Gaj. Could this monster elephant, with its great domed head the likes of which even the local people had never seen before, possibly be a throwback to the mammoths of prehistoric times?

My wife Avril and I have known John, or, as many of his friends prefer to call him, 'Blashers', for a number of years. He is the only man I know who sends my wife and I postcards from Outer Mongolia by 'runner' (what a wonderfully old-fashioned word!) or by riding a yak to the nearest post office many, many miles away, for the card to eventually reach us safely here in leafy Surrey.

We have many common interests as conservationists and lovers of the wilderness, not least our passionate love of elephants, and so I was honoured to be invited to write the foreword to this book which he and Rula have written of their attempt to unravel the mystery of Raja Gaj and the beasts of Bardia. Surely none is more qualified to write about these experiences in such an exciting way.

Should we not leave certain things to the imagination? Do we have to have the answer to every surprise that Mother Nature is still capable of springing upon us? If it adds to our knowledge and therefore to our ability to conserve what is left of this beautiful planet and the creatures that share it, then the answer must be 'yes'. For, above all else, this book will be of enormous value to the cause of the Asian elephant. So much publicity and attention has rightly been given to their African cousins over the years, the elephants of India have almost been forgotten and they are, like so many other species, on the very brink of extinction.

The book is also about many personal friends of mine, such as Billy Arjan Singh. He is one of those all-too-rare dedicated conservationists who are fighting to save the few remaining tigers left in the world. Billy invited me to stay with him at Tiger Haven, a remote little paradise on the edge of the Indian plains almost in Nepal. It was here that Billy showed me my first wild tiger and it is in this, one of the last remaining wilderness areas in an overcrowded country, where the tiger has possibly the last chance to survive in the wild.

Whether or not the elephants of Bardia are genetically connected to fossils found in the area – throwbacks to prehistoric times – they are the subject of a cracking good yarn which is not only an exciting tale of adventure but will bring to the reader the desperate plight of so many species which share this planet with man, the most greedy and dangerous animal on earth.

DAVID SHEPHERD, OBE FRSA FRGS

# PROLOGUE

The ice-cold lager swilled down the last of the *chara ko masu* as a smiling Nepalese girl deftly cleared the plates. It was September 1987 and we were the only diners remaining in the Sun Kosi Restaurant but, being about to start a very long trek into Tibet, I savoured the precious moments of relaxation. The ceiling fan hummed gently as John Edwards refilled my glass. From the busy street came the sound of motor horns and the bustle of people, but here one might have been in a peaceful oasis. I stretched out my legs as coffee arrived and John lit a cigarette.

'I have a little mystery that is right up your street,' he said with a sly smile. My eyebrows raised in interest. 'There are reports of a strange mammoth-like beast living in a remote stretch of forest alongside the Karnali River,' went on my old pal. 'I'm not kidding.'

The air, still warm and humid from the monsoon, brought a bead of sweat to my forehead. 'He's pulling my leg,' I thought, and retorted, 'Rubbish, mammoths are extinct.'

'Of course, but something big is frightening the pants off the locals and messing up their crops.'

I grinned as he recounted some pretty tall tales about a massive creature that was only seen at night when it emerged from the dense forest to feed on village gardens, trample irrigation ditches and smash down the heavy mud walls of houses as if they were delicate pottery.

'Get a few facts and we might look for your giant one day,' I laughed as we strolled into the glare of the afternoon sunlight. 'God willing, I'll see you in a couple of months' time if I don't freeze on this ruddy mountain.' So saying I set out for Mount Xixabangma in Tibet.

\*      \*      \*

Although at this time I had dismissed John Edwards' story, I could not get it out of my mind and in fact it led to a quest that has occupied much of my life since. I love animals and have always been intrigued by mysteries and the suggestion, however unlikely, that there might be a living mammoth or at least a recognizable relative of these colossal creatures stomping around in a little-known Nepalese valley, had whetted my appetite for an investigation.

To search the vast area for the beast would need expert trackers and, to guide our teams, I chose skilled, sharp-eyed Nepalese as boatmen, elephant handlers, and naturalists. The teams themselves were to be composed of professional men and women, drawn from all four corners of the globe and all walks of life, and ranging in age from twenty-five to eighty-two. They were rather older than the youngsters I had been taking on expeditions hitherto, but all shared a desire to tackle something adventurous and different, most were conservationists and many were passionately fond of elephants. None more so than the remarkable actress I met in 1987 in Perth, Western Australia. The Operation Raleigh flagship *Sir Walter Raleigh* was in port for a stopover during her circumnavigation, which happily coincided with the Americas Cup races. Rula Lenska and Dennis Waterman were appearing in a play at a local theatre and kindly invited our crew to the show. Afterwards they joined us at a party on board our ship, where Rula talked to me with enormous sincerity and concern about the plight of the world's wildlife and especially the elephant. Her work for endangered animals was already well known and thereafter she did much to encourage the Scientific Exploration Society to tackle worthwhile conservation tasks. It was almost inevitable that she should become a key player in this extraordinary quest that has attracted so much interest.

To operate in this far-flung corner of Nepal has meant using inflatable boats, porters, domestic elephants and vehicles, making it a costly venture. Those who take part can only spend a certain time away from businesses or families so we have had to mount a series of short expeditions. Most of us would admit that the occasional close call and the thrill of working amongst large and dangerous wild animals, with nothing more lethal than a Swiss Army penknife for defence, has been an added attraction.

Each year we have added to man's knowledge of these mysterious creatures and discovered new clues to their origin. The story is not yet over and indeed it has become an ongoing project which hopefully will continue to focus attention on the need to protect one of the most magical areas on earth and the beasts that live there.

## Chapter One

# THE BEAST OF BARDIA

DAWN was breaking as we drove out of Kathmandu. In the sprawling outskirts, bundles of rags huddled around dying fires, dogs barked, cocks crowed and the mist hung on the terraced fields. Jim Edwards of Tiger Tops fame had loaned us his Range Rover. It was to be our last taste of comfort, for beyond the hill village of Lamosangu the road had disappeared. Where it had been was now a jumble of broken rock, boulders and grey mud leading directly down into the swirling water of the Sun Kosi river. The monsoon always caused landslides, but in 1987 the rain had been torrential and for the last twenty miles to the Chinese border the road was blocked or totally destroyed.

The policeman who waved us down was polite. 'Namaste. Where are you going, sir?'

'Namaste,' I replied, 'Tibet, if I can.'

He made a little sucking noise and shook his head. 'Then you'll have to walk, but the rain has stopped and you should reach Tatopani tonight,' he grinned.

We unloaded our rucksacks and, with a wave to Jim's cheerful driver, started up the narrow path that a thousand human feet had already worn in the soft soil.

The air was clear and through gaps in the hills we glimpsed the mighty Himalayan peaks rising jagged over the glimmering perpetual snow. The higher we climbed the more we saw of the glistening white slopes of Dorje Lakpa towering above us on the frontier, and soon I was fumbling for my dark glasses. These mountains are totally awe-inspiring. It is a treat to watch them in the late afternoon when the sun dips and the summits turn strawberry pink as the shadows slide across the snow fields.

There is real magic here, for it is not only a place of frightening beauty, but also a land of mystery and myth. Indeed, the particular mountain for which we were heading was Xixabangma, 'The Abode of God', which rises to over 26,000 feet on the very edge of the Roof of the World – Tibet.

Our trek across the treacherous landslides led us puffing and panting upwards over a region once regarded as an impassable obstacle that separated the rich trading centres on the Silk Road to the North from the sun-baked plains of India.

Names like Kashgar, Lhasa and Dunhuang had beckoned the invaders and merchants from the South just as the peaks challenge the mountaineers of today.

'I've read somewhere that the Nepalese brought elephants up here to invade Tibet,' smiled climber Julian Freeman-Attwood, trying to cheer me up as I struggled for breath in the thin atmosphere.

'They must have been bloody big, strong elephants,' muttered another colleague and, to keep my mind off every painful step, I began to think about elephants.

My first encounter with these great beasts had almost been my last when, in spite of a warning to stay in the Land Rover, I'd foolishly tried to approach a large and apparently docile tusker browsing quietly in Kenya's Masai Mara. I was about forty paces from his backside with my camera raised when he spun round, his ears came forward and with a raucous trumpet he headed straight for me at a frightening speed. The vehicle was moving as I hurled myself in through the open door. Lesson one: elephants can move surprisingly quickly when they want to.

At another encounter I was even luckier. Exploring the Zaire River in 1974, I heard that a Pygmy tribe in the Ituri Forest had captured some okapi. This creature was only discovered at the beginning of this century. Found solely in the dense tropical forests of eastern Zaire, this member of the giraffe family is striped like a zebra on its buttocks and legs but has a body shape resembling a giraffe with a short neck.

Driving 350 miles towards the Mountains of the Moon, we met Pygmy hunters who, sadly, had captured two fine bulls which they hoped to sell to a zoo. They were too precious to kill, explained the hunters, although in the old days an okapi skin was treasured. It was supposed to ensure an endless supply of beautiful and co-operative women to anyone who sat thereon!

Hoping to film these rare and gentle creatures in the wild, we marched deep into the twilight forest with our tiny guides. We were closing with an okapi that was moving ahead of us along a game-trail when there was a sudden commotion ahead. Then the leading Pygmy raced back down the track, going like a rocket. Immediately I saw the reason, for close behind him came four very angry elephants. Squealing and trumpeting they rushed at us, scattering the vegetation. We dived for cover behind trees as they crashed past, their trunks swinging like cudgels. When they had gone our somewhat shaken group emerged and compared notes. The jumbos had seemed rather small. Later we realized that these were the dangerous and much feared forest variety of elephant that the Pygmies have hunted with poison-tipped spears for 3,000 years. It was small wonder that they attacked humans on sight. Lesson two: elephants are masters of concealment.

In the early 1980s I had an amazing experience in Kenya. Mount Elgon, an extinct volcano on the Kenyan–Ugandan border, is known to be the home of wild elephants. This was discovered earlier in the century when a farmer by the name of Renshaw Mitford-Barbeton had been exploring and found himself in a cave called Kitium under Mount Elgon. It was an eerie place and he made his way through the low entrance cautiously, stumbling over fallen rocks and aware of avoiding narrow crevasses and hidden pools of dripping water. About to retrace his steps, it dawned on him that some other living being was in the cave with him. Summing up all his senses, he could hear low rumblings and shufflings, accompanied by flapping noises and puffing. Feeling trapped and uneasy, he peered into the gloom and with the aid of his torch-light, was just able to distinguish some huge rock-shaped forms. Straining to see further, he realized they were moving slowly – swaying and rumbling. They were elephants! He crouched in the darkness for what seemed like hours, waiting for the creatures to move. When eventually they made their way out of the cave, Mitford-Barbeton was able to trace the well-used path the elephants had made into the cave, but the reason for the journey remained a mystery. Why should such large animals squeeze themselves into such a small, inaccessible place – and how to investigate further when any use of lighting would scare them off or, indeed, cause them to panic.

When I was in Kenya with Operation Drake we had time to look into this story and took a group to Mount Elgon to investigate. Before entering we checked carefully to ensure the cave was empty and then, leaving an armed guard, inched our way into the darkness. Immediately overcome by the strong stench of decaying flesh, we were able to quickly identify the origin – deep down in a crevasse lay the remains of a baby elephant that had fallen to its death in the gloom. Moving on into the bowels of the cave we disturbed thousands of fruit bats hanging from the roof and walls – the smell of their droppings overpowering us and making us gasp for air. Evidence of fresh elephant manure was all around, but still we could not understand the reason for their presence.

The Wildlife Department planned to open the area up to visitors and we had agreed to cut a path up to the entrance and erect a viewing platform. We were also anxious to further survey the cave and discover more about the elephants' movements. As an engineer I had noticed with intrigue that the roof seemed to be supported by a central pillar about twenty feet thick and made of the same mineral salt as the walls. There were only old tusk marks on it substantiating the theory that elephants are great engineers and would know this support had to be left. Some time later an earthquake occurred at Kitium and the pillar and roof collapsed, trapping and crippling an elephant that was quickly put out of its misery by a courageous warden who risked his own safety to go into the cave and shoot the poor beast.

Lesson three: elephants are highly intelligent. But all these examples involved the African variety. Those used in Tibet would have been Asian, smaller and perhaps hardier.

In 1975, Jim Edwards, who had spent a short time at my old school, Victoria College, Jersey, strolled into my office in Whitehall. Safari expert, explorer and hunter turned conservationist, Jim was already well known for the extraordinary Tiger Tops Lodge that he owned in the Chitwan Valley of Nepal.

'I've got a river that I'd like to open up for tourism and local traffic,' he explained. 'It's pretty rough, a few rapids; but nothing compared with the Nile or the Zaire.'

'Where is it?' I asked, my interest immediately drawn from the mass of Army paperwork that littered my desk.

'It's called the Trisuli and it runs from Tibet to India, through Nepal.'

Edwards lay back in the deep armchair. His off-white safari suit was in no way out of place as he sprawled, surrounded by the photos and maps of a score of expeditions that adorned the walls. 'By December the snows will have melted and the river will be low; you could have a good look at the rocks,' he continued. Jim has a flair for inspiring others to help in his projects and an impressive track record. These attributes, combined with good looks and embarrassing generosity, make him a persuasive fellow.

'Haven't been at home for Christmas for . . .' I muttered.

'Bring the family, be my guests. It's great fun, we have a huge party at New Year,' interrupted my long-legged friend. 'I need someone with a sound knowledge of rivers to tell me if this idea is feasible, and you'd love to ride my elephants.'

So in December that year, after the descent of the Trisuli, we spent a week ambling around Chitwan on Jim's elephants.

We saw and sometimes disturbed groups of deer, peacocks and even rhino. The elephants gently made their way through the undergrowth, sometimes heavily wooded, sometimes open grass-land, feeling the ground before each footfall with their trunks if they were at all unsure of it. Each foot was laid quietly down on the exact spot touched by the trunk, then the back foot was placed exactly where the front foot landed. This makes tracking easier, as you only get one left and one right foot mark, the two feet superimposed on the same spot. The huge animals negotiated the steep descents to the river bed with extreme care, often going down on the knees of either their front or back legs to keep their backs relatively level so we didn't fall off. The drivers used their feet to put pressure on the tender flesh behind the elephants' ears to guide them and egg them on with a kicking movement, whilst using a stick in each hand to ward off branches from flicking into our faces. Meanwhile the elephants amused themselves as they walked along, pulling branches off trees and munching away at them.

I have never got over this first experience of working with elephants and my amazement at their willingness to accept orders from a mere man.

K. K. Gurung, the great Nepalese naturalist whom I first met in 1975 when he was managing Tiger Tops, wrote:

> The most fascinating thing about an elephant is its readiness to co-operate with man. That the biggest animal on earth should be willing to work with puny humans is somehow tremendously attractive. If it so wished, an elephant could kill its keeper with one blow of its trunk, and if it did not want to work, no human being could make it. Yet the fact is that most elephants not only co-operate, but seem positively to enjoy their association with man. They recognize their keepers easily and if they ever need surgical treatment, they seem to realize that it is for their own good. Conversely, their keepers become extremely fond of them; some men sing to their elephants as they go along and others believe that the great beasts understand not merely the twenty or thirty routine words of command, but everything said to them.*

The humbling experience of communication with such a gigantic animal led to my deep affection for them and the idea of an elephant-mounted expedition began to take on tremendous appeal.

I vaguely remembered reading that on a visit to England, the Maharajah of Cooch Behar had been disturbed to discover that Queen Victoria possessed few blooms from his jungles. Her Majesty said she would be delighted to receive some specimens for Kew Gardens and the Prince returned home post haste. There he assembled an expedition of four hundred elephants complete with a mounted quartet to play his favourite Gilbert and Sullivan airs. He also obtained the first ice-making machine in India to keep his champagne cool and, with a team of gardeners, set off to collect orchids and rare plants. Standing on the elephants' backs, the gardeners reached into the forest canopy with long

---

* K. K. Gurung, *The Heart of the Jungle* (André Deutsch/Tiger Tops, 1983)

clippers to gather the rare specimens. By all accounts, the Queen was extremely pleased with the results of this unusual botanical safari.

Whilst not in a position to mount an expedition of such an exotic nature, nevertheless my aim became something of an obsession. With each encounter, my love and admiration for this majestic beast grew. At the same time one could not help but be acutely aware of the terrible plight facing them.

Visiting an Operation Raleigh team in the Zimbabwean bush I had seen a cloud of vultures flapping about a large rock. As our Land Rover approached, the grotesque birds shuffled away into the scrub and the most sickening smell I can ever remember struck us like a solid wall. The 'rock' was in fact all that remained of an elephant. Streaks of bird droppings ran over the putrefying carcass. The face had been pecked clean and the tusk sockets bore the marks of an axe; splintered bone and ribbons of skin lay scattered on the blood-soaked ground.

Putting a handkerchief to my nose and mouth I advanced, but was stopped by a swirling cloud of bloated flies. 'Bloody poachers,' exclaimed the game warden who was with me. 'They kill one of the noblest animals on earth just for a hundred pounds' weight of ivory.'

'Then it gets used for a Chinaman's chop [a personalized stamp or seal] or a mantelpiece ornament,' I replied, turning away from the horrific scene. 'What a waste.'

Driving home we reflected on the tragic way man is destroying the fauna and flora of the planet and especially the greatest mammal of all. Illogically I could accept the death of a snake or a rat but somehow an elephant was different. I felt a very close bond to these gentle giants.

Back on Xixabangma, I was still pondering how elephants could have marched up these mountains into Tibet when we caught up with our supply chain. Because the road had been swept away we had 178 porters carrying four tons of stores. I met them winding their way barefoot over the landslide, each man under a large box bearing an ICI logo in honour of our major sponsor. Filing up a narrow mountain path, we came upon some elderly tourists who stood aside to watch the procession.

'Tell me, sir,' said a white-haired American gentleman. 'What is "Icky"?'

Somewhat puzzled, I replied, 'Icky?'

'Yeah, Icky on each box.'

I quickly explained that ICI (Imperial Chemical Industries) make, amongst other things, fertilizers and explosives.

'Looks as if you've enough to fertilize the whole of China, then blow it up,' he remarked.

Then Corporal John House of the Devon and Dorsets walked past carrying an eight-foot steam lance which he intended to use to drill holes for scientific measurements in glaciers. The vicious-looking device bore a strong likeness to a futuristic weapon from *Star Wars*. On it were stencilled the words MADE BY BRITISH AEROSPACE, another of our sponsors, who also manufacture missiles. To add to the confusion, John wore a T-shirt inscribed THE EMPIRE STRIKES BACK.

'I get it,' the American winked. 'The CIA has companies like Icky. Good luck to you, young fellow.'

Perspiration poured off us as we continued the ascent of steep slopes, picking off tenacious leeches that dropped from every tree, bush and shrub. It was a fit, lean group which finally reached Tibet. They must have been very tough elephants to have made this climb – perhaps they were giants?

Out on the high plateau, gazelle, wild ass and rodents were the subject of our studies, whilst powerful yaks carried our stores. Our task was to conduct botanical, geological and zoological surveys. When our camp was almost buried by an unseasonable blizzard sweeping up from the valleys of Nepal, reference books helped to pass the time spent huddled in our tents.

'You're not likely to see elephants here,' teased Emma, my 23-year-old daughter, a nurse in the team. Too engrossed to reply, I had already learned that unless something quite extraordinary existed in Nepal, there are only known to be two species of the largest living land animal still in existence: the African and the Asiatic elephant. The African species lives throughout the continent south of the Sahara and has two sub-species, the savannah and the rather smaller forest type. A fully grown African bull can reach well over twelve feet at the shoulder and weigh over seven tons, whereas his Asian cousin rarely exceeds ten feet and five tons. The huge ears of the African are the shape of the map of Africa and both sexes have tusks. The Asiatic beast is essentially a forest dweller and has smaller ears, more like the outline of India, and its back is higher than its shoulders. Tusks are only found on bulls, but it is quite common to find a tuskless male; cows usually have short 'tushs', an undeveloped form of tusk. There is also thought to be a pygmy elephant in West Africa, around six feet in height, but this has yet to be accepted by science as a separate sub-species.

The largest recorded kills were an African bull shot in Angola in 1955, which reached a shoulder height of twelve feet six inches, and a giant Asiatic elephant felled in 1882 by W. H. Varian whilst hunting in Sri Lanka. Measurements of the carcass on the ground showed it to be eleven feet one inch at the shoulder. It seemed this was the largest Asian elephant ever recorded to date. It probably weighed around seven tons.

It is difficult to say which species is most closely related to the mammoth. There are skull features that seem to indicate the Asiatic elephant is the nearest relative, but DNA tests are in progress to test whether this is correct. Skeletons and frozen carcasses of mammoths have been found in many parts of Russia and fossil remains are not uncommon world-wide. I wondered if there were any remains south of the Himalayas that might be linked to living creatures.

Man has been training elephants since at least 3500 BC and over the years they have been used for engineering, transport, hunting and in battle. Few schoolboys have not heard of Hannibal's epic crossing of the Alps in 219 BC with his war elephants, although these were thought to be trained Atlas elephants, now an extinct sub-species. Hannibal realized the value of such ferocious-looking monsters in his army for, although they are naturally gentle and slow moving, their sheer size and threatening tusks made them a pretty intimidating sight. It is doubtful whether the Carthaginians got more than a few of their thirty-six pachyderms over the Alps, but their appearance was enough to put the fear of the devil into the Romans, and much of the success of the campaign may have been due to the terror of the Roman cavalry horses.

In the thirteenth century Kubla Khan used a massive mobile fort carried on the back of four elephants. From its ramparts his archers sent out showers of arrows as they plunged into the enemy lines. Of course, once the opposition learned to attack the beasts' weaker spots, they would flee out of control into their own army, causing havoc. There were plenty of tales about the use of war elephants along the Himalayas and the story of the Nepalese invasion of Tibet using huge tuskers could well be true. The great gates of Indian cities are often adorned with three-foot-long spikes, fitted to prevent elephants battering them down with their heads.

It is quite wrong to think that African elephants cannot be domesticated. The large head allows space for a fair-sized brain. I'd already experienced their intelligence. The Belgian colonists had a tame herd in the Congo for logging and a few of these are still alive today. However, the Asiatic elephant is usually the one carrying man or doing his bidding and these are found in four distinct sub-species. The Indian is the commonest and the beast found in Malaysia is the hairiest. Indonesia has the highly endangered Sumatran variety, whilst the herds in Sri Lanka have the fewest number of elephants with tusks.

The use of elephants for hunting was a long-established tradition in Nepal. In 1961 one of the greatest assemblies took place at Chitwan when 376 elephants were brought in from throughout the Terai. A report of the day says, 'nose to tail they would have stretched for over two miles!' The reason for this incredible gathering was a grand shoot organized by the King of Nepal for Her Majesty Queen Elizabeth II and His Royal Highness the Duke of Edinburgh. Never was there to be another such spectacle.

The task of preparing the camp was given to the Nepalese Army. Using bulldozers, they built a road to an attractive spot on the banks of the Rapti River. An airstrip was cut out of the forest. Where the tents would stand the top soil was scraped away to a depth of two inches, then coolies carried away every bug and scorpion in baskets. The ground was sprayed to kill off flies and mosquitoes that might carry malaria to the royal guests. Next, specially selected turf was laid and flattened by steamrollers before the Kathmandu fire service arrived with their engines to water the grass. (What happened to the luckless population of the capital in the meantime is not recorded.)

The camp was a mile square, with hundreds of tents for courtiers and other staff, and in the centre was a splendid scale model of Mount Everest, built of stone. Tented palaces were erected for the Queen and the King; Her Majesty's quarters consisted of two bedrooms, each with its own bathroom and drawing room so the Queen and Prince Philip had their own suite. King Mahendra was especially concerned about the toilet facilities and ordered that there was to be an efficient system of flushing. No doubt His Majesty had heard of an unfortunate oversight during an earlier visit to India by King George V and Queen Mary. A modern loo had been erected for the Royal couple, but the water supply had not been connected to the cistern. As a result, a servant was made to stand above the contraption with a bucket of water, and through a spy hole would watch for the regal hand upon the chain. At that precise moment he would pour in the contents of his bucket. There was no such problem with the Nepalese loo, for a well had been specially drilled.

The day before the Queen's arrival, engineers dug up flowering trees from the forest and transplanted them to decorate the avenues running through the camp and linking it to the airstrips. Almost fifty tons of fridges, furniture and fittings were shipped in from Hong Kong and, in spite of the Indian Customs and Excise, not to mention floods, it all arrived safely at the jungle camp three days ahead of the Royal party.

Riding in a wonderful gold and silver howdah on a specially selected elephant, Her Majesty and Prince Philip set out to inspect the mounts. It was a magnificent sight. Most of the great creatures were decorated, and with uniformed phanits, mahouts and pachwas on their backs, the beasts lumbered forward in procession toward the jungle. In howdahs rode ordinary people and retainers, and there were even elephants for the press. To slake the thirst of the visitors, bar elephants loaded with drinks ranging from chilled beer to iced champagne moved along the line.

Eventually the column reached the area where tiger had been located by the King's shikaris. There the elephants formed a line and encircled the unfortunate cats. White cloth a yard high was dispensed from two more elephants that rode around the ring erecting a fence. The circle was now a mile in circumference.

Prince Philip had an injured finger and could not shoot, and by all accounts the marksmanship of the other guests was not spectacular. Happily it meant that rather more tiger and rhino survived than might have been expected. Her Majesty filmed the hunt and is remembered for having raced her husband back to camp on her elephant.

When it was time for the Royal party to leave, the 376 enormous animals lined the route. Carrying their ornate howdahs, the richly decorated elephants raised their trunks in solemn salute as Her Majesty drove slowly past, telling King Mahendra that it was one of the most exciting days of her life.

Now the rapid depletion of wildlife has led to a ban on hunting and we shall never see such a sight again.

'Giant creatures are usually represented in art,' pointed out my friend Percy Trezise, when we had been exploring the caves of northern Queensland some years earlier. Percy, author, painter, pilot and one of the greatest authorities on the art of Australia's first people, was as tough as a dingo and burnt the colour of old mahogany. He was a real expert on that little-known, north-eastern corner of the continent. Every stream, water hole and rock face had been visited by this remarkable man. Once settlers and miners had combed the wilderness for gold, but Percy sought different riches. His quest was to find the paintings of crocodiles, kangaroos, serpents, people, emus and echidnas on the walls of hidden caverns. Black silhouettes of hands and figures of men and women painted in blues, ochres and white are frozen in time. The paintings record the stories and culture of a people. Frequently they are powerful symbols of love and hunting magic as well as sorcery.

'The aboriginals used to exaggerate certain features when depicting animals,' explained my friend, pointing to the prominent toes, whiskers, tail and testicles on the drawing of a diprotodon, a rhinoceros-sized wombat.

If the aboriginals did this, perhaps Asian artists might provide a clue to the mysterious beasts of Bardia in western Nepal. Indeed, elephants are well represented in both African and Indian art and, judging by the distribution of cave paintings, occupied a far greater area than today. They also appear in carvings and castings, while ivory seals and coins commonly depict elephants.

There were religious portrayals too: the Hindu god Ganesh has the head of an elephant on the body of a plump little man. So we began to build up a portfolio of drawings, amongst which was a mammoth drawn by prehistoric man on a cave wall at Les Eyzies and an engraving on flat ivory found at La Madeleine, both in the Dordogne region of France. These pictures showed a creature with a huge domed head and a sloping back. A similar beast was featured on Roman medals struck in AD 197, though in this case the shape of the ears suggested that the animal was more akin to the African elephant than the Indian.

I was hoping we might find some more recent references to a monster. Delving back in history there were accounts by Aristotle in the fourth century BC and, seventy-seven years after the birth of Christ, Pliny wrote that elephants were 'especially fond of water, and wander much about the streams'. Many of his observations hold good today and he even noted 'these animals are well aware that the only spoil that we are anxious to procure of them is the part that forms their weapon of defence.' Pliny went on to point out that when elephants lose their tusks they bury them and he commented that when surrounded by hunters, members of the herd with the smallest tusks were used to screen the better prizes. I had certainly heard tales of such behaviour in Africa.

One remark caught my eye: 'Large teeth (tusks) are now rarely found, except in India, the demands of luxury having exhausted all those in our part of the world.' So even 2,000 years ago the African elephant was threatened, whilst there were large tuskers in Asia.

Accounts of pachyderms on display are contained in stories of circuses and zoos. In 900 BC Middle East potentates had them tamed for entertainment and the Romans' exhibitions of live animals are said to have included elephants captured in the war with Hannibal. Some of these were to die in gladiatorial bouts, but others were trained for circuses. In the last century, the showman P. T. Barnum claimed to own the largest tusker ever captured. Declaring its height to be twelve feet at the shoulder, he refused to permit independent measurement. As it was an African elephant, he may have been correct.

Back in Britain in 1989, I had stopped thinking about elephants when a dreary winter's day in my London office was brightened by the arrival of a bouncy brunette who had once worked with me in Papua New Guinea. Sara Bampfylde was just back from Nepal where she had been with Jim Edwards' Tiger Mountain organization. My assistant, Sally Cox, brought in mugs of coffee and, bubbling with excitement, Sara told us her tale.

During a recent fishing expedition on the Karnali, she and an Icelandic chum were drifting silently down a shallow tributary of the great river that passes through the Royal Bardia Wildlife Reserve. The mahseer, for which the river is famous, had eluded her. The Icelander was hauling in these thrashing silver and golden fish over the side of the Avon inflatable in fine style but, try as she might, Sara had caught nothing and her interest turned to the sandy, jungle-topped river banks.

Brahminy duck rose quacking from the water's edge, parakeet flitted through the bombax trees and a solitary langur on sentry duty eyed the boat with suspicion. Otherwise nothing stirred and only a faint breeze moved the warm afternoon air. Sara yawned as she reached for an apple from the ration box, but her hand stopped halfway. She gave a little gasp of surprise, for right ahead the forest was moving. Then the trees parted and the strangest creature she had ever seen came into view. By its gleaming yellowish tusks it was clearly a bull elephant – of sorts. But it was quite different to the domestic tuskers Sara knew well at Tiger Tops. This lumbering beast was massive. His head was topped by a huge pronounced dome, the grey body was gross. As he came forward, a long, ribbed, almost reptilian tail twitched from side to side.

The Icelander's line drifted downstream as he followed Sara's gaze. 'What a monster,' he hissed.

'I think you're right,' whispered Sara, 'this must be the creature all the villagers are talking about.'

For several years the Tharu people living around the Royal Bardia Wildlife Reserve had reported raids on their crops and houses being destroyed by an aggressive giant animal that came without warning from the forest, usually at night. Few had ever seen it but the vast footprints and the trail of damage it left were firm evidence of its existence. Originally it was thought to be a rogue rhinoceros, but at the Karnali Lodge the staff spoke of an enormous wild bull elephant coming after the female pachyderms they kept for visitors to ride.

It was even said that the tusker had taken off one of the female elephants, who had not been found for two days.

As they drifted close, the beast ignored them and, lumbering to the river's edge, knelt down on his hind knees, supporting his mountainous bulk on his forelegs. Sucking up water with his trunk, he drank deeply.

Now only a hundred yards away, through the camera's long lens Sara could see the small, inquisitive brown eyes watching their every move. Knowing that she was one of the few to see 'the beast of Bardia', she tried to take in as much detail as possible. Suddenly the muscles of the animal's huge body flexed and, heaving himself erect, he turned away, ambling slowly back into the green wall of vegetation.

I met this tale with a look of sheer incredulity, but, unfazed, Sara delved into her bag and produced a box of colour slides. 'I thought you would like to see these,' she chuckled. Holding the transparency up to the light, I was amazed to see a picture of a massive elephant-like creature with a great domed forehead, sloping hindquarters and an almost reptilian tail. I was flying off to the Explorers Club annual dinner in New York in a couple of days so I pushed the transparencies into my briefcase and decided to seek expert opinion once I was in America.

'Could be a mutant,' guessed one of the scientists to whom I spoke, 'it looks really deformed.' A surgeon who examined Sara's photographs thought a bullet lodged in the skull might have caused a growth, perhaps affecting its glands and producing the huge girth. But this did not explain the ribbed tail. And then, for the first time, we noticed the folds of skin resembling enlarged glands at its rear end.

I talked to wildlife experts and zoologists. All agreed that its profile was remarkably mammoth-like, but reckoned it was an odd sort of elephant. 'You'll have to get more facts about this thing before anyone can give a considered opinion,' they advised.

I heard that Peter Byrne, a Club member who had for many years hunted big game before turning his attention to conservation, had been working in the far west of Nepal. Peter, a true adventurer, had started life in Dublin and served in the Royal Air Force in World War II before becoming a tea planter in Bengal. We had not seen each other for some years since meeting at a party given by an eccentric Texan in Houston; Peter had been asked to collect flora and fauna including rare penguins, but we both harboured doubts about our host. Our old hunting instincts were not wrong for the Texan was to end up in prison. I remembered Peter's Irish charm, his love of Nepal and his dedication to wildlife, so I phoned him at his home in Oregon.

Whilst on safari in the White Grass Plains area of south-western Nepal, Peter had found a really massive bull elephant which he had named 'Tula Hatti' (Big Elephant). The creature was thought to be around eleven feet tall, weighing an estimated seven tons. By all accounts Tula Hatti was not a good-tempered beast, as Peter describes in his book, *Tula Hatti, the Last Great Elephant*.

He had had several encounters with the huge tusker and on one occasion, video camera in hand, Peter found him in a thicket. A sixty-foot sal tree with a fifteen-inch trunk suddenly crashed over in front of him. No ordinary elephant could cause that and indeed, as Peter suspected, it was Tula Hatti. Knowing that wild tuskers will remain still and concealed for many hours, Peter waited. 'The elephant stayed in the thicket for about five minutes. Then I heard him move. I could not see him when he was in the thicket eating at the tree he had pulled down and I could not see him when he started to move. But a murghi (jungle fowl) suddenly dashed out on the left side of the thicket directly in front of me and, with a loud cackle of alarm, went racing off on foot into the undergrowth. Immediately afterwards, slowly, majestically, massive head nodding to the rhythm of his stride, Tula Hatti appeared from behind a big jamun tree and began to walk directly toward me. As he approached, I saw something that sent the hair on the back of my neck prickling and my heart pounding. On either side of his face, halfway between the eye and the ear, a stream of black mucous fluid streamed down in a delta-shaped flow. The stuff was rutting fluid; the bull was in heat.'

A hunter knows well that any elephant in this state of musth is a highly dangerous beast and can attack at the slightest provocation. With his heart pounding, Peter filmed the monster, but as he came closer, discretion overcame valour and Peter tried an old trick. An elephant's sight is surprisingly poor and it depends to a great extent on hearing and scent to detect intruders. Peter was crouching only twenty-five feet from Tula Hatti's trunk as it swayed back and forth trying to identify whatever was there. Most animals dislike sound or smell associated with man and will usually retreat when meeting them. In Africa I'd used a high-pitched squeak to clear inquisitive buffalo from the path. Squatting in front of the moving grey mountain, Peter gave a short cough, not quite a human sound, but one which would make the giant wary. Tula Hatti stopped, yet did not retreat. Possibly the faint hum of the video camera or maybe the thumping of Peter's heart or his scent alerted the great elephant. He took another pace forward and was now only seventeen feet away. Fearing he was about to be trodden into the ground, Peter coughed again. At once, with an ear-splitting trumpet, the monster turned, crashing off into the thicket. But not for long, for within a few seconds he decided to be rid of this annoyance.

Peter recalls, 'He came out of the thicket of greenery like an express train. The sound of smashing and bursting shrubbery was accompanied by a series of powerful screams and the ground trembled under tons of angry elephant. His huge trunk lashed from side to side and his enormous head bobbed up and down in time to the piston-like pounding of his twenty-two inch feet.'

An inexperienced person would have run in blind panic, but Peter Byrne knew that the chances of outstripping an enraged tusker in musth, even in jungle, were pretty slim. His only chance was to get out of his attacker's line of sight. He walked – yes, walked – to one side, looking around for a place to run to in the last resort. Tula Hatti stopped after a short charge. The man had gone, so he used his thick trunk to wrench out a tree stump and, with a shriek of frustration and rage, hurled it from him. Having taught all concerned a lesson and demonstrated his enormous strength, the mighty fellow stalked back into the all-concealing greenery. Peter had some incredible video footage and was very lucky to escape.

If the giant of Karnali was similar to Tula Hatti, I knew I'd better be well prepared.

Sally was filling a large box with 'miscellaneous information on giant elephants' and I started reading *Elephant Bill* by Colonel

J. H. Williams. The mysterious creature of the Karnali Valley was becoming an obsession. 'Well, at least there is a clear photo of this thing,' said my wife, Judith, urging me on, 'which is more than exists for the Yeti or the Loch Ness Monster.' But was the strange elephantine creature that Sara had seen the monster that was terrorizing the people of the Bardia area?

*Chapter Two*

# THE QUEST BEGINS

HAVING spent six years travelling the world, overseeing the projects undertaken by the young pioneers on Operation Raleigh, in the summer of 1990 I was faced with a new challenge: leading a group of 'wrinklies' – many of them sponsors and bosses of the young Raleigh venturers – across the Kalahari Desert and through the Okavango Swamp of Botswana in dugouts. By putting them through the same sort of experience as the youngsters, our purpose was to 'stimulate and re-motivate' a group of rather worn executives who had been winkled out of their offices to undergo 'management development'.

An expert on leadership in management, Professor John Adair, with whom I had taught at Sandhurst, suggested that by taking executives overseas to undertake challenging projects they would return to their desks revitalized and better able to cope with the day-to-day stress and pressure of the commercial world. Having acquired confidence and proved themselves in situations which involved teamwork, decision-making, problem-solving and creative thinking, they would thus become more effective and valuable members of their workplace.

There were twenty-four members of our first 'Executive Expedition', ranging in age from twenty-seven to sixty-nine, including a solicitor, a midwife, and a sprinkling of chairmen, managing directors, company secretaries, bankers, and chartered accountants. Requests to join came from all quarters, including a secretary who begged me to take her chairman to the North Pole for a year!

The challenges were many and varied; the value of the whole

experience was well summed up by John Campbell, our management trainer, in his report on the trip:

> The scale of everything you undertake is so much bigger on an
> expedition to a remote place; the distances are longer, the scen-
> ery more magnificent, the flora and fauna more exotic, the very
> timelessness of it. And so it is with the experience. There is no
> doubt that management development using the outdoors is
> immensely successful in Britain – mine and other companies
> can testify to this. But there is something very different about
> doing the same work in the wide open spaces of the Kalahari,
> perhaps reviewing the day under a baobab tree, or examining
> leadership styles after some key decisions around a camp fire
> in the Okavango Delta. The reality of the situations, the need
> for decisions and the interplay between people is inescapable.
> There is no hotel room to retire to in comfort and hide away,
> there is just the reality that tomorrow is another day when
> tasks have to be completed and the journey continued. So, from
> a management development viewpoint, it is an exhilarating
> environment in which to work. People do learn, do discover
> new resources in themselves and new perspectives on a wide
> range of issues. It is not an experience from which people return
> unmoved. In many ways it is this personal quest which partici-
> pants will value most on reflection, the fact that they have had
> a good opportunity to reconsider their priorities and recharge
> their batteries and all this on top of examining their leadership,
> decision-making and interpersonal skills.

We had certainly provided a different landscape and scope for
character development, and within a few days of returning I was
having to write articles for the press and to think of where next
to take a bunch of executives who were far more keen to face
the challenges of the great outdoors than sterile and introverted
in-house training.

It occurred to me that searching for a giant jumbo in a Nepalese
forest would be an ideal project to rejuvenate tired and listless
industrialists, and so began our expeditions to Nepal, the first in
1991. Several team members have joined me on more than one
of these ventures and over the years our relationship with the

river boys, elephant teams and naturalists of Tiger Mountain has developed into a strong friendship. Nepal, always a seductive country to the traveller, never loses its fresh charm and every Christmas I am impatient to be off again to breathe the fragrant, warm, dusty air of our river campsite in Bardia.

In 1846 the Ranas, the ruling elite of Nepal, set up a royal hunting preserve at Bardia, some 250 miles west of Kathmandu. The area encompassed around 130 square miles of forest, grassland and swamp. Being such a long way from the capital, it was used rather less than the more conveniently situated Chitwan. Thus in 1976, when it was declared a wildlife reserve, there was a reasonably healthy population of animals. By enlarging it to over 370 square miles in 1985, even more favourable conditions for wildlife were created.

The great Karnali (or Peacock) River forms the western boundary. On the eastern edge is the main road from Nepalganj to the hill town of Birendranagar. The northern limit crests the Siwalik hills and from here the reserve drops steeply for 4,000 feet to the sal forest sloping away gently into the Terai and India.

The dry, deciduous hardwood forest with its termite mounds, streams and ravines provides a perfect refuge for several species of deer, porcupine and sloth bear. At the lowest levels the jungle is more dense with areas of towering cuckoo grass, swamp and open grassy phantas where villages once stood. Rhino, leopard, tiger, jackal, monkeys and wild boar are common. Prolific bird life, crocodile, otter and even the rare Gangetic dolphin are found along the Karnali and its side streams. It was here that Sara Bampfylde had seen the strange elephantine creature.

Tiger Mountain had built a lodge just outside the reserve and moved six female elephants up from their base in Chitwan. These would prove invaluable in covering the ground, although what these well-behaved ladies would do if and when they met our quarry was anyone's guess. However, my previous experiences on foot encouraged me to put my faith in the domesticated elephants.

Information on the giant was scarce so I assumed he had not come from a populated area. Perhaps he originated north of the reserve in one of the wooded valleys, although I doubted if he would have ventured far into the mountains . . . but then elephants had been to Tibet. To be certain, we could start off by checking the Bheri River, travelling by Avon raft, then turning south through the Chisapani Gorge into the reserve.

In the period from January to April the rivers would be dropping but quite navigable and the temperature would be moderate. With little rain, there would not be too many bugs about. This seemed the ideal time for our expedition. With a team of seventeen we should be able to do a pretty thorough fact-finding and reconnaissance expedition in three weeks. Already volunteers were coming forward, but I've always selected expedition members with care and this one was no exception.

So it was that I found myself in the bar of the Frimley Park Hotel, Camberley, greeting Robert Brown, managing director of an auto electrical parts company, with a zest for sailing, riding, shooting and fishing, who had read about the project in the *Sunday Times*. Next in was Cynthia Campsall, a teacher at a comprehensive school in Rotherham, who enjoyed a wide variety of outdoor sports and had fished for salmon in Alaska.

Then Philip Downer, a staff and training director with Our Price Music Ltd, asked to join as he was keen to test his leadership skills, and John Hunt, the marathon-running General Manager of Marks and Spencer stores in Northern Ireland, came as a result of his wife calling me.

We recruited three more managing directors, a banker, a county education officer, a remedial teacher, a technical officer from ICI and a mother who walked guide dogs for the blind. 'A promising bunch,' murmured John Davies, our doctor, as we had a last glass at the bar when the evening briefing was over. 'The next twenty-four hours will tell.' John, who had accompanied me on many expeditions, was noted for his dry wit, shaggy dog stories and quiet professionalism. He was also a good judge of character.

My love of sappering had started here at Hawley Lake, thirty-seven years before, when as a young cadet I had learned a thing or two about demolitions, bridge building and boating. Now a greying Colonel, I stood on the bank watching our mature explorers trying to build a bridge of barrels and planks on a cold November weekend. All day they had engaged in team-building exercises, paddled assault boats and listened to briefings on every aspect of the expedition. Mark O'Shea, our red-haired reptile expert, had talked about the wildlife and brought along a ten-foot python to test the resolve and courage of the volunteers. He looked quite disappointed when everyone was able to handle the snake. 'It's like holding a child, not at all slimy and slippery,' commented one lady.

When night fell, tents and rations were issued and we set up camp on an exposed hilltop, the nearest I could get to conditions in Nepal. They cooked rabbits and rice over open fires before setting off to locate boxes of stores said to have been parachuted into the darkened woods at precise locations. The boxes made up a rescue and medical kit to use on a casualty from an 'aircrash'. It was all good Boy Scout stuff, but the most important part was simply to get them working together as a team under slightly adverse conditions. For a fifty-year-old executive, sleeping in a tent with a stranger on a winter's night when they're both damp and tired, can be quite stressful. The presence of the 'staff' who, although they did it with great diplomacy, were obviously assessing the individuals, did not seem to upset anyone. There were no complaints, even though the temperature was near freezing.

Next day a dip in the Sandhurst baths proved they could all swim two hundred yards. Back at Hawley the final session required everyone to say what they wanted from the project, what they brought to it and what they had learned from the weekend. To this, Chris Burke, who ran his own industrial cleaning company, said, 'I discovered how useless I am,' and Robert Brown reckoned, 'We've got a lot to learn.' Clearly the experience had been more humbling than I'd imagined, but the fact was they were a good team and I told them so. John Campbell, the management trainer, was already at work building up self-confidence, counselling and encouraging, whilst my assistant, Sally Cox, was busy with the administrative detail. Responsibilities were shared out and everyone had a job to do. Philip Downer became entertainments officer and produced a portable tape player, John Hunt was to make a video film, Libby Smith, the guide-dog walker, would handle the bird counts and Michael Edwards, the educationalist, would keep the records. Lastly, each person had to find £5,290. Elephant expeditions are not cheap. Any funds remaining at the end would go to Operation Raleigh to help the less fortunate young.

I spent that Christmas reading every book available on West Nepal. Not knowing the area, I felt uneasy and was reminded of the epic Darien Gap Expedition twenty years before, when I'd taken on a hellish challenge in deep jungle and based my plan on the reports of others. We only just pulled that one off and I did not want my quest for a monster to be such a close run thing.

Sally sounded upset. 'You're not going to believe this, John – Royal Nepal Airlines have gone on strike.'

'How dare they,' I roared, 'the ungrateful . . .' But it was true and there was nothing I could do. The next flight was a week later, but by some miracle Sally had got us all on Bangladesh Biman and we'd fly in via Dhaka, arriving at Kathmandu only a couple of days late. I went off to revise our plan.

The first airline to have wide seats and leg room for large passengers ought to be rewarded with a world monopoly. Alas, Bangladesh Biman was not in this class, although they did their best to make us comfortable. Ten hours in a pre-natal position did not impress the members of our team and on arrival in Dhaka they dived into the transit bar to be thoroughly ripped off for beer, milk and tea. Interestingly, more passengers seemed intent on transferring to flights heading elsewhere than staying in Bangladesh. The flight to Kathmandu was heavily overbooked but Sally, who had worked for Gulf Air and was brilliant at handling airlines, got all of us aboard and most upgraded to first class. Mark's snake-catching stick aroused interest and passion, and was impounded as an offensive weapon to be returned to him on arrival. So the gallant band flew on in luxury with flowers, fine food and the *Bangladesh Times*.

The rapid descent through the mountains and into the smog of the Kathmandu valley brought us to the new red-brick airport. Nepal lives on tourism, so entry is easy and the Tiger Mountain bus soon had us on our way to our accommodation.

For first-timers this capital city was a complete culture shock with its grimy houses, surface drainage, teeming masses of people and ubiquitous children. For those who do not know the East, the poverty was mind-blowing, but the Manaslu Hotel was an oasis of calm. And it was here that we held our final briefing, in the garden, sipping tea. That evening we strolled into the city, dilapidated but a hive of industry. Bicycles everywhere, used by locals and foreigners alike, weaved in and out of the market stalls, porters and domestic animals, whilst sacred cows scratched themselves on gate posts, and pigs, chickens, dogs, cats and even great flying foxes circulated amongst the houses.

The tiny shops, besieged by ragged children with runny noses, sell bracelets, brooches, ornaments, sweaters, T-shirts with bright, instantly embroidered designs and the used gear of impecunious trekkers. Fruit, that can ravage a European stomach if eaten unwashed, is piled high, and small boys peddle snuff and vicious-looking kukri knives to tourists.

Rickshaws and battered, three-wheeled scooter cars jostle for space in the narrow alleys with ancient crones laden with bundles of firewood that would defeat a six-foot Englishman. Electric cables and telephone wires enmesh with each other, draped like jungle creepers from leaning poles and balconies. Demented drivers hammer their horns. The resulting cacophony mixed with a thousand other noises makes Thamel, the shopping centre of Kathmandu, seem like a great chaotic fairground, through which the population scurries or strolls without a care.

I could see the American Ambassador thought me mad as we discussed the possibility of there being a monster lurking in the jungle when we met at the house of Lisa and Tensen Choegyal that night. However, diplomatically, she did not make any critical remarks and the gathering gave the team a chance to meet local dignitaries and wildlife officers before setting out. They were all polite, but then Kathmandu has long been the starting point of famous quests. Forty years before, those who aspired to climb Everest had been tolerated with a similar degree of patience.

On my first visit to Nepal, I had met the legendary Boris Lissane-vitch. Son of a wealthy Tsarist family, this engaging eccentric had made his home here and had become something of an expert on the Abominable Snowman or Yeti. Although Boris never saw it, he interviewed many reputable folk who claimed to have done so and as a result was prepared to accept that an unknown animal could exist. So certain was he that he had a Yeti-gun known as 'Alka Seltzer'. Presented to him by a Texan hunter, this was an early dart gun and with it came two unmarked bottles. Unfortunately Boris had lost the instructions, but he knew that one contained a powerful tranquillizer to send the Yeti to sleep, whilst the other was a stimulant intended to arouse it. Boris dared not use the weapon for fear that he might fire the wrong drug into the Snowman and have to face an over-excited Yeti. It is rumoured that female Yetis have an insatiable sexual appetite, so Boris was not encouraged to set out on a hunt. However, as he pointed out, a live giant panda had not been captured until 1936 and there could well be other animals, unknown to science, in remote parts of Asia. But could a six-ton creature exist?

Next morning, a flat tyre on our minibus delayed our start by half an hour and then we were off through the city, past the stadium where swarthy soldiers did their PT, and out on to the new road heading west, already crowded with hooting buses and overladen lorries. Signs proclaiming 'man at work' warned of road-widening projects where we passed hundreds of dust-covered labourers running about like ants to carve away the living rock. Drivers of oncoming traffic, reluctant to concede, still managed to smile pleasantly as we drew level. 'We could learn something from these people,' commented Michael Edwards, who was keeping the log. Stops at police checkpoints and villages opened our eyes to the real Nepal beyond the capital. Bazaars stacked with fruit and vegetables and garment sellers' stalls were alive with shoppers and bystanders, children hawking, pleading and smiling, and old soldiers who insisted on saluting. An air of industry and tolerance was the main impression.

The sun peeped over the mountain as we reached the Trisuli River and peered down at the first set of rapids. The colour of the river water is remarkable; an icy, milky bright aquamarine, and throughout Nepal the sand glitters with tiny grains of mica. Sixteen years before I had broken my nose here whilst pioneering rafting in Nepal with John Edwards and American explorer Vince Martinelli. Now, looking down at the relatively easy white water of 'Snell's Nose' it was hard to see how I had made such a stupid mistake.

At noon we came across an horrific accident. A 'public carrier' truck had crashed head-on into the end of a box girder bridge. Although it had happened a week before, the whole community was out still trying to prise the stricken vehicle off the bridge. We stopped. English conversation flowed. 'Five dead,' sighed a grey-haired old fellow. 'The truck was flying, a cyclist caused it all.'

That night was spent at a rather charming lodge near a Tharu village. This was a last little touch of luxury and it seemed a good place for John Campbell to start the management training. So, seated on cosy chairs in a fragrant garden, we did a spot of self-analysis. The team responded enthusiastically and by the flickering light of the Tilley lamp we discussed interpersonal relationships and Belbin's tables.

A mouth-watering curry supper washed down with cold beer put us in the mood for dancing. It was also the banker Stewart Purton's birthday and Libby surprised us by producing a freshly made cake. So when the village troupe arrived, we joined in, whirling with clicking fingers and swirling hips around the central fireplace.

The moon had risen and there was a chill in the air when we turned in, but the beds were comfortable and, apart from a vocal contest between the village dogs and a jackal, all was quiet. I flicked on my small radio for the BBC World Service news. A voice like that of an old Pathé news announcer told that Iraq was pulling out of Kuwait. That all seemed a very long way away.

We breakfasted before dawn on scrambled eggs and miniature Nepalese sausages, whilst a vigorous thunderstorm rumbled and crashed across the Terai. The lightning display was impressive and when the rain struck the lodge it fell in rods, creating streams and pools from which frogs and lizards hopped and scuttled. By 6.30 a.m. the tempest had passed and we were bouncing along in our solid-seated bus. The distant deep grey mountains loomed out of the clouds and, as the sun beat down, the temperature reached 80°F. Occasional comfort stops (boys to the left, girls to the right) and a few running repairs to the vehicle gave us some leg stretches. A picnic lunch with the invariable hard-boiled egg, bread, butter and fruit filled a gap. Mark O'Shea managed to catch his first snake by the side of the road.

At Nepalganj, a sprawling town on the India/Nepal border, we found a medicine man selling cure-alls and aphrodisiacs. He was drawing quite a crowd by putting large scorpions on his tongue until Mark fearlessly picked up a large black specimen, saying, 'Simple, quite safe: their stings have been removed.' The salesman glowered.

A stroll around the houses, decked in red-and-white Congress Party flags set up for pre-election campaigning, gave us a chance to stretch our cramped limbs before we turned north and, leaving the flatlands, followed a deteriorating track into the steep, tree-clad hills.

As night fell we reached our first campsite on the north side of a tributary of the Karnali. The Himalayan River Exploration team we were using for the rafting phase had gone ahead. Tents were up, water was sterilized and supper was ready. For cheerful efficiency in the field it is hard to equal the Nepalese. Their leader, Mash Thapa, had already established a reputation as an expert on the Himalayan rivers and in perfect English he briefed us on the journey ahead. With the sound of the rushing water in our ears and the haloed moon overhead, we crawled happily into our sleeping bags.

My log for the morning of 28 February read: '0700 Reveille, but most of the team rose early. Hearty breakfast followed by allocation of crews to boats and safety briefing. Sent final sitrep* back to Kathmandu with returning bus, to be telexed to Britain. Started out 0945, hit first rapid, a grade two plus after thirty minutes. Next came a grade three, an hour later, but quite exciting. Big stopper wave.'

In fact it was an excellent shakedown day. John Hunt was hurled out in an early rapid and the boatman went overboard in another. Both were gathered up undamaged. The abundance of white water, tossing waves, the narrowness of the valleys gave us a fast and sporting ride. The photographers had a field day and by the time we made camp everyone was in great spirits, even if one or two had bruises.

We landed on a virgin beach at 5.45 p.m. having run nineteen miles of the river. Mash and I had chosen the spot because of a

---

* Military abbreviation for situation report

small lake tucked in the valley above the river. A shrine to a Hindu god was said to exist there and game had been reported. There would certainly be hunters in the area and if anyone knew of strange creatures it would be them.

With a crackle of static Big Ben's slightly tinny chimes rang out from my radio, and the BBC brought news of a cease-fire in Iraq with Saddam Hussein's army largely destroyed. Around our campfire a cheer went up, and we cracked a bottle of J&B.

The hidden lake was a beauty spot, prolific in wildlife; fish and frogs abounded and we soon found the shrine to the jungle god. A simple stone structure, it stood in a grove of trees on a small island. On the shore, tracks of deer and small cats were plentiful. A group of three stayed out that night using an image intensifier, kindly loaned to us by Pilkingtons to watch for wildlife. They only saw a deer. On the next night one of the watchers was stricken with squitters and the resultant noises scared everything away.

I met three hunters clutching ancient muzzle loaders, but although they talked of tiger, no one knew of any elephant in the area. They were so thin and emaciated that I didn't think they could be very successful. A visit to a hamlet called Similpali produced great excitement. We were certainly the first white folk they had met, but the people had not seen elephants. However, one bandy-legged old man with deeply wrinkled skin said, 'You should ask the Raji.'

'Who are they?' I said, turning to a muscular boatman named Megh Ale.

'I think he means a tribe of hunters who used to live in the forest on the Karnali,' replied Megh who, like most raft commanders, spoke good English. 'Since the trees have been cut down their hunting ground has gone and now they are very poor,' he explained. Megh, an ardent conservationist as well as a skilful rafter, was to become a very useful member of the team and a good friend in the years ahead. He was also pretty handy with his kukri and, to the dismay of the ladies present, took the head off a goat that had been accompanying us with a single swipe. The carcass was then prepared and roast goat followed for supper.

After supper, Philip, doing his duty as entertainments officer, produced the karaoke machine which his employers, W. H. Smith, had lent. Whether it was this or the goat I know not, but Mark got an attack of verbal diarrhoea and talked all night.

By 4 March we had completed our survey of the area, Mark had netted a fine collection of fish for the Natural History Museum in London and even spared a couple of mahseer for the pot.

Only small rapids lay ahead and the crew had to paddle rather more often to maintain our progress. I noticed Mash was keeping guard at night. 'The people here may not be so trustworthy,' he confided, 'there is marijuana grown in this area.'

By now we were getting to know each other pretty well; however, all tents looked identical and you had to remember which one was yours. Stewart recalled one embarrassing incident in his diary: 'I shared a tent with Adrian Thorogood and early one morning I returned from a call of nature, still somewhat sleepy, and by mistake entered the wrong tent. Crawling in I looked up to find Sally getting dressed. All she said was, "Does Adrian wear a bra?" as I reversed at speed.'

I had brought a lightweight waterproof bivvy bag and decided to try it out by sleeping outside. At 4 a.m. the skies opened and I awoke when a cold trickle of water ran down my back. After several good oaths, I wriggled out of my sodden bedding and dug in my rucksack for dry clothing. As I pulled on my clean underpants, I discovered they had been well and truly eaten by rats. Sitting huddled in Henri Lloyd's best Gore-Tex anorak whilst thunder roared and lightning flashed, I brooded. It was not going to be a good day. However, the boys produced a splendid breakfast of pancake, scrambled egg, baked beans and toast. Spirits rose. Our joy was short-lived for no sooner had we cast off than the wind got up and down came the rain again.

Some only had thin clothing on and Stewart Purton had turned a shade of blue. Everyone was thankful when we pulled in to the shore. As if by magic, a villager appeared and, to revive us, lit a fire in the open space beneath his hut. Someone found a bottle of vodka and we donned dry clothing. With lunch came the sun and soon after we reached the junction with the Karnali. On the shore dark-skinned men and women panned for gold and we were able to trade a little tobacco with them for some of their necklaces. The washerwomen nearby sang and smiled sweetly as we climbed back into our boats.

'Hold on tight, watch for the whirlpool,' cautioned Megh at the meeting of the rivers. Sure enough, turbulence had us in its grip and spun the Avon around twice before sending us on our way into the great Chisapani gorge.

High above the river a suspension footbridge was alive with schoolchildren. 'Namaste! How old are you?' they shrilled, ever keen to practise English. The towering sides of the gorge closed in rapidly around the hissing water. On the west bank ran a track that had been used for centuries by traders heading to and from Tibet. Mules and packgoats carrying salt could be seen trotting along, leaping from rock to rock, as small boys herded them forwards.

Mash had a line out and soon produced a fine mahseer. Watching him land his catch we almost missed a pair of twelve-foot gharials, fish-eating crocodiles, sunbathing on a secluded beach. A fleeting glimpse of a man-eating mugger sliding into the shallows reminded us that swimming might be hazardous, but Megh, in his wetsuit, wanted to cool off and went in anyway. 'It was only a little crocodile,' he laughed as we cruised by jumbled boulders on which monkeys played happily.

'What's the difference between these crocs?' asked Sally, remembering the first time she had accompanied me overseas. Having mentioned that she didn't like boats, she had found herself in a leaking dugout on a Kenyan lake. A storm blew up and waves had slopped over the gunwales. My new assistant didn't speak for quite a while until a crocodile surfaced beside us. Looking down its jaws all she had said was, 'Oh! Really!'

Pulling on the oars, Megh explained that the thin-snouted gharial is well equipped for sweeping up fish with a sideways flick of its head. Its streamlined body, webbed hind feet and long, powerful tail are perfect for underwater hunting. It can grow to over twenty feet in length. Predators and humans had taken such a toll on them that extinction was likely until the Frankfurt Zoological Society had funded a rescue programme and, after captive breeding, the reptiles had been reintroduced to the wild.

'They don't attack man,' grinned Mash.

'What about women?' queried Libby.

'You have only to worry about the mugger,' replied Megh. 'In spite of their bulky appearance they are extremely agile. They will lie still for hours, but if an animal or a human gets close, they will attack with incredible speed.'

I remembered my own battle with a Nile crocodile that had tried to eat me in Ethiopia. The mugger looked very similar.

Megh went on to tell how this croc, although smaller than the gharial, would drag its prey down into the river and drown the victim, then let it rot for a while in its underwater lair before tearing it apart, swallowing great chunks of flesh without chewing.

'Charming,' said Sally, dipping her paddle into the stream as if to push us on a little faster.

Above us the weird rock formations twisted and turned their way up the near vertical cliffs. 'Look well,' said Mash, flinging his spinner. 'If the dam is built this gorge will become a lake.' He was talking about the proposal to construct a hydroelectric power dam almost 900 feet high across this natural wonder. It could be one of the largest hydro-systems in the world, capable of producing more power than all the United Kingdom's nuclear power plants. The project would cost £4 billion and no one was sure how Nepal could pay such a sum unless it was given substantial loans and help by India. Indeed, the country does not need so much power, but the economists see a way of selling it to their electricity-hungry neighbours. The disruption to human and animal life in the area to be flooded was considered less important. We argued the cases for economic necessity and progress against preservation, whilst our bulbous grey inflatable drifted lazily through the shadow-filled canyon. As if to remind us of that other world, a motor boat carrying Japanese construction engineers appeared from a bridge site ahead. They roared past, shattering the peace. No one waved; we just scowled in disapproval. Further evidence of the destruction of the environment was seen on the beaches, where piles of firewood were ready for ritual cremations. 'What a waste of trees,' said Libby.

A northerly breeze sprung up in the afternoon and Stewart used his Midland Bank umbrella as a sail, while the other boats had shirts and anoraks up for the same purpose. A race was on. Although morale was pretty good I thought a little treat would do the team no harm, so instead of camping on the beach we pulled into Tiger Mountain's tented camp. No visitors were staying and the staff were delighted to have some thirsty customers. After a warming curry, a few beers and a chance to dry clothes, the team was in even better spirits and well prepared for the rigours of the morrow.

The Bardia forest extends up to the southern face of the Siwalik hills, and the reserve boundary runs along the crest. Here a few villages look out over the braided Karnali and the jungle where our quarry was said to roam. By walking the ridge line 4,000 feet above and talking to the hill people, we might pick up some clues. We split into two groups; the slightly older members would make the ascent with Doc John Davies and me in the cool of the morning. The younger ones would search for specimens with Mark and John Campbell and then tackle the climb in the afternoon.

Forty-four porters of assorted age, sex and size had arrived, but unlike their eastern cousins these folk had never been part of a shikar (hunt) and lacked experience in carrying awkward loads. However, after much discussion we got under way. The first four miles went up a winding trail to 3,000 feet. We took it very gently, with frequent stops for water. 'Is it always as hot as this?' enquired Cynthia as we collapsed in a grassy clearing to eat lunch and enjoy a superb view of the great river spreading out beneath us.

On reaching the crest, we halted in a hamlet of low mud-walled houses named Gaynekanda. Water was very short up here and we dozed in the grass until the exhausted porters struggled in.

By 4 p.m. there was no sign of our second group and I was becoming concerned when John Hunt arrived to announce that several were suffering from heat exhaustion and Adrian was quite poorly. Apparently they had shunned the porters and tried to carry their own packs up. Cursing their foolishness, the Doc seized his medical kit and moved back down the mountain at best speed. By dark all were gathered in and received a stiff lecture on heat-related illness from John Davies. Mark was elated as they had seen civet cats and deer and had a brush with three sloth bears that had come tumbling across the track. This bear can be an evil-tempered fellow and I hoped we would not find many on the narrow hill paths.

Our sirdar had not organized the porters particularly well, and when he produced soggy rice and under-cooked potatoes for breakfast, he got the sharp edge of my tongue. However, the fantastic sight of the snow-capped Mount Api and the Western Himalayas in the golden light of sunrise took our minds off our stomachs and we set out along the ridge path. A gentle stroll soon turned into a challenging scramble as the track rose and fell with sheer drops on either side. To the heavily laden lowland porters it proved a daunting challenge. Suddenly a cry rent the still air and I knew at once that someone had gone over the edge. A series of crashes, as the body plummeted down, down through the undergrowth, was sickening. John Campbell was first on the scene. A barefoot lad had indeed fallen, but only a few feet. The crashes had been Doc John's medical rucksack going down. It was only recovered after a long climb by the bearer and the contents had suffered badly. The pay for these poor fellows was pretty miserable, only 27 rupees for a day's work (and the exchange rate at the time was 67 rupees to £1). This helped us to forgive the unfortunate boy for dropping John's rucksack.

The night campsite was in a flat field beside the village with uninterrupted, spectacular views north and south; it was overlooked by a small shrine with the usual bronze bell. Whilst John Campbell conducted a management development discussion, I talked to the local people. A wizened old chap with a frightful wheezing cough and bloodshot eyes said he had lived in the valley as a boy, but his community had been moved out by the government when the area became a reserve. His only regret was the loss of good farming land and the fact that life was harder in the hills; water was a problem and, as it was forbidden to cut trees in the area, firewood was scarce. 'There is a track you can take down the mountain and through the valley,' he stated, waving his wrinkled hand in a southerly direction. 'Tomorrow I will show you.' He had used it often, though now it was overgrown in parts and there were dangerous animals in the forest. He described leopard, tiger, cobra and hyenas, but my ears pricked up as he mentioned 'the creature that you do not see'. Bringing out my mammal book I flipped through the pages as he tapped the picture of each one he had seen. When he came to the rhino he jabbered with excitement, 'Tula, Tula – big, big,' then we got out the sketch-pad and finally agreed the monster was a kind of giant rhino with a bump in the middle of its back. He admitted all this was hearsay, adding that as the beast moved by night, few had ever seen more than the damage to houses and trees it left in its wake. But he did give me one interesting clue. 'It makes a call like the bark of a dog,' he said. I returned to the fire in a pensive mood and joined in the limerick competition that Philip had organized.

At first light I yelled out, 'Wakey, wakey, rise and shine, you've had your sleep and I've had mine.' Bleary eyes peered out of tents and gradually the team emerged, shivering in the dawn. The entire population turned out to watch us leave; it was a very special occasion. Foreigners, and indeed Nepalese from far afield, had never visited their village before. As the old trail dropped steeply into the jungle we ran into a layer of hot, humid air rising from the vegetation. In no time our clothes were drenched in sweat and, as fast as we drank, liquid streamed out of our pores. Most of the trees were sal, a hardwood that grows to around 100 feet. Although a deciduous variety, it never loses all its leaves and the gentle scent of its cream-coloured flowers gives the forest a most pleasant smell in the spring. It is a valuable commodity and used extensively in building. There were many locals who would prefer to harvest the Bardia forest than leave it for wildlife.

I had wrenched a tendon in my foot, making the descent slow and painful, and when we reached the valley and the wide boulder-strewn stream, I plunged the limb into the icy cold water to reduce the swelling. Small fish nibbled my toes and Mark soon had some for his collection. By mid-afternoon it was 85°F but with high humidity, conditions were becoming exhausting. Philip leant on a rock looking like a beetroot. His fair skin was on fire. 'God, this heat! I never imagined it would be like this,' he groaned as Doc forced him to drink another pint of liquid.

All day Mahendra, our cook, had led a rather attractive goat which skipped along happily, munching on choice shrubs and grass. When we stopped at the stream, I heard the rasp of his cook's file as he put a razor edge on his kukri. The ladies were all bathing or fishing, so with luck no one would see the planned execution. In fact, all we heard was the swish of the blade and the spattering of blood upon the rocks as Mahendra decapitated it with a single blow. Whatever our finer feelings, the dish that followed was delicious, greatly improved this time by the boning of the meat.

Even before we reached the camp we could smell the elephants. Their heavy scent hung in the tangled bushes at the side of the path, pressed flat by their wide footprints. Here and there a torn branch revealed where they had snatched a mouthful of leaves. A mound of khaki-coloured dung balls was placed neatly in the centre of the trail – almost as if it had been put there by hand. Then I saw her. Madu Mala Kali was standing very still in the deep shadow. She had come from a bath and her wrinkled skin still shone with water. One brown eye, strangely small in the great head, stared unblinkingly at me. Then, satisfied that I posed no threat, she fanned herself with her dappled pink ears and, flicking her ridiculously short tail, she cleared away a small cloud of flies. Plucking a trunkful of vegetation with the ease of an experienced nibbler at a cocktail party, the lady opened her huge jaws and savoured the morsel with her soft wet tongue.

'Be careful, this one is unpredictable. She can be very danger-ous,' cautioned Mash, who had come up behind me.

Madu Mala Kali (or Honey Blossom) was the matriarch of the little herd of domestic elephants. Standing eight and a half feet at the shoulder, she was about forty years of age, very experienced and the least likely to panic in the face of a charge by rhino or tiger – or anything else for that matter. She did have one or two drawbacks. As I was soon to discover, riding her was like travelling in a car with a missing spring and she was slower than her four colleagues, but when aroused she could be ferocious, as her unfor-tunate attendant had discovered some years before. Chan Chan Kali, Sundar Kali and Champa Kali, all young girls, were already powdering themselves with fresh, fine dust, greying their brown hides so they blended easily with the forest. At the far end of the clearing was another large lady, Luksmi Kali. Always apart from the others, she nonchalantly crossed one hind leg around the other, but her gaze never left us. Later we were to see that female jealousy can be as strong between elephants as it is in humans.

Kamal, a swarthy tracker, was in charge of the elephants and was to be our leading naturalist. Once we had unpacked our gear and drained several mugs of welcome tea, he briefed us on our beasts. Saddled with a square wooden cage or howdah, Champa Kali (Flower) ambled forwards and, flickering her long eyelashes, squatted down like some gigantic dog in front of us. 'Elephant will carry four people in a howdah and there are two ways to mount,' he explained, going to the rear end. 'For bigger people it is best to climb up the back.' So saying he formed a loop with Champa's tail, creating a step in which John Hunt, hardly able to contain his fascination for the big mammals, placed his foot and pulled himself up on the crupper rope into the howdah.

'What's the alternative?' asked Libby Smith, the guide-dog walker from Harrogate.

'The elevator,' grinned Kamal and, turning to face the elephant, barked, 'Utha.' Obediently Champa Kali put out her trunk, forming a hook with the tip. Kamal seized the ends of her ears and the elephant lifted him effortlessly on to her head. All were impressed. Amazingly these gentle creatures do not seem to mind people climbing all over them.

Kamal explained how the phanits (drivers) controlled their beasts sitting astride the elephant's neck. Steering was done by body language, with the feet being pushed forward behind the ear or pressed back against the shoulder for reverse. To stop his mount the phanit will lean back and to make it kneel he will lean forward and press downwards on the head. Otherwise it was all by voice commands in Hindi.

Night fell quickly, but all one needed was a thin sweater after sundown. Mash produced a bottle of Kukri rum which he added liberally to our tea and then traditional dhal bat was served for supper. An army sergeant commanding a small anti-poaching section joined us and told of a large, wild tusker that had been seen nearby. He had no doubt it was an elephant and would show us tracks at dawn. John Hunt rewarded him with a 'Belfast 91' flag, saying it would protect him from things that go bump in the night. The sergeant looked puzzled but accepted it graciously. The next day it was flying above his camp.

It was chilly and damp as we ate breakfast, but by 7 a.m. we had mounted and set off in two teams. Five elephants advanced through the dew-drenched forest with less noise than a single man. Only the occasional crack of a branch being broken disturbed the silence in the eerie dawn. As the light increased, inquisitive sambar deer, their distinctive big ears twitching, watched us moving through the bush. Peacocks screeched and flapped out of the way as langur monkeys rushed down the trees. Why they came down when danger threatened instead of staying up in the branches out of harm's way, I couldn't understand. There was fresh tiger spoor only 100 yards from the camp. Green doves and white crested kingfishers flitted along the river bed. We found wild elephant prints in the mud, but they were old and not unusually large.

We plodded on in silence, three or four to an elephant, rocking from side to side in the howdah, eyes straining into the twilight forest. The occasional flicker of a chital or spotted deer and the scamper of a muntjac kept the teams alert, but an elephant moves with an unusual rhythm and the bouncing, rocking motion can induce sleep, as some of us discovered when the temperature rose. Branches and vines that threatened to catch the passenger were deftly moved aside by our mounts. They seemed to know exactly how much extra to allow in terms of height and width for us to pass safely through the trees. Only occasionally did the elephants make a mistake or disobey an order; for a small fault there was a whack with the phanit's stick, but for a greater error the steel ankush was used. The sound of the blow always made me cringe. Having been brought up to train animals with kindness, to strike a lovable creature went against the grain, but as Kamal pointed out, 'Elephants are big, strong beasts, and if you do not handle them firmly you will regret it, for they can be as cunning as they are clever. If they feel they can get the better of you, they will soon become uncontrollable.' I consoled myself with comparing the thickness of an elephant's skin and the great bone structure of its head with the flank of a horse, on which I had no hesitation about using a riding crop, but still I winced whenever the ankush was used.

When the sun was at its height we stopped to rest, taking a light lunch and, most enjoyable of all, bathed the elephants. The girls, or 'ladies' as we now called our mounts, were unsaddled and wandered happily into the shallows. Catfish fled for cover as they lay down to get the maximum amount of body into the cool water. The phanits climbed on to them, scrubbing their hides with sticks and stones, changing the dry grey skin to wet ebony. Chan Chan's head submerged, leaving only the tip of her trunk playing like a curious serpent above the surface and then spurting water on all concerned. Sundar blew bubbles with an almost musical note and, as if to answer a challenge, we stripped to our pants and jumped in to join them. The phanits urged care in scrubbing the highly sensitive trunk and ears. As soon as one side was finished the phanit cried 'Theeray' (turn over) and the ladies rolled on to their other side. Then the process was repeated. Champa was the cheeky one. 'Ow!' cried Avril as she felt something plucking at the pants of her costume. The phanits roared with laughter and gave the young elephant a slap of rebuke. We also discovered that several had ticklish feet. 'Be careful, they can kick,' warned Kamal, 'and don't laugh at them or they'll spray you.' It seemed odd that being unable to laugh, elephants disapprove of it. Then I remembered my mother's warning to me as a boy. 'Watch out if he grins,' she said of my pet monkey, 'it means he's afraid and might bite.' One day I ignored her advice and got a bite that almost severed my jugular vein. Perhaps the contortion of the human face means something different to a jumbo.

I have never seen animals so blatantly enjoying themselves. Only Luksmi washed alone; she had a strong dislike of Chan Chan and kept away from the group, like the dignified old lady that she was. As Honey Blossom was the 'command' elephant I rode her with Kamal, and she seemed to accept me quite happily. 'Talk to her, sahib, then she will know you,' he advised. We also discovered how our mounts talked to each other in low rumbles, seeming to come from deep in their bellies, which made their bodies shudder. However, when they became excited they would throw up their trunks, flap their ears and let out an ear-splitting trumpet.

The afternoon search produced no new sightings and it was a weary team that climbed down when we returned to camp. Seven hours in a howdah leaves one stiff and aching. However, Mahendra's chicken curry soon cheered us up and a three-man team went out with the image intensifier to see if they could spot the tiger. In camp the rest of us enjoyed a restful evening. Bent over his microscope, Mark examined the day's collection, giving a running commentary on his observations. Suddenly he spotted a variety. 'Quick! Who's got the Dichotomous Tables?' he yelled in excitement. 'Never travel without one,' yawned investment expert Chris Mitchinson, who was repairing his pants. Ignoring the remark, Mark returned to his world of field zoology.

The night was noisy, with the racket of frogs, toads and night birds interspersed with the occasional trumpeting from our ladies. Perhaps there was something disturbing them, I thought, just before I slipped into oblivion. I woke once to hear the distant roar of a tiger, but he was far away.

At dawn we discovered one of our ladies had done a runner, much to Kamal's consternation, but before we set out to search, she had returned looking most apologetic. It was late morning when we found what we were seeking. Flattened grass, broken trees and droppings showed where wild elephants had been.

'How old?' I asked.

'Two or three days,' muttered Kamal. 'They are heading west.'

The footprints were ill-defined and around sixteen inches in diameter. That meant we were tracking elephants only eight feet at the shoulder, I calculated, using the formula that gives the approximate height of the elephant as six times the diameter, or twice the circumference, of the forefoot.

By now we had learned to watch for spoor, droppings, scrape marks, scratching on trees and shelters. With the help of the Nepalese naturalists, who were the real experts, we began to identify various creatures from these tell-tale signs. To interpret pug marks and some faint traces of movement took years of training, but it was surprising how quickly our eyes, used to straight lines and strongly contrasted patterns, were adapting to the confused and shadowy world of the jungle. We saw how on soft earth or mud the tracks were exaggerated and for a more reliable spoor one must look on solid ground. If a beast was running on sand its feet were spread wider to give it more support and thus the tracks looked larger than usual.

We learned to tell the difference between various types of deer and wild boar; cats have retractable claws so it is easy to identify them, whereas the track of canids, such as fox, jackal and hyena, all show claw marks.

Small mammals were more difficult. Kamal and his shikaris (hunters) took great pains to explain everything and encourage us. In no time our ears were able to distinguish the various alarm calls. The 'dhank' of a startled sambar, the hoarse alarm coughs of the langur or the piping whistle of the spotted deer all told us something. Sometimes whole flocks of peacocks would join in shrieking chorus until the whole forest resounded. At night the tiger's deep, booming roar sent shivers up my spine, but not as much as the rasping growls of the leopard that sounded so like a bow-saw on hard wood.

I've always had a good sense of smell, and being allergic to cats can soon detect when one has marked its territory with spray from an anal gland. The tiger's scent is strong stuff, but nothing compared to the stink of a civet. The longer one spent in the jungle the more one's senses developed.

The next day we moved our base westwards, watched by herds of beautiful spotted deer whose pale brown coats flecked with white blotches blended them into the forest. The graceful stags, standing around three feet at the shoulder, displayed their sweeping antlers whilst guarding the elegant, long-necked hinds and Bambi-like fawns. In herds of around a dozen or more they roamed everywhere in the reserve. 'Tiger food,' muttered Kamal.

Our new camp was at the edge of a large clearing. Water was short and, as the heat of the day rose and sweat poured out, we found rhino tracks and tiger spoor. By now we had given our quarry a name and called him 'Maila', but although we found some eighteen-inch footprints, of the creature there was no sign.

Jungle living was taking its toll. John Hunt had a tick in his groin, John Campbell was suffering from the runs, Mark had a fever, but he still managed to go out on a night hunt for specimens with his spot lamp.

'Maila is across the river,' shouted the runner from the lodge. 'He was seen by villagers this morning.'

Our spirits rose as we moved further west. Perhaps it was the onset of drier weather, but near the Karnali the game was more numerous. A female nilgai antelope was seen and many types of deer, including whole herds of spotted deer, swarmed around us. Jackals scampered away through the grass and we found tiger tracks everywhere. That night we slept in the comfort of the Karnali lodge and Mark caught a common shrew in the bar.

The next day we decided the Karnali was low enough to try a crossing with our elephants and, in a line, we marched towards the river. Moving through the twenty-foot-high cuckoo grass, we crossed the dried-up marshland, flushing a herd of swamp deer and scattering a gaggle of peahens. At the water's edge the bank was vertical and at least ten feet high. Honey Blossom stopped at the edge and her huge shoulders heaved like pistons as she pushed down the cliff, creating an earthy slope. Then, sinking on to her back knees with legs tucked up under her belly, the lady tobogganed down. The current was slack on this side, but the water rose rapidly until it almost touched the howdah's footrest. Step by step the great cow advanced, feeling the river bed carefully with her feet and, as the flow speeded up, leaning upstream. Like five cruisers on a naval exercise, the line of massive animals waded on slowly, remorselessly, with Luksmi bringing up the rear, urging on the younger beasts.

'We have never taken an elephant across the Karnali before,' confided Chandra.

'Now you tell me – blimey, I thought you did this every day.'

No one had a life jacket. Although we could all swim, I began to wonder what would happen if a jumbo capsized in this fast-flowing, icy waterway. Elephants swim well and would get out, but we'd probably be swept downstream into a series of shallow rapids. However, I need not have worried for without a hitch we reached the far side where the ladies pulled down the bank to make an exit.

All day we searched the tree-covered island for Maila without success. A boatman drifting downriver told of a house in Gola that had been badly damaged two days before by a 'monster elephant' seeking salt. 'It came at night, there was no warning.' Suddenly the wall had collapsed and the trunk came through the gap, 'just like big snake', found the salt bag, tearing it open as the inhabitants fled. Furthermore a watchman asleep by a paddy field had been attacked and seriously injured by the 'devil animal'. We decided to visit the village.

With their usual intelligence, our jumbos again found the easiest way out of the river and heaved their bulky bodies up the bank on to the flood plain. The local children, who had watched our approach in awe, fled screaming towards the houses. They had good reason to fear elephants.

Gola was a linear settlement with thatched houses and farms spread out along the one dusty, tree-lined road. Tulbahadur dismounted and led the way carefully, guiding us through small gates, avoiding damage to irrigation channels. By the time we reached the headman's house the people had become bolder and came close, the children's wild eyes taking in everything about this strange collection of foreigners bedecked with binoculars, notebooks and cameras.

Then Honey Blossom spied a tasty bush and her great trunk rolled out to seize mouthfuls. 'Naughty, naughty,' cried the phanit, whacking her with his cane. Honey Blossom looked forlorn and gave vent to a long fluttering fart. The children bolted in terror. A few minutes later, to make up for her bad behaviour, the old girl picked up the lens cap Chris had dropped and passed it up to him with her trunk.

It was a real relief to stretch our legs and the villagers were eager to show us the damage done by wild elephants and rhino. So, like some royal commission, we strolled into houses, visited the little shop and the mill where an attractive young woman in a bright red sari operated the grain crusher with her foot whilst her children played with a dead chick on the earthen floor. We saw broken walls and fences at which the people pointed, crying, 'Hatti, Hatti.' There were large footprints, although very old, in the paddy fields; undoubtedly some were elephants' but others were rhino. 'Hatti, Tula Hatti,' they kept saying, pointing at the forest. 'Maybe Maila there,' shrugged Tulbahadur, unconvinced by the villagers' vague directions. However, we continued the search.

First we had to cross over to the other side and here the Karnali was wide and fast. The ladies hesitated, Chan Chan trumpeted and dithered. Clearly they didn't like the idea. However, raising her trunk, Honey Blossom, the matriarch, slapped Sundar Kali's backside and purring loudly urged the herd in. 'Get on, you silly things,' she seemed to say. 'We can't hang around here all day.'

The current was swift and as we edged forward it eddied around the elephants' thighs, getting deeper as the water built up against their bellies and they leaned into the flow. Downriver a set of rapids boiled and tumbled. 'Ever tried white-water rafting on an elephant?' enquired John Hunt. We were in line ahead, in midstream, when we came to a halt. By now the water was up to Sundar's eyes and her trunk was acting as a snorkel. The ladies held a conference, discussing the problem in throaty rumblings.

'What's up?' I asked.

As if to answer, Sundar's phanit called back, 'Quicksand, quicksand, go back.'

There was no panic and we reversed out of harm's way. 'Elephants swim, but dangerous for passengers,' said Chandra as we climbed the steep bank.

Out in the flow, a smooth, grey-green creature surfaced. Its pea-sized eye seemed to stare yet I doubt it saw us. Then the Ganges River dolphin slid gracefully below the surface. We were most fortunate to have seen such a rare creature.

The snow-clad Himalayan peaks were easily visible to the north and our attention turned to photographing this incredible sight. So much so that we did not notice the movement on the edge of the jungle to the south. It was Sally who saw it first. 'What on earth's that?' she hissed, pointing to a great dark mound half a mile downstream.

Through the binoculars I could see two big bulls munching away on an island and our much discussed approach plans swung into action. We could not cross the river at this point so, like soldiers stalking the enemy, we used the sparse cover as best as possible, moving downstream to reach a point opposite the tuskers. Three hundred yards and they were still there. At two hundred yards one bull looked up, raised his trunk and sought our scent. His tusks gleamed white in the afternoon sun. Then the shrubs and grass ran out. The last hundred and fifty yards would have to be over open ground and through the river. 'I never saw these before,' whispered Tulbahadur, who was standing at the back of my howdah.

Chan Chan Kali was the first to react to our quarry; her ears came forward as she listened and trembled. Then a deep purring rumbled through her whole body. Across the water the big males browsed on unconcerned. I was about to send our two fastest elephants in an out-flanking movement when something extraordinary happened.

'Look,' said Libby, who had been watching the bulls through her binoculars, 'it's a man.'

Sure enough, a Nepalese in a tattered green shirt and pants was ambling casually over to the huge beasts, carrying a short stick.

'My God, they'll kill him,' muttered John Davies but, as he spoke, the newcomer walked straight up to the biggest elephant and, with a sharp command, demanded its trunk. In a flash he had been lifted up between its gleaming tusks, on to its head.

'Government elephants,' sighed Tulbahadur, and we turned for home.

Passing the Park Warden's headquarters, we popped in to see the crocodile-rearing programme. Mark astounded the warden by vaulting over the barrier and seizing a young man-eater, holding it aloft for all to photograph. Then the three-foot mugger woke up and surprised our herpetologist with a show of its true strength. Mark leapt aside, narrowly escaping its snapping jaws and looking suitably chastened.

Our time in Bardia had run out and all that remained to be done was the 'school photograph'. So with the elephants bathed and decorated with chalk patterns and the humans in relatively clean clothes, we assembled on the lodge lawn. The Nepalese love being photographed and volunteered to take pictures for us; Hari, the barman, proudly took their cameras from each person and stood out in front. Now it was a question of getting the elephants to raise their trunks and everyone to look at the photographer. Instructions in English, Nepalese and Hindi (for the jumbos) went out, and chaos resulted. Sensing the fun, Chan Chan began to trumpet and the others took up the call. The noise was deafening; so much so that the team seated below the bellowing beasts had to cover their ears. 'Film all finished, sahib,' Hari grinned, handing back the cameras.

It had been a memorable trip. The team had worked together

extremely well, the management development had been a success and we had a mass of scientific data on fish, flora and birds. We had measurements of some huge footprints, but we had not seen a single monster.

*Chapter Three*

# THE PEACOCK RIVER

A fEW weeks later I met John Edwards and told him what we had discovered, which was not much.

'Have you ever seen wild elephant in Bardia?' I asked. 'Only once,' he replied thoughtfully, 'that was some years ago when there were few motor roads west of Chitwan, so it took four days of rough travel to reach the Karnali Valley.'

John is a keen angler and a champion mahseer fisherman. Believing that the mighty Karnali River held some whoppers, he set out with his friend, Nick van Gruisen. Going after this great sporting fish is not unlike tiger hunting in that one must stalk one's prey. So it was that John and Nick floated downstream in a canoe with a couple of Tharu boatmen. At a likely stretch Nick hopped out and set to work whilst John and the boatmen waded back upstream in the freezing waist-deep water, pushing the boat up a small rapid. They were aiming for the top of the broken water where an eddy circled back on itself.

Standing well out in the river, John braced himself and then with all the power he could muster, sent his lure looping skyward and watched it drop into the deep water. He started to reel in the line when his hand froze on the wheel, for there, standing right in front of him at the junction of jungle and river, was the biggest tusker he had ever seen in all his years in Asia. He could hardly believe his eyes.

The huge creature had been watching the approach of the boat. It did not move an inch. Indeed, elephants often do this to avoid detection, but the arrival of a twenty-eight-gram Toby spinner within fifteen feet of his trunk was too much. The bull probably thought it had been aimed at him and decided to show these impudent interlopers who was the boss. With a shattering bellow and ears extended, he came charging at them. Water sprayed around his thundering feet. 'Run, sahib, run,' screamed the boatman. Below the rapid Nick had already taken to his heels and John, deciding to abandon his expensive kit in favour of being able to buy a spinner another day, struggled for the canoe. Tumbling in, the brave anglers shot the white water in record time, leaving the angry beast behind. As it stomped back into the forest they had a good look through their binoculars.

'This was no ordinary elephant,' said John. 'What struck us was the very size of the creature and the peculiar dome-shaped head, giving it the appearance of an ice-age mammoth.'

'But where can something as big as that hide?' I asked.

'We searched miles of that jungle,' John smiled. 'There are a thousand square kilometres of forest and high grass in which a hundred elephant could be hidden – and remember, very few Nepalese go into that area, let alone Europeans.'

I realized then that if we were to find the elusive Maila I needed to do a much more detailed study of elephants and their habits. At the same time we started to recruit a new team to return in 1992. Clearly I needed the most experienced Nepalese naturalists and trackers, and John kindly agreed to get us one of the very best, Pradeep Rana. Like Peter Byrne, Pradeep was a hunter turned conservationist; having lived all his life in the wild he knew the Terai and the jungle like his own back garden. His powers of observation and his tracking ability were second to none. 'He thinks like an elephant,' John said, but it was some time before I was to meet this living legend.

To cast our net wider, it was decided to come into Bardia via the Karnali in the hope that we might meet the lost tribe of hunter gatherers known as the Raji, and glean information from them. To get to the river we would drive to Birendranagar in the foothills, then trek with our boats and equipment for three days over the mountains. Although from January to March the water is usually low, it can still be a challenge and so we needed good boatmen too. Mash would come and bring Megh Ale, one of the few who had rafted the powerful river.

I felt a little incentive might prove useful, so we offered the people living around the Bardia reserve a reward for information leading to the discovery of the strange creature. Having laid our plans, I turned my attention back to organizing expeditions for the young with Operation Raleigh.

Raleigh had been run very successfully since 1984 and over 8,000 young men and women had taken part, but, though I found it immensely satisfying, I needed a new stimulus. Working behind a desk soon sapped my enthusiasm and being due to retire from the army in 1991, I had to decide on my future. While lumbering along on Honey Blossom I had time to think.

Back in Britain I lunched with my friends Graham Walker, now Chairman of the Raleigh Trust, and Harbourne Stephen, who was a Trustee, and they kindly invited me to continue directing the operation after my service career ended. It was a tempting offer. Ten years of hard work had gone into this unique enterprise. However, throughout my life I have always been something of an entrepreneur, or maybe a maverick, and having got a project up and running I have moved on. Raleigh was in good shape and it was time for me to find a new challenge.

'But why give up the organization you've spent so long building, now it is well funded?' I pondered. Sitting by the flickering fire with a whisper of the night breeze in the sal trees, I was in a pensive mood. Kipling's 'The Explorer' is the one poem I've read a hundred times:

> Thought to name it for the finder: but that night the Norther found me –
> Froze and killed the plains-bred ponies; so I called the camp Despair
> (It's the Railway Gap today, though). Then my Whisper waked to hound me:–
> 'Something lost behind the Ranges. Over yonder! Go you there!'
>
> Then I knew, the while I doubted – knew His Hand was certain o'er me.
> Still – it might be self-delusion – scores of better men had died –
> I could reach the township living, but . . . He knows what terror tore me . . .

But I didn't . . . But I didn't. I went down the other side.

'The railway' was coming up behind me and somewhere in this dark forest I knew there was something, some incredible beast that I had to find. So I decided to found a new organization to work closely with the Scientific Exploration Society, involving older people in worthwhile challenges. Thus Discovery Expeditions was conceived.

By November we had nine executives looking for a spot of excitement. In fact, two, Chris Burke and John Hunt, had been with us the previous year. Sally marshalled us all to the usual preparatory weekend at Hawley Lake.

Doc John, John Campbell and Mark O'Shea also joined us again so, in the end, the group was fourteen strong. All came from Britain except John Cochrane, a well-built Zimbabwean businessman who, having seen most African game, was keen to meet some of the Asian varieties. Rod Barnes, landlord of the Jolly Woodman at Burnham, adored dolphins and was eager to see the rare Ganges River variety. Janet Charge, a management consultant, was a reptile enthusiast and would assist Mark. Sheena Cox managed a string of Our Price record shops for W. H. Smith, and fair-skinned accountant Ian Mitchell was determined to catch a mahseer. Malcolm Procter, a cheerful, blunt, northern company director, loved mucking about in boats and would become our 'Admiral'. The ornithologist was to be Inspector David Warren of the Humberside Constabulary. Sally, helped by Janet and Sheena, would do a study of the women living along the river. Our ages ranged from thirty-one to fifty-five, but there was a spirit of youthful enthusiasm and great optimism. I felt that if anyone could solve this mystery it would be this group.

In tackling the Karnali and the long march to the river, the expedition was going to be more demanding than the previous sortie, so we had selected personnel with care. Throughout the winter I jogged around the muddy Dorset fields and, when in London, swam at the Royal Automobile Club. By mid-February I felt pretty fit and all was set. As the river would be at its lowest in the first three months of the year, I calculated it should be reasonably safe to take comparative novices down it, although we would need experienced boatmen. Reaching Bardia in March, the grass cutting and burning should be over so the chances of finding undisturbed game were good.

'I simply can't believe it,' Judith was saying as she hung up the phone.

'What's up?' I enquired.

'That was Sally. Royal Nepal Airlines have gone on strike again, but she has it under control.'

Sally was at her best in a crisis and had adeptly managed to re-book us on Emirate Airlines. My old pal, Simon Ames, met us at Gatwick to tape an interview for Radio Mercury before we embarked and, sensing our frustration, the Emirates cabin staff did all they could to make us comfortable and after a glass of wine, passable by any standards, I heaved my bulging briefcase on to my lap.

I never have enough time to read and long air flights are the ideal opportunity to catch up. So as we droned above the endless expanse of cotton wool our researcher's meticulous notes took my attention. In the next seat Sally was dozing. Nearby, Mark O'Shea's tales of extraordinary reptiles and his hair-raising close encounters were entertaining some of the team and clearly worrying an old nun who sat fidgeting with her rosary.

The researcher had done a good job. Quotes from *The Asian Elephant – Ecology and Management* by Sukumar and *The Guinness Book of Animal Facts and Feats* were all neatly arranged for me to digest.

As far as giant Asian elephants were concerned, some of the largest beasts had been seen in Sri Lanka. William Murray, a police officer, killed a notorious rogue elephant in March 1882. On examination, its head and body were found to be covered with healed bullet wounds. No fewer than seven rounds had penetrated the poor creature before the fatal shots. No wonder it was bad tempered. Its left tusk had been broken off in a fight with a rival five years before its death and was found in the jungle by natives. Although this piece of ivory only had a circumference of thirteen inches at the base, and the elephant's height had not been measured, he was clearly a big fellow. But as I had already discovered, the record of eleven feet and one inch had gone to Mr Varian.

Researching Nepalese accounts of giant elephants, I read that a captured tusker named Hari Prased had been owned by the Maharajah of Nepal and was recorded in 1957 as measuring ten feet and nine inches at the shoulder. In the only picture I found, Hari Prased's head was hidden beneath layers of ornate decoration and the fact that the photograph had been taken from ground level made it impossible to distinguish the shape of the body.

Yet despite the historical evidence, contemporary experts on wildlife were sceptical of our chances of finding mammoth in Nepal. One person who knew more than most about wildlife everywhere, but especially in Nepal, was my old friend Dieter Plage, a top wildlife cameraman with Survival Anglia. Looking at Sara Bampfylde's photos he had shaken his head. 'I've been to Bardia several times to film tiger,' he said, 'but I've never seen anything like this. I don't think there are even any wild elephants there.' Alas, Dieter couldn't join us and sadly we never met again. He died two years later falling from a small airship whilst filming rhino in Indonesia.

The new airport at Delhi was a great improvement but still required patience to survive it. In theory, the system is that on arrival at the gate, transit passengers are met by a representative of the airline on which they have arrived who should gather those going directly to Nepal into a waiting area at the foot of the stairs. 'For Pete's sake don't go through health and immigration,' John Edwards had said in his last phone call. 'Wait in the seated area at the foot of the stairs. On no account must you enter India.'

A helpful Emirates lady took us to the stairs, smiled sweetly and left. We watched anxiously as the hall emptied; there was no sign of officialdom, no baggage, no airline staff, only Mark describing a meeting with a rattlesnake in the West Midlands Safari Park at the top of his voice. Finally, a weary Sikh in a blue uniform strolled into view and seated himself at a nearby desk. 'Passports,' he groaned, and we queued up.

'Where are our bags?' I asked.

'They will come sir, never fear,' he said.

The expedition members were now growing anxious. Thoughts of weeks in the jungle without a change of pants were flashing through the ladies' minds when a couple of dishevelled porters wheeled in the baggage. By a miracle it was all there. Fanning ourselves with our passports and bleating 'Kathmandu, Kathmandu' we trooped to the Royal Nepal check-in.

'Make sure all batteries and penknives are in hold baggage,' John had cautioned. 'Indian security officials are convinced anyone with batteries of any sort is a potential bomb maker.' So there was some hurried repacking. We were still grumbling about the stupidity of all this when who should appear but John himself. Being due to go to Kathmandu, he had got on our flight and soon we were on the final leg of the journey.

'What news from Bardia?' I asked as we squeezed into seats designed for a Nepalese dwarf rather than a beefy Britisher.

'Well,' yawned John, 'there is a story of a village house being attacked and a farmer who got in the way of the beast being crushed. Also the tiger population is increasing and several females have cubs. You will have to be careful.'

At Kathmandu the smiling faces of Mash and Megh gladdened our hearts. 'Namaste, John, namaste!' they cried. 'Welcome, everyone.' Traditional garlands of sweet-smelling flowers were draped about our necks and spirits rose; it had been a long haul.

Ever since my first intercontinental flight I have been fascinated by mountains. It is not so much a longing to climb, but the sheer pleasure of gazing in awe at their beauty and majesty. So it was that February morning in 1992, as we watched the procession of icy ramparts sliding past the Boeing's windows. I could feel the cold rising through the floor and the biting winds seemed to chill me. I shivered and shook my head, muttering, 'incredible', even though I had been on the early-morning scenic flight to Everest before.

Take-off had been delayed by mist but now the air was crystal clear and the jagged peaks of the mountains stood out in stark outline against the deep blue sky. A plume of snow billowed from the top of Mount Everest as our cameras clicked away. There is something wonderfully inspiring and refreshing about the Himalayas. It was a splendid way to start an expedition and we all felt the curtain had been raised on a great adventure.

Briefing and shopping over, we enjoyed the almost traditional get together. Lisa again laid on everything at her house. How her sons, Sangay and Rinchen, had grown! Their wicked, enticing smiles bewitched us as they passed around the cocktail snacks. Other old friends were there: Gurkha Captain Pratap Singh Limbu, who had led us through the infamous Darien Gap in 1972, was as tall and straight of back as ever, author Toby Sinclair, who had done so much to help me organize Operation Drake in 1978, and Lisa's sister Joanna came with fascinating tales of India. Once again I felt they were all being too polite to express doubts about our quest. Indeed, I might have felt easier if someone had said, 'Mammoths? You must be out of your mind!' Also at the party was the legendary Pradeep Rana. A striking, well-built man with aristocratic features and manners, he exuded confidence and was comfortable in his executive role. He spoke rapidly, his eyes darting about like the animals he knew so much about. There was an air of professionalism about him that I liked.

It was more likely that the Paludrine tablets had made me feel sick than the supper at Rum Doodle's in Kathmandu, and I made a note in my log to suggest to ICI that they coat these anti-malarial pills with sugar. However, by the time our bus reached the Blue Heaven Café on the banks of the Trisuli next day, I felt better. This watering hole boasted loos, although the bushes offered distinctly preferable facilities with a lovely view of the river and the mountains.

That night's stop at the Tharu village, with the usual dancing, was accompanied by Doc John and Sally discussing the local women's habit of serving food to their men with their feet. This strange custom goes back to the time when most of the Tharu husbands had been killed fighting the Moslem invaders in Rajastan. Their women had fled for safety to the northern jungles of India and here, in desperation, they had married their servants. The habit of serving them with their feet is said to be a sign of the higher status of the women.

The Tharus are a fascinating people, for they live in one of the

most unhealthy parts of Nepal, the Terai, known for the high
incidence of malaria throughout most of the year, but they are
said to have developed immunity to the disease. Sadly, the malaria eradication programme has had a detrimental effect on the
lives of these simple, gentle people for, as the disease has been
stamped out with DDT, so hill people have moved in and virgin
forests have been replaced by fields of crops. Thus their remote
homeland is being opened up day by day. In spite of appearing
to be undernourished, they are surprisingly strong people and
capable of great feats of endurance. It was the Tharu who became
skilled at capturing the wild elephants that live in their Terai and
it is therefore natural that most mahouts, or phanits as they are
called in Nepal, are Tharus.

As one might expect, they have a host of tales to tell. In 1844
a huge rogue elephant was reported to have taken at least a
hundred human lives in the region. A Nepalese Army expedition,
equipped with two six-pounder cannon, was sent to destroy it,
but after a disastrous meeting the soldiers fled, leaving the giant
tossing their artillery around the forest. Greatly perturbed, the
King asked Captain Thomas Smith of the British Resident's Guard
to kill the creature, warning him it was a shaitan (devil) and he
should not get too close. Up to that date no Westerners had been
permitted to hunt in the Terai, but the gallant captain set out
with a powerful muzzle loader and a good supply of powder and
shot. Using Tharu trackers and riding a tame elephant, he soon
found evidence of the 'devil's' work.

At the edge of the forest he came upon the mutilated remains
of an unfortunate Brahman, pounded to pulp. Shortly afterwards
the monster turned up, coming on them in a rush, attacking
Smith's elephant. A terrible battle took place, the two great beasts
crossing tusks and pushing each other like infuriated rams. The
rogue soon got the upper hand and the captain, having lost his
mount, was left to continue the fight on foot. For several hours
they circled each other in the humid sal forest, hunter and hunted
frequently changing positions. Firing and re-loading the heavy
musket, bleeding from cracked, parched lips, Smith prayed that
his adversary would retire and allow him rest. But although blood
was pouring from a dozen wounds, the enormous animal continued to stalk him until finally a heavy musket ball penetrated

a vital organ which brought the tusker to his knees. The King rewarded Smith with a splendid khilut (coat of honour).

There were also vague accounts of massive tame elephants being used by one of the Rana family to carry building material up into the mountains where he was creating a palace, but at this time I could find little to substantiate the story.

However, in my researcher's notes I read that in 1938 a tiger hunt was arranged for His Highness the Maharajah of Nepal with the Viceroy of India, Lord Linlithgow, and his guests. On 5 December a huge bull walked into their camp. The next morning he was there again but, being left in peace, returned to the jungle. Later, a band was asked to play before the Viceroy's tent. The sixty musicians paraded up and down and then marched off to their own encampment, their 'rompy-pom' music echoing through the forest. Rounding a bend in the trail they came face to face with the huge tusker, which blasted them with a shrill trumpet. Those at the front cried, 'Back', and those at the back cried, 'On'. As a result the entire party became a solid entangled mass of men and musical instruments. The elephant looked on in surprise and, when a group of orderlies arrived, it was standing, its head slightly cocked to one side, gazing at the writhing mass. Then, giving a loud rumble, it ambled off into the cover whilst the bandsmen fled.

There are even earlier accounts of problems with elephants: in the seventeenth century, Tavernier, a famous Grand Jeweller to the Indian Emperor, recorded an incident on his trek to Tibet during which his caravan suffered much from the overgrown nature of the track and the large number of wild elephants. 'The merchants got little sleep at night and were obliged to surround themselves with fires and to frighten off wild beasts by loosing off their muskets.'* An amusing description is given of an elephant which marched noiselessly upon the caravan, not for the purpose of doing any harm to men, but to carry off the stores, such as bags of rice or flour or pots of butter.

Another note told me that earlier in the same century a certain Father Gruebar recorded that the King of Morang had paid the Mogul Emperors a considerable annual tribute and seven ele-

---

* Percival Langdon, *Nepal*, vol. 2 (Constable, 1928)

phants. I learned that the Kingdom of Morang had protruded from Nepal into Tibet. Perhaps some descendants of these elephants had survived at high altitude, I pondered. If so, could they, like the wild yak, have developed hair?

Further study revealed the account of a Gurkha army invading Tibet in the eighteenth century. They took along tame elephants and after their surrender handed these over as a tribute. Perhaps these were the ones Julian Freeman-Attwood referred to when we discussed it on our march.

It was a damp misty morning as we pulled out of the Tharu lodge. Five punctures and several hours later, our bus turned north at the border town of Nepalganj. Crossing the Bheri River at last light, we drove up into the hills. It was after 8 p.m. when we reached Birendranagar where the road ended. As we climbed out of the vehicle, winking lamps and flickering fires showed the outline of a large sprawling town. The raft crews had gone ahead.

Cramped and stiff from the journey, it was joy to find the tents were up. Mash greeted us with hot tea and chocolate laced with rum, followed by a tasty stew and perfectly cooked rice. He had even remembered my favourite sauce – chilli garlic. The monsoon makes trekking almost impossible in the period from June to September when the rivers are in dangerous spate. Insects, especially the mosquitoes, are present in swarms at this time. But from December to February the trails are dry, rivers moderate, skies clear and, although the nights can be cold, the temperature at lower altitudes is like a late spring in Britain.

Again a cool misty dawn greeted me as I unzipped the mosquito net and crawled from my tent at 7 a.m. Glancing at my pocket thermometer, I saw the air temperature was 47°F. Thanks to barking dogs and long-distance drivers summoning their passengers by continuous hooting, little sleep had been possible after five, but a shower in the tepid water of a nearby holy spring raised morale. Beneath a vast banyan tree was a steaming, man-made pool inhabited by large, fat carp. Water spilled out through ornamental lead pipes on to the bathers who had come to cleanse themselves in the sacred waters. Said to be one of the King's favourite places, Birendranagar is the regional capital with extensive shops and an army unit whose bugle call was sounding as we packed up camp.

The porters were slow in getting organized but the first few hours of the trek are often frustrating; it is then that one remembers all the items that have been forgotten. There was apprehension about the climb ahead, but it was too late to change plans and we marched off towards the hills, passing a funeral procession at the edge of town. The mourners seemed pretty cheerful, showing little emotion as they swung along with the corpse slung from a pole.

We headed northward along a good trail climbing up through groves of eucalyptus, sal and pine, and each group prepared its own map which would later produce a trekking chart of the area. The porters forged ahead of us carrying the Avon rafts, rations, tents, and kit. As the day wore on it grew hotter as the mist evaporated and from a ridge at 5,000 feet the view was magnificent. John Hunt, as fit as ever, and Mark raced ahead like boys on a school outing. John found the ruins of an old fort and, near the village of Ramdikhana, we saw a strange, inscribed pillar dating back to the tenth century. Camping on some terraces that night, we sang around the fire – 'Land of Hope and Glory', 'Jerusalem', 'The Road to Mandalay', 'On Ilkley Moor' . . . and many more old favourites. Lubrication with a little J&B Rare did wonders for the voice.

One or two of us, including myself, had the runs and out came the Lomotil. The next day I marched with a roll of loo paper to hand.

Pradeep Rana's expert knowledge of the flora and fauna added interest as we clambered up and down the slopes. He also demonstrated how to recognize animals from their tracks and claw marks on trees. It was a long and tiring day, but the next was even harder and hotter. Several of our team found the going tough, but we helped each other and greatly appreciated a little tea house at Chanteri, where we rested in the shade of a convenient pipal tree. Here we lunched before making the final descent. Lying full length in warm sun I thought how often I had blessed these shady trees that one frequently finds at the top of a steep ascent. Sometimes stone platforms or chautaara are built around the trunk to provide a cool bed for tired travellers. These are kept clean and in good repair by local people who receive what amounts to religious goody points for the service.

The Lord Buddha is said to have gained enlightenment whilst resting beneath a pipal tree. After a long and exhausting haul up a slope, the sense of relief and wellbeing on reaching these stopping places does induce a sort of euphoria. In a few moments I was sound asleep and, according to my friends, snored loudly and contentedly for ten minutes.

These places can also be a meeting point for a village and traditionally it is a favourite spot for young lovers. There is often a banyan tree next to the pipal. Indeed, at the start of our climb at the holy spring in Birendranagar there was such a combination. The banyan's round leaves are said to represent the female whilst the pipal with its pointed leaves is the male. Local gods are said to dwell in the chautaara and the goddess Lakshmi and her husband Vishnu are supposed to visit them.

The pipal is sacred to the Hindus and infertile women pray at it. Many that I had seen on my treks in Nepal had been anointed with rice, flowers and vermilion. The banyan is also worshipped and to cut either tree would cause instant ill fortune.

'Listen,' said Mash, as the wind rustled the leaves over our heads. 'They say that is the movement of invisible spirits.'

I felt totally revived and uplifted when we started out again.

As we crossed the ridge, the turquoise blue ribbon of the Karnali or Peacock River came into view, winding through a rocky canyon 700 feet below us. As we paused to drink in our first sight of the impressive waterway we had come so far to ride, two tiny women marched toward us carrying enormous bundles of wood. We tried to lift one and could hardly shift it.

Later, camped on the soft, fine sand beside the river, we broke out the fishing gear. The Shakespeare Company had kindly provided us with telescopic rods, and Farlow's had given us accessories which helped us to supplement our diet on this and many expeditions in the future. The light went early in the gorge and we pulled on sweaters and long pants to shut out the evening chill and the sandflies. Ahead of us lay eight days rafting the tumbling rapids of a river that few foreigners had seen and a journey through a sparsely populated pristine wilderness.

*Chapter Four*

# KARNALI CAMP

PRADEEP was examining tracks along the water's edge when I went out for an early morning stroll.

'Tiger?' I enquired.

'No, just otter,' he grinned, pointing out the details of the five webbed toes and claws in the mud.

The dew was still heavy on my tent as we struck camp. It would be several hours before the sun peeped into the canyons. The boat boys had walked down the bank to assess the first rapid and, standing on the polished black boulders, they pointed and gesticulated. My mind went back sixteen years, to the time when I brought the first white-water boat to Nepal. Rafting was unknown in the Himalayas and few Nepalese could even swim. After a near capsize whilst running the Trisuli River, the two Sherpas John Edwards had brought with him waded ashore, took off their life jackets and announced, 'Everest any time, but this is madness!' Yet now there were dozens of skilled Nepalese rafters and men like Mash Thapa, Megh Ale, Tej Rana and Sundar Thapa, rated amongst the best in the world.

In under an hour the camp had disappeared into deep rubberized kit bags and watertight boxes. 'This is not like the Bheri; although the river level is down you can expect some big waves,' cautioned Megh, our sailing master, as he briefed us on the perils and techniques of white-water rafting. 'Technically it is going to be difficult. We must manoeuvre the boats quickly to avoid rocks.'

'What's the largest rapid?' asked John Cochrane.

'Grade five plus, I expect,' smiled Megh.

'What's above that?' enquired Sheena.

'Six – and that's almost impossible,' came the encouraging reply.

The crews needed no second bidding to secure everything well and check waterproof bags and camera cases. Last of all we donned protective clothing: spray suits, bulbous life jackets, helmets, gloves and canvas shoes. Some wore lightweight wet suits but I reckoned these would prove terribly hot once the sun reached into the gorge.

John Hunt checked his video camera and Malcolm Proctor, assuming his role as 'Admiral', got us aboard. Sally looked apprehensive; she was not fond of boating.

Settling into the bow of Megh's Avon, I stowed my main camera equipment in the waterproof plastic barrel lashed securely to the boat and adjusted the strap on my helmet. Although we were still in shadow, it was already boiling hot in our spray suits and life jackets. Like a pilot doing pre-flight checks I went through the navigation and recording gear: binoculars – waterproof Bausch & Lomb, compasses – Silva sighting, map case, camera – Nikon AF35 waterproof, sunglasses – unbreakable, notebook – also waterproof. Everything electrical and mechanical had to be sealed in plastic bags to keep out water and, worse still, the fine silica dust that got in through the smallest joint.

'Let's go,' sang out Megh. 'Let's go,' the raft boys echoed. 'Cast off,' commanded Admiral Procter and the grey boats slid effortlessly into the turquoise torrent. I felt a small surge of excitement; it was always the same at the start of a rafting expedition on a new river. 'Just like going to the moon,' I thought. 'There's no turning back; you can't paddle upstream.' Memories of that day twenty-four years before when we had started the Blue Nile Expedition in Ethiopia came flooding back. Then we had outboard motors, but even they could make no headway against the turbulent current that had borne us into the black basalt gorges.

'How about a bearing then, John?' chided Sally, sitting poised, the ever efficient PA, even if she were now swathed in waterproof clothes and crash hat.

'Two hundred and seventy-five degrees to the lone tree by the square black rock on the left,' I replied.

'Four hundred yards,' cried Malcolm, estimating the distance on the first leg of our traverse that would eventually become the authoritative chart of the river.

'Rapid coming up,' warned Megh, muscles flexing as he angled the stern across the current. Ahead a thin line of white marked the start of a cataract. Approaching the lip, the water slowed and for a few seconds we peered into the swirling, tossing waves. We were perfectly positioned. 'Hold on tight,' yelled our skipper as, lifted by some invisible force, the craft hurtled down the slope straight at the curling stopper waves. We struck them head on and icy green water cascaded over us. More than a pint must have gone down my collar. 'Damn,' I swore, having forgotten to do up my Velcro neck-fastener. But now we were through, bumping along among smaller waves as we shot downriver, the self-bailing floor draining the surplus water away, but always leaving some in the bottom of the boat. 'Grade three plus,' called Megh, pulling us into an eddy by the bank. There was just time for me to get my long lens out of the barrel and use the motor drive in my Nikon to cover the passage of the following raft. Paddles flashed, 'Yippee' they yelled like excited children as they broke through the foaming water.

White-water rafting is one of the greatest thrills, whether one is careering down the mighty Zaire or drifting silently past a herd of hippo on the Zambesi. The advantage it has over skiing or rock climbing is that anyone can take part and you don't need weeks of training. With the protection of life jacket and helmet, you don't even have to swim. 'Bad swimmers make good boatmen,' muttered veteran rafter Jim Masters after a splendid day on the Colorado River many years ago.

There are many types of rig; some paddled by all the occupants, possibly with a stern-mounted helmsman on a pair of long oars, and others where all the work is done by a centrally seated oarsman. The latter type is ideal for parties such as ours, engaged in mapping or scientific observation. Whatever the arrangement, the skipper or helmsman is in command and his orders have to be obeyed instantly. To position a raft to safely navigate a boulder-strewn rapid or to avoid a gaping hole in the river requires good prediction and strong muscles. Once you are committed you can't go back, so teamwork is all important. But the real skill is to be able to read the river and to recognize danger signs. Whilst rafting is exhilarating, it is not dangerous. Compared with mountaineering or skiing, there are far fewer accidents and injuries. Having been over the side myself a few times I have never felt seriously at risk and the only damage I sustained was due to my stupidity in accidentally wedging an oar between two rocks on the Trisuli, which resulted in my broken nose. Indeed, you don't have to be especially fit, although I always make an effort to get myself in shape before an expedition because I then enjoy it more.

Being tossed out in a Nepalese river can leave you jolly cold, but all you need do is float downstream on your back with your legs up to fend off rocks. You will be surprised that once out of the full power of the rapid, you move quite slowly and can usually swim to the side. However, it may be difficult to climb out on the polished rocks and it is more usual to be picked up by another boat.

The morning passed quickly with some sporting rapids and by noon we were ready for lunch. The boys found a beach of virgin sand and we tucked into a delicious salad and pasties which seemed to have appeared from nowhere. 'How on earth do they do it?' queried our ornithologist David Warren, a youthful Hull police inspector, as he took a second helping. Inspector Warren's bird list was growing by the minute as we all reported sightings.

As the day wore on, the rapids increased in severity and at 4.30 p.m. we hit a grade four in the deep shadows of a sinister canyon. The sun had long gone and we shivered from the drenching as we set up camp. It had been a long day and by 9.00 p.m. most of the team was asleep. Only Sally and I struggled on, plotting the day's run in the chart record.

It was the sort of night entomologists dream about; every shape and size of flying creature seemed determined to commit hara-kiri on our hurricane lantern. At the same time, they tried to make a meal of us and I gave up in despair, retiring to the protection of my mossie net.

'Happy new month,' cried some joker as I tipped a mug of icy water over myself at dawn – it was Sunday, 1 March.

The gorge seemed to be closing in. 'There's a big rapid coming up, shortly after we get to Junglyghat,' confided Megh. 'We call it the House of God.'

Reaching Junglyghat, it made a change to see people again for although the hillsides echoed with the sound of communicating whistles we could rarely make out those responsible, concealed amongst the vegetation. At the village we bought a rather thin chicken which perched itself happily on top of the waterproof bags in the stores boat and rode through the rapids without a care in the world. 'I suppose it's enjoying its last few hours,' grinned John Cochrane, who guessed correctly that the chicken was to be our supper.

Back on board, the roar from the House of God was clearly audible as we rounded the bend. We pulled in and went forward over the jumbled rocks on foot to recce. Megh and his boys deliberated long and at last said, 'Too risky – we'll line it.' We could see their point; there was a massive boulder mid-river with a huge hole behind it where the entire flow seemed to sweep down into the abyss. I doubted if we could avoid this hazard.

An excited band of locals had come down from the hills and was squatting on the bank in anticipation. 'Raji?' I asked an old man with a face like a walnut. He waved his hand downriver, but his response to 'Hatti?' (elephant) was a shake of his head, so I turned my attention to photographing the operation of lining through the rapid.

The boys had run out an old climbing rope along the bank and hitched each unmanned raft to it with carabiners. As the restrained boats slid downstream, the crewmen leapt like young antelope from rock to rock and whenever a vessel seemed likely to snag, they rushed into the shallows to push it clear. Megh's powerful voice yelled commands above the roar of water and the first two rafts bounced safely through. 'They certainly know their job,' commented Malcolm, sitting beside me on the warm basalt. But the stores boat seemed to move more slowly, possibly due to its extra weight. Suddenly a carabiner caught on a knot in the line and before anyone could free it, the craft had swung sideways into a powerful stopper wave. Pounded by tons of icy water and held back by the line, the inflatable thrashed wildly in the tumbling waves. A red plastic bucket broke away from the cargo and bobbed downstream. Soon it was joined by an oar, a spare life jacket and a pair of boots. 'My God, she's breaking up,' cried Malcolm as we watched impotently.

Through my binoculars I saw Megh and Mark O'Shea running into the river. Both were clad in wet suits, but to leap into this torrent was a very risky business. However, Megh's pride would not allow him to lose a boat, and anyway, a new one would cost several years' pay. I saw his muscular legs bend and flex as he catapulted himself into the current and struck out for the raft. Up to his neck at the water's edge, Mark pulled in what slack he could on the line and then Megh was aboard, wrestling with the slings. Suddenly the boat was free and through the stopper. Riding it like a runaway horse, Megh brought it safely into the bank. 'Phew, that was close,' muttered John Hunt, who had videoed the action.

Drifting round the corner we came across a pack of rhesus monkeys bathing. Their yellow-brown coats glistened with water and their pink faces made them look like overclad holidaymakers paddling on the beach at Brighton. Like the langur monkeys we had seen earlier doing acrobatics in the trees, they took little notice of us. Clearly man was a rarity here, for the monkeys showed no fear of us.

By the time we made camp most of the items lost in the accident had been recovered; the raft itself was hardly damaged. The Avon really deserves the description we gave it on the Blue Nile: 'the toughest boat in the world.' Tragically, however, the plastic container of Kukri rum had leaked. 'Why don't they fit airtight zips to the thwarts as we did on the Nile?' I pondered. 'Then we could stow kit in them and reduce the risk of losing stores in a capsize.' I scribbled in my waterproof notebook to remind myself to raise this with Avon Inflatables.

That night, Megh gave me more names for the grade three plus rapids: 'Humans for Lunch', 'Flip and Strip', 'Juicer', 'Freight Train', and for some strange reason, 'Jailhouse Rock'. Gone are the days when mountains and rivers were given noble titles or named after men of great deeds!

In spite of our precautions, the exceptionally fine dust on the beach was getting into everything, especially cameras, and it was irritating our lungs; many of us had developed coughs and colds by the time we reached Totalighat. Here a well-built suspension footbridge spanned the Karnali and we paused at a cluster of mud brick houses. The whereabouts of the Raji was still 'downstream', but when I said 'Hatti?' hands pointed south over the mountains. We waved farewell and sailed on into an uninhabited canyon of red rock, through which the river hissed and swirled as it passed between cliffs with tumbling, picturesque waterfalls.

The Red Gorge, as we called it on our map, ended at the junction with the Seti River, one of the Karnali's main tributaries. We stopped here for lunch, the fine sand baking hot under our feet as we hauled our gear up the pristine beach. Pradeep managed to obtain some rakshi, a local liquor made from fermented rice and millet, which gave us frightful headaches, and he also got us a goat and some chickens.

The valley had opened out and with the full benefit of the sun, the temperature had soared to 86°F. While the gear was being mended, we lazed and relaxed, watching the parade of colourful birds flying low along the river. Megh beheaded the goat with one slice of his razor-sharp kukri and, to appease the squeamish, John Hunt stuck its head back on by reversing the video film.

We stayed at this spot for a day, to examine the flora and fauna, while Mark netted fish to add to his collection for the Natural History Museum. Two groups set out to explore the valley. Guided by a villager, we puffed and panted up the slopes to see our first evidence of game – tracks of deer and pig. Then, pressing on through the forest, we heard someone banging on a tree. 'What on earth's that?' I started to say when David Warren pointed excitedly ahead. An enormous grey bird wobbled awkwardly through the trees with a strange cry like 'we-kuk-kuk-kuk'.

'It's a great slaty woodpecker,' cried the policeman, as if he had caught a much-wanted villain after a long hunt. 'They are very scarce.'

At Papighat, a hamlet on the south bank, we came across a crop of marijuana and found the people using many herbal medicines; they took acacia juice as an antiseptic, the bark of the sal tree as a painkiller, and we learned that the 'tatoru' could produce hallucinations. There were also some fascinating craftsmen at work. We saw a blacksmith sitting on his heels, spinning a four-spoked bicycle wheel with one hand to drive a small encased turbine. This blew air into clay bellows, from which it exited through a two-inch hole on to a bed of white-hot glowing charcoal, in which the smith fashioned sickles, adzes, ploughs and the like.

But there was still no sign of the lost tribe nor any strange giant beasts. That night Janet Charge produced a bottle of Drambuie and taped music which, after the rakshi 'paintstripper', was a real tonic. Crawling into my tent to listen to the BBC news, I unzipped the padded bag which carried the radio. To my surprise something scuttled out and ran on to my sleeve. It was a two-inch, black and very agitated scorpion. The important thing was not to provoke it for, unlike the one Mark O'Shea had picked up in Nepalganj, this fellow's sting was completely intact. Venom from it paralyses and kills any prey the scorpion captures with its claws. The victim is then torn apart by the jaws and eaten piecemeal. I'd learned this from my friend the naturalist K. K. Gurung at Chitwan years before. Watching the evil-looking creature perched on my shirt with his tail erect and threatening, I tried to remember what else KK had said. All I could recall was that, when mating, the happy couple dance round pincer to pincer until the male guides the lady to his sperm sac, which he has deposited in front of her like some tempting titbit. Mating often ends with the female consuming her partner. 'Just like some couples I've met,' I thought as I watched the beast. He hadn't moved, nor had I. I was thinking that whilst it might make biological sense it was pretty hard on the male who has to sacrifice his body to provide loads of protein to bring up the brood. His only recompense is that his genes get passed on. At that moment my head torch flickered and died. The battery had given up. 'Bugger,' I swore, under my breath so as not to disturb my visitor.

The tent door was zipped up and it was pitch black inside. 'Now what?' I wondered. The scorpion wouldn't kill me, but it would be a bloody painful sting and it was only ten inches from my face.

At that moment a light appeared outside. One of the boys was carrying away the Tilley lamp. 'Just stop there please,' I said firmly. Thankfully the light halted. 'Hold it a moment, my torch has gone out,' I explained. Then with my free hand I reached for my canoe helmet and very, very slowly lowered it on to the beast. I hoped he would hop into the interior of the headgear but through my thin shirt I felt him turn. He was still on my arm.

'Keep the light steady,' I implored my unseen helper, removing the helmet. Next I picked up a jungle boot and offered the open end to the pincers. Scorpions love hiding in boots so perhaps this would work. To my dismay it began to back away under my arm, so in desperation I lifted up the J&B bottle and with finger and thumb unscrewed the cap. Then I very gently poured a few drops of the precious spirit on to my sleeve. Nothing happened for a moment then, very slowly, and I really think slightly unsteadily, the creature crawled off my arm and on to the floor of the tent where I quickly encased him in a Tupperware box.

'Are you all right, sir?' said a voice.

'Yes thank you,' I replied and, having taken the beastie out into the bushes, had a glass of scotch myself.

Thursday, 5 March 1992, dawned warm; '55°F', I scribbled in my log. The river was easier now with rapids graded one or two and we drifted on down the widening waterway. Monkeys were seen frequently along the banks.

Sally saw them first. 'Look!' she cried, 'these people appear quite different to the ones we've met so far.' A group of darker-skinned men, women and children in colourful clothes were smoking fish over wood fires at the river's edge. They had a pitiful appearance and their eyes seemed to plead with us. Pradeep went up to one of the men and exchanged greetings. Then he turned and reported, 'They are Raji.'

So these were the folk we had sought and now we had to find out what they knew of the mysteries of the forest. There were five men, the oldest aged between 40 and 50, three women and two young children. They told us the main village of their tribe was Solta, further downstream. Sitting amongst these shy, simple people we produced sweet biscuits which were clearly appreciated. I noticed how the mothers took a small bite and passed the rest to the children. Their religion is a form of Hindu and strangely they consider it taboo to grow crops. Since the forest had been destroyed, their hunting grounds had gone, and they were forced to give up their nomadic hunter-gatherer exist-ence. Now they lived mainly on fish from the river, often selling their labour to buy food. The problem was, they owned no land and did not understand cultivation. Alcoholism was a growing problem and they pleaded with us to represent their difficulties to the Nepalese government. This I promised to do and then we talked of 'hattis'. There were many large animals in the forest, they said, but few were dangerous. These people had lived in peace with the beasts, only killing for food, but now the jungle had been cleared the wildlife had moved south. Yes, they knew of a giant creature, but were unclear about its description. Apparently it only came out at night and was usually found near the river. Much encouraged by this information, we waved farewell. 'Please tell the government about us – for our children's sake,' they pleaded.

One of the most magnificent sights on the Karnali is a set of weathered rocky outcrops rising skyward like spires of a great church. We decided to call them the Cathedral Rocks and Sheena made a note for the map. The river was deep and slow and only the occasional raucous quack of a brahminy duck and the creak of the oars broke the stillness.

Most people have a private ambition on an expedition: perhaps to see a tiger, or make new friends, to have time to think out personal problems in peace and quiet, or just to enjoy themselves. Accountant Ian Mitchell's ambition was to catch a mahseer and, as we floated along in the gentle current, he optimistically put out a line astern, towing a spinner.

A faint breeze stirred the water's surface as the fish struck. Ian's line went taut, Megh stopped rowing instantly and everyone's attention focused on a patch of sunlit water into which the line led, jerking and straining. 'There,' cried Rod Barnes, whose eyes constantly scanned the water, searching for one of his beloved dolphins. We all saw the splash as the mahseer's beautiful silver and gold shape broke through.

'Looks a good one,' encouraged Megh, bringing the boat into the shore. 'Keep the line tight.'

Twenty minutes later, we came to the conclusion it must be a monster. Ian was playing it from the bank now, gradually coaxing it in. We had no landing nets, so, with a final flourish, he heaved the wriggling beast up the sands.

'Six point four pounds,' proclaimed Mark, reading the scales.

'It feels like sixty,' smiled Ian, looking as pleased as punch.

Mahendra nodded admiringly and popped it into the cooks'

box. 'To hell with the museum collection, this one's for us.'

At Solta we found more Raji people. They too were fisherfolk, but thought longingly of their lost forest homes and spoke of the time when many elephant moved west to east along the foothills and tiger hunted high up on the slopes. They mentioned some areas of jungle remaining along the tributaries to the Karnali. 'Oh Lord, we can't go back now!' I thought, wondering if we should have spent longer examining the Seti Valley. I was still mulling this over when we reached the whirlpool at the Bheri's junction. The vortex swung the fleet around before the great Chisapani gorge closed in on us.

As we emerged, the familiar sight of the grubby little town greeted us. The ferry still plied across the river, but it would soon be replaced by the enormous suspension bridge that even now was inching out from the east bank. I doubted if the people of Chisapani would miss the endless queue of buses and trucks that blocked their narrow high street, belching black fumes every time they shuffled forward a few paces. As we rowed past, the stench of diesel was heavy in the air. Perhaps progress has some benefits.

A huge fish-eating crocodile watched us cruise out of the chasm and into the jungle-covered valley. The last few miles were hard work; a south wind tried to blow us back into the canyons and the river was low, necessitating frequent disembarkation to push the Avons through the shallows. But it was all worth it when we rounded the final bend to meet Mash standing by a line of tents on the top of a high bank overlooking the water.

The setting was idyllic, in a grove of rosewood and acacia trees, looking out over a tributary to the great Karnali River. Each tent had its own bathroom arrangement: a washstand complete with bucket, bowl and towel rail. The dining and seating area was furnished with three log benches and some canvas easy chairs round an open fire. Small coffee tables gave a further touch of comfort and a well-stocked bar provided solace. Hari, the barman, who mixes the finest Bloody Mary in the world, was awaiting us.

As the sun set we met our five lovely ladies coming up from the river. Honey Blossom and her sister Luksmi, with three younger elephants, were to carry us on the next phase of our quest. With raised trunks they sounded a welcome. In the days ahead these lumbering jumbos would transport us through the dark forest. Man Dhoj Rai, Honey Blossom's phanit, nodded a solemn greeting from his position on the cow's neck. A quiet, serious man from east Nepal, he was an experienced hand in his late thirties and, in spite of difficulties of communication, he inspired a feeling of confidence.

'You need a cold beer,' called Megh.

'Too bloody right' shouted big John Cochrane, whose thoughts had often strayed to that very subject over the past ten days.

Pradeep Rana was clearly in charge now, rapping out orders and making sure all was to his liking. The raft boys took a back seat and, watching wide-eyed as the phanits tended their elephants, they fingered the howdah chains and the ankush with respect. This was not their world, but natural curiosity made them eager to ride the big beasts and I promised to take some with us in the morning. As the moon rose over the mountains, Pradeep called 'Dinner' and the Tharu mess staff, brought in from the Karnali Lodge, spread out a mouth-watering selection of dishes on the bamboo serving table.

Well filled, we sank into our canvas armchairs for the evening conference, the Tilley lamp casting deep shadows on the trackers' faces. Our offer of a reward for information leading to a sighting of our quarry had produced results; a spindly-legged farmer had come in with news. Pradeep interpreted, 'Only last night a big elephant destroyed a banana plantation two hours from here.'

'How big?' asked John Cochrane.

'The footprints are very large. You must see for yourself,' said Pradeep.

'I'll go,' volunteered the enthusiastic Marks & Spencer man.

'Any snakes?' enquired Mark hopefully.

'Too cold yet, perhaps a little later,' the Nepalese assured him.

Mark looked sad. 'I'll pay fifteen rupees to anyone who can take me to a snake,' he said. A ripple of interest went through the elephant boys crouching behind us in the darkness. Fifteen rupees was a good incentive. 'But please don't touch it,' went on Mark. 'Leave that to me.' The boys' eyes flashed in the firelight. I guessed Mark would get his serpents.

One by one our team turned in and, as the camp fire died, the moonlight cast deep shadows across the beach. Hari poured me a Scotch and said, 'Goodnight, sir,' then, apart from the glow-worms, I was alone. 'No firm clues to the mystery beast, but we have navigated sixty-eight cataracts, made the first chart of the lower Karnali and produced a mass of information on the fauna and flora. And we found the Raji,' I wrote in my diary.

I was about to turn in when Pradeep appeared from the elephant camp where he had been conferring with the trackers. 'Have a drink,' I offered, but he refused politely and sat down on a log. He looked slightly worried, which was unusual in him. 'Any problems?' I asked. For a moment he was silent; clearly something was on his mind. He was about to answer when Honey Blossom gave a piercing call, fit to waken the dead. We both shot to our feet and looked towards the elephant lines. I could hear Man Dhoj scolding her and after a couple more blasts the old lady quietened down. It was as if we were all on edge, wondering what on earth we might discover in the forest.

'No problems,' grinned Pradeep, tossing a branch on to the fire.

'Tell me about Madu Mala Kali's past,' I said. 'I gather she has a reputation for ill temper.'

'Like most of our elephants, she was born in India,' he replied, 'probably around 1950 – I think she is forty-three now. In the late Seventies she was at Tiger Tops. There was another elephant there called Kristjen Bahadur.'

'Of course,' I interrupted, 'I remember Kristjen Bahadur – he carried my daughter, Emma, and me to meet George the rhino.'

'Well,' continued Pradeep, 'Madu Mala Kali always fought with Kristjen Bahadur and so she also disliked those who worked with him. Elephants can be insanely jealous and if they smell the scent of a rival beast on a man, they will react. One day a mahout named Sankar Kummel walked over from Kristjen Bahadur to do something for her and, without warning, her trunk flashed out like a cobra striking. She hit him a terrible blow, breaking his back. Your friend, Dr Dan Osman, was there. He did all he could for the poor fellow and we evacuated him to India, but eventually he died. Honey Blossom was sent to Bardia; there are not many people here.'

Dan Osman, who had been with us on several expeditions, had told me this sad tale, but until now I had not realized that the aggressor was Honey Blossom. Pradeep poked the fire and a shower of sparks rose skyward. 'She also injured Bhakta Badur Magar and a Tharu as well as Bahadur Tamang,' he went on. 'She is most unpredictable.'

'Well, it's nice to know I'm riding a killer,' I retorted.

'But she is fearless and steady and even if the others bolt, Madu Mala Kali won't let you down,' Pradeep reassured me.

I went to bed thinking about this. There was a tale in India of a Maharajah's favourite elephant seizing its mahout during a parade and stamping him to death. Then the animal had sucked up the bloody mess into his trunk and shot it out all over the startled Maharajah. Apparently the tusker was only saved from execution because the other mahouts in the great man's employment pointed out that the dead man had been incredibly cruel to his elephant and deserved his fate.

Bill Williams, the elephant expert, tells of a tusker killing his rider and then guarding the body for a week, allowing no one near it. However, when the remains had decomposed he lost interest and thereafter behaved perfectly. He was not even on musth.

Another bull gored to death nine riders in fifteen years until Elephant Bill sawed off his tusks as short as possible. Although the operation must have been unbelievably painful, the elephant was allowed to live and became totally placid and well behaved.

In the early part of the night I slept fitfully, constantly awoken by Honey Blossom's insistent calls. To make matters worse, the rest of the ladies took up the bellowing. In the wild, elephants will sound off to protect their calves from marauding predators. If a mother gives birth, a herd will not move on until such time as the new-born calf is strong enough to travel with them. During this period, they will always surround the nursing female and her calf, forming a tight protective ring around them at night. Unable to sleep any more, at 4 a.m. I lit my candle and re-read some of *Heart of the Jungle* by K. K. Gurung.* He told of an extraordinary event at Tiger Tops:

> Domesticated working elephants do not seem to breed very well. At Tiger Tops sporadic matings have been observed over

* K. K. Gurung, *Heart of the Jungle* (André Deutsch/Tiger Tops 1983)

the years since 1965, but only one calf has been born – and that took everybody by surprise. Until the baby actually arrived one night in February 1980, nobody had known for sure that its mother, Durga Kali, was pregnant. Her breasts had been swollen for the past three months, but there had been no other indication that a birth was imminent.

The birth took place soon after midnight. Unfortunately no human saw it, but the whole elephant camp became aware of the new arrival and tremendous trumpetings started. Rup Kali, a close associate of Durga Kali, broke loose from her chains and was evidently most anxious to be near the mother; she was chained back to her own post after great difficulty.

In a wild herd, where all the females are related to one another, some have been known to assist the mother in childbirth. It seems most unlikely that Durga Kali and Rup Kali can be related, so their behaviour was as puzzling as it was interesting. No one could tell if Rup Kali was reacting instinctively, or whether it was sheer curiosity that made her so frantic to be at the mother's side. To this day, she stays close to the mother and calf whenever possible and behaves like an aunt in the wild.

Now the calf is causing problems in his own right. For three years he has kept his mother from working. Soon he will have to be weaned and sent to be educated at the Government elephant camp at Sauraha in the east. No matter how quickly he learns, he will not be fit to carry tourists until he is about fifteen. Only then will he have the physical strength and the nerve to stand his ground in the face of an angry tigress or a charging rhino – and by then he will have cost a great deal of money. With luck, his working life will last at least forty years, from fifteen to fifty-five, and he should live on in retirement for another ten years after that.

The question of what to do with aged elephants also poses difficulties. On moral and emotional grounds the park staff would find it very hard to shoot one. Yet equally, they cannot turn an old stager loose, for an elephant so familiar with human beings might prove a danger to villagers.

I wondered if all the noise heralded a birth and with the book still in my hand fell into a shallow sleep. Honey Blossom's trumpeting cut through my dreams. There was something massive, something malignant, perhaps even supernatural, always lurking just beyond vision in the dense vegetation. What on earth would the next day bring? Perhaps Honey Blossom was having nightmares, too.

## Chapter Five

# SNAKES AND MONSTERS

CLUTCHING his tape measure, John Hunt left at dawn and, moving on foot through the dripping grass, soon picked up fresh tiger pug marks and the spoor of a large rhino. Then his tracker pointed out a vast circular print in the mud. 'Hatti,' he hissed. It was very fresh and water still oozed into the impression as they measured its diameter. 'Twenty-one inches, multiply by six for the shoulder height ... wow, that's ten foot six,' whispered John, calculating the height of the animal by the tested formula. 'A very big elephant.'

Nearby, a thick branch had been wrenched down from a kapok tree, the tender leaves methodically stripped. 'Hatti eat here,' muttered the Tharu, moving cautiously through the tangled undergrowth. It was as well, for only yards away a big black boar was watching them from a patch of shade, his evil eyes unblinking. Fortunately, the fearless four hundred pounder decided they posed no threat and turned away, trotting off with tail erect and hackles bristling. There are few more cunning and dangerous creatures in the Asian forest than a wild boar at bay. Their courage and ferocity is legendary. Some years before, we had just finished dinner at Tiger Tops Lodge when the bell in the bar rang, signalling that an old and sickly goat, tethered as bait, had met its end. Slipping off our shoes, we tiptoed up the covered way to the hide that overlooked the bait, now illuminated by a spotlight. Thirty yards away a large leopard sat with the kill between its paws. Just as it started to feed a black shadow appeared at the edge of the clearing. The cat turned its head, but before it could move I saw the gleam of tusks and a huge boar hurtled across the open ground. Snarls and snorts mingled as the two collided, fur and hair flew, tusk and claw flashed in a furious struggle, but it was the boar that won. Twice the leopard tried to regain his dinner, only to be driven off by its much heavier assailant. Eventually the evil-looking beast settled down to consume the goat, its teeth creating a spine-chilling sound as it ground the bones.

The big footprints led into a grassy phanta beside the river. Not far away a rhino chuffed. The Tharu listened and pointed left, then continued following the massive tracks. By 9.30 a.m. John reckoned they had covered ten miles. The ground game was retreating into cover as the sun's heat grew more intense. Peacocks called and monkeys chattered, but the big animals would now be resting in the shade.

'Twenty-one-inch spoor,' reported John, gulping down a large glass of water. 'Heading east.'

'We'll find Maila tomorrow,' stated Pradeep. 'I'll keep trackers watching the area to make sure we know if he moves.'

The hunt was closing in and I felt our luck was changing. Indeed it was, for Mark acquired his first reptile, a slow-moving water snake trapped in the fishnet.

'Deadly poisonous?' queried Chris Burke, fascinated by Mark's work.

'Mildly,' smiled Mark, handling it with care.

Meanwhile Rod was building a blind from which he could watch for dolphins and, at night, using the image intensifier, he hoped to see other animals coming down to drink in the river. There was a great air of anticipation in the camp as we checked cameras. Every movement in the surrounding bush aroused interest and even the small herd of picturesque spotted deer caused a flurry of excitement.

At moonrise, Rod and Sakali headed off to the blind. 'Don't get eaten or sat on,' we called. It took about half an hour for the publican's eyes to become fully accustomed to the dark. Nothing stirred, but as the camp noises died away and the temperature dropped, he shivered. Quietly opening his hip flask he took a nip of brandy to revive his spirits. Sakali declined, he was listening intently for any tell-tale sounds of approaching game. Across the river an owl hooted, 'zee-gwat, zee-gwat', then all was silent.

Eyes tire fairly quickly when using an intensifier, so they shared the job. It was well into the night when Sakali touched Rod's shoulder. The moon was shrouded in cloud, but the Nepalese was pointing to the right. Now Rod could hear a soft crunch, crunch on the gravel. Something was coming, very near, very slowly, very cautiously. Rod wondered whether the flimsy grass wall of the hide would give any protection. Unable to view the ground to their extreme right, they could only sit tight and wait.

The noise got louder and a pebble rattled. He looked at Sakali appealingly, but the naturalist just put his finger to his lips. Whatever it was, it was extremely close when Rod put the image intensifier up to the observation slot. He could see clearly for fifty yards but there was no sign of an animal.

Ten paces away and just out of view, a two-ton Indian one-horned rhinoceros stood silently scenting the air. He had come for a drink at his pub, little knowing that the landlord of the Jolly Woodman at Burnham was lurking there. Standing over five feet at the shoulder, the ponderous beast remained quite still for several minutes, then decided it was safe to proceed. It passed very close to the slot and Rod almost died of fright. 'All I could see was these enormous armoured plates of its huge body as it crossed in front of the lens,' he gasped when he reached camp. Luckily, the rhino had not seen Rod.

It had been a day of thrills. As I closed my eyes, I prayed the next would not prove too exciting. Pradeep had never really given me a straight answer to my question, 'What will our tame elephants do if they meet a wild tusker?'

'Five-thirty, sahib,' came the voice that brought me back to reality. The waning moon was still reflecting off the river, but Honey Blossom, who had as usual trumpeted through much of the night, was quiet now. A small brown gecko watched me with interest as I squatted on the camp loo. I resisted trying to catch it for Mark because it would probably have dived down the hole and besides, it might be a good omen.

Mash kicked some life into the fire as we sipped hot tea and filled our water bottles. In the elephant lines our large ladies burbled and grunted as they munched their breakfast sandwiches. The phanits chatted to their charges as they heaved on the harnesses and howdahs. Pradeep emerged from his tent, donned his Akubra and camouflage jacket, slung his binoculars round his neck and said, 'Let's go.'

Man Dhoj had Honey Blossom groomed and saddled in the lines. His jungle green uniform had been freshly laundered and his jet black curly hair was neatly combed. 'Namaste,' he smiled, touching my hand. It was good to find I had this reliable phanit with me again. Honey Blossom rumbled a greeting as I heaved myself up by her tail. The day before, we had briefed newcomers on mounting procedure, so all went smoothly and in five minutes we were aboard. Silence was the order of the day; only Pradeep and his men would speak from now on and then only in brief, hoarse whispers.

Turning south, we moved out in line ahead with only the soft shuffle of the elephants' feet, the occasional slap of their ears and the rustle of the passing grass to announce the passage of thirty people and twenty tons of jumbo. Sly rhesus monkeys slipped down the tree trunks, and with raucous cries the peacocks flapped away in ungainly flight. From our lofty seats, we viewed the scene above the tall grass and undergrowth. Riding in a howdah gives one an entirely new perspective of the surrounding area and a feeling of invincibility. I would not have been so happy to meet wild elephant, rhino or tiger on foot.

At the first water, the ladies drank deeply, watched from a branch by the yellow eyes of a crested serpent eagle looking for his breakfast. Feeling cooler, Honey Blossom quickened her pace. Elephants don't perspire but cool themselves by flapping their ears or using their trunk to take saliva from their mouth and spray it over their belly and sides. Sometimes the ladies would pile leaves on their heads to protect them from the sun.

'Tell, tell, tell,' rang the alarm call of the spotted deer. Man Dhoj lowered his head to look under the trees.

'Tiger,' muttered Pradeep, standing like a coachman at the back of my howdah. Not our business, I thought, although a sighting of the big cat would have enlivened the hunt.

At 8 a.m. the sun was coming up above the forest, but early morning mist still hung in the trees when we spotted the tracks that John Hunt and the Tharu had seen the previous day. They meandered across a patch of sand and on into an isolated copse.

Without any command, Honey Blossom stopped. All the ladies followed her example. Their ears came forward like parabolic reflectors and they started a deep rumbling purr. It seemed to come from down inside their stomachs, but this was not their digestive juices at work. I knew this noise and the accompanying low frequency, subsonic sounds that are the elephant communication system at work. They were talking about something, or to something. Usually this sound is pitched too low for the human ear, but it can carry for many miles in the forest.

Honey Blossom raised her trunk and scented. Pradeep had his glasses up scanning the tree line, Man Dhoj was looking straight along the trunk. 'In the trees,' whispered Pradeep, but the sun was in our eyes, reflecting off the mist, and we could see nothing. Then David, our sharp-eyed policeman, spoke quietly: 'I think I have it.' He pointed ahead. We still saw nothing, then through the swirling mist the grey that I had assumed was sky beyond the trees began to move. It looked like a jumbled pile of smooth, rounded rocks sliding silently through the forest. Suddenly a massive domed head appeared from behind a tree. I could not believe my eyes. The great tusks and colossal body that followed gave the creature the appearance of a fat old gentleman with spare tyres and a double chin. Snake-like, a thick trunk sought our scent. No one said a word, but our elephants trembled and our cameras clicked into action. 'My God,' gasped John Cochrane as I reloaded my camera. Looking up, to my surprise I saw a second grey mountain sliding into view, even more massive than the first. Its enormous ivory curved upwards and its huge head carried an even higher dome than that of the first animal. 'At least seven tons,' I thought.

'What on earth is it?' whispered someone.

'Mammoth?' hissed another. Now I could see how the legend had come about.

Flapping their ears, the ghostly apparitions approached, pausing to pluck some choice branch or seize a trunkful of grass. They were only fifty yards away and our mounts were shaking with fear. They too had never seen anything like this before, but their phanits spoke gently, coaxing them to retreat slowly across a dry river bed. By backing off, we hoped the giants would follow and give us the opportunity to get good clear photographs and video footage. For a while they followed on slowly, but at the edge of the wood they halted; perhaps it was too hot in the sun.

'We must lure them out, and preferably with the sun behind us,' I hissed.

'Chan Chan will give a mating call,' said Pradeep, and snapped an order in Nepali. The young lady's shrill cries would have woken the dead, but had no apparent effect on the tuskers.

'Just our luck to find gay elephants,' mused Sally.

'Let's leave them in peace,' urged Pradeep. 'They won't go far in the heat of the day and I'll leave someone to watch them. We can track them again later.'

We turned back and looked for earlier footprints to get an accurate measurement. A sandy area provided what we needed and, dismounting, Pradeep and I took the tape to six well-defined sets. The huge pad showed faint marks of toes, five on the circular forefoot and four on the hindfoot. This is an elephant's fingerprint by which a phanit recognizes his own mount when he seeks it in the jungle. The large prints were between 22½ and 24 inches in diameter, whilst the smaller read 21 to 21½ inches. Taking the lower reading in each case, this made the heights of these strange beasts eleven feet three inches and ten feet six inches respectively.

'It's only an approximation,' I told the team, 'but the big fellow is two inches taller than any Asian elephant ever recorded, and the second one is a good size too.'

'How old d'you think they are?' asked John Campbell, who had been studying the pigmentation on their heads and ears.

'About fifty and forty,' said Pradeep.

'I don't know much about elephants, but they look in magnificent condition,' said Mark.

John Hunt was checking his video. 'It's all there,' he reported proudly, as we headed back to camp.

Over the scrambled eggs, beans and chapattis, we talked like excited children.

'We can't have two Mailas,' pointed out Sheena. 'What shall we call them?'

'Any ideas, Pradeep?' I asked, taking a second helping.

Our mentor stabbed a sausage. 'We should call the taller one Raja Gaj,' he said quickly. 'That means King Elephant – I've never seen a bigger animal. And the other had better be Kancha, which means youngest.'

So the giants were named.

'Where are their cows?' asked Janet.

Pradeep shrugged. 'Who knows – somewhere out there. There is a thousand square kilometres of this jungle.'

The game scout was breathing deeply as he ran in to camp. Pradeep listened to his report.

'This man has just seen Raja Gaj only half a mile away, on the island.'

Following the great footprints earlier in the day, we found they'd crossed the river, raided fields near Gola and then turned north. Now they were right on our doorstep.

The light was still bright as we mounted up, but to allow for the movement of my elephant and that of the tuskers, who might well be in deep shadow, I loaded one camera with a roll of 1000 ASA colour print film and wrapped a towel round the wooden rails of the howdah to cushion my forearms during the hot pursuit. Man Dhoj said, 'Aghit,' and we were off.

The river was shallow and, as a hornbill flew overhead, the ladies made light work of the crossing to the island, heaving themselves up the steep bank. Then, in a line abreast, we began to sweep towards the bulls. Pradeep hissed, 'There he is – the big one.' Raja Gaj was standing in tall grass, but even so his mountain of flesh stood out clearly. If he saw us he showed no sign and was more concerned with his toilet. His enormous ears flapped as he sniffed up trunkfuls of dust with which to powder and cool himself, then he moved on to feed at a new spot. His towering convex back sloped steeply away to the strange ribbed tail, but it was the majestic sweep of his tusks and his huge domed head that made him look so remarkable. Through my binoculars I tried to study every inch of him as he moved in and out of the grass.

'Kancha,' warned Pradeep, and there suddenly, coming up behind us, was the escort to the king. 'Back, back, back,' urged the phanit and Honey Blossom reversed quickly from the bush. Without unseemly haste we divided our force of five elephants and outflanked Kancha.

'Try to get the sun behind us,' I whispered.

Softly Pradeep gave a command and Man Dhoj urged Honey Blossom on through the tangled growth. A tawny jungle cat broke out at our feet and a hog deer scampered away, but now our one aim was to get the tuskers into a good position for a definitive photograph.

At the south end of the island a dry watercourse strewn with boulders formed a natural barrier. Picking our way across, we lined up on the bank beyond. 'Perfect,' muttered John Hunt with his video camera ready. Indeed it was; from here we could look down on the two large gentlemen in the open clearing. Raja Gaj was still in the high grass, but Kancha stood on guard and watched us with an aggressive pose. I didn't feel concerned as I doubted he would cross the watercourse. A courageous tracker dismounted and went forward on foot to test reactions. He soon got one as Kancha, ears extended and trunk waving, advanced. The Nepali retreated and remounted fast. Having seen off the threat, the younger bull stopped and for minutes the elephants remained still. Cameras clicked, the video whirred and pencils scratched on notepads.

All this industry was suddenly upset by the most fearful racket. Trumpeting and charging, Luksmi, her pent-up hatred boiling over, rammed Chan Chan, bulldozing her and her terrified crew headlong through the bushes. The little elephant screamed. 'Bloody hell,' cried Doc John. Pradeep cursed and the phanits wielded their steel ankush to bring the elephants under control. Out in the clearing, the bulls looked on with mild curiosity as if to say, 'What on earth are you silly women up to?' Kancha came forward and, to my surprise, picked his way carefully over the boulders. As before, we separated, confusing the tuskers with trumpet calls and playing a strange slow-motion game of cat and mouse until the sun turned orange and started to set.

What a day! We now had evidence of their existence, but what sort of elephants were these giants? We would need the help of scientists to work it out.

At dawn Mark's snake catchers went to check the drift fence they had laid to entrap small reptiles on the island. It consisted of plastic buckets buried at intervals along a low canvas fence. The idea was that snakes and lizards would run into the fence, move along it and drop into the smooth-sided buckets. To their astonishment, the whole contraption had been uprooted and was festooned in the trees. Each bucket had been pulled out of the ground and smashed. I'd often heard that wild elephant would not tolerate manmade items in their territory. Apparently they account for many milestones that go missing from jungle roads. 'I'm one bucket short,' moaned Mark, retrieving his kit. 'Look out for an elephant leaving a footprint reading ADDIS.'

We decided to let the tuskers rest and browse in peace for a few days, while we took the opportunity to visit Sukla Phanta, the white grass plains where Peter Byrne was studying his own big elephants. Suffice to say it was a long and tiring journey on the Chisapani ferry and along the King Mahendra Highway in a very decrepit Land Rover. Bridges spanning the many rivers flowing from the Himalayas were only partly constructed and their piers had subsided, leaving the roadways contorted in silent death throes. 'What a waste of money,' remarked Sheena, as we spluttered and coughed our way through clouds of choking dust. Sakali had brought with him a young boy whose major task was to test the depth of the rivers ahead of the vehicles. Malcolm christened him Dipstick.

'What happens if there's a crocodile in the river?' asked Sheena.

'We look for another boy,' groaned a car-sick member of the team.

It was dusk when we reached the reserve and, as this was one of the poorest parks in Nepal, it had few facilities. Eventually we pitched our tents at the rangers' elephant camp, which made us feel a little at home. At least the elephants here were quieter than Honey Blossom, and only the clank of their foot chains mingling with gentle munching made us aware of the presence of three rather sad pachyderms.

The park is on the India–Nepal frontier and is much smaller than Bardia. In 1992 it had only fifty visitors, but it is famous for its herd of swamp deer and has much open grassland. There were plenty of cattle in evidence and no one prevented them from coming in to compete with the wildlife for food. There was much talk of poaching; a large bull elephant had been killed some years previously. The resident Nepalese Army patrols told us proudly how they had shot four poachers in recent months.

Peter Byrne was at home in America and his big elephant was said to be on holiday in India. We sipped lemonade with his friend, a very charming retired Nepalese Colonel named Hikmat Bisht, in his camp, which was the only comfortable place for overnight visitors. I felt sorry for the park staff and their supporters. It is a sad place that will need much help from Kathmandu if it is to survive.

The return journey to Bardia was no improvement on the outward trip and when we reached Chisapani a traffic jam stretched for over a mile from the ferry. The town planner had designed the main street for one and a half vehicle widths. As this was currently the east–west highway the blockage to the ferry can be imagined. Sakali looked resigned to a very long wait, but seeing that most ferry crossings only carried one large truck and there was ample space to add a Land Rover we drove on, horn blasting, shouting, 'Airport, airport,' in the hope that this would be interpreted as, 'We have a plane to catch.' Amazingly, the congested street opened up like the Red Sea in front of the Children of Israel and we drove on to the next ferry.

Mark had a growing collection of reptiles by the time we returned, but his water snake had escaped from the lab tent and presumably wriggled back to the river. Since he now had a highly venomous Russell's viper and a deadly krait, I hoped they were in more secure containers. Rod was in seventh heaven as he had seen a dolphin. Otherwise the only new animal on the sighting list was a mongoose that had cavorted along the river bank.

Our task now was to locate any wild elephant cows that might be associated with Raja Gaj, so that evening I briefed David Warren to take a group eastward to search the Babai Valley.

I woke at 2 a.m. with the wind shaking my tent. It was coming straight out of the Chisapani Gorge and in minutes it had reached gale force. A shout of alarm indicated a tent was going over and I suddenly remembered the snakes in the marquee. Leaping up, I seized a torch and ran out, but Mark was already there carrying his venomous collection to safety as the canvas thrashed wildly in the tempest. To my surprise the storm did not worry the ladies one bit. As the rain swept over them, they simply turned their huge backsides into the wind and went on munching contentedly.

At first light we surveyed the damage; it could have been worse. The wind dropped and we decided to continue our search, so we mounted up and moved north-east in two groups. It was still quite dark in the jungle when we picked up Raja Gaj's spoor. He was trundling eastwards. Stripped bark and broken branches marked his progress. He was alone; perhaps he had become separated from Kancha in the storm. Then we saw him a hundred yards away, standing very still in a patch of open woodland. Honey Blossom halted, trembling. She had sensed him long before and as she purred, so the enormous bull swung his head towards us. While we watched he became agitated, casting about as if looking for his escort. Being unsure of his intention, we prepared to fall back as he lifted his trunk to scent us. There was no sign of Kancha. 'Wait,' said Pradeep, 'keep very quiet.' Closer and closer came Raja Gaj until he was only fifty yards away. Honey Blossom trembled, her big sleepy eyes met his and he quickened his pace. 'Go,' snapped Pradeep, and Man Dhoj dug in his toes, urging our mount into a near trot. The old boy followed for a while and then, losing interest, settled down to browse.

'Was that aggression, curiosity or lust?' I asked Pradeep.

'Sex, I think,' he grinned. 'The King seems to like Honey Blossom.'

'He must be so lonely,' said John Hunt, who had become deeply interested in the elephants and was to join the elephant boys' camp that night so that he could learn the art of being a phanit himself.

On the way home we came to a steep-sided ravine that the trail crossed by way of a wooden bridge. Honey Blossom stopped and looked uneasily at the decking, then put out her trunk and pressed downwards. Some of the planks were loose and moved at her touch. Man Dhoj swung down via her ears and inspected the bridge. Finding the rest of the structure sound, he remounted, muttered a few words to the old girl and over we went, avoiding the defective part. 'Bloody marvellous,' said John Cochrane. 'If only we could get African elephants to do that.'

\*       \*       \*

Next day the spoor told us Raja Gaj had moved west. Pushing aside the smaller trees, we followed him on to a small, overgrown island in the mass of streams that fanned out from the gorge. The footprints were fresh. 'Early this morning,' announced Pradeep. 'We must be careful; the cover is thick and he might be difficult to see.' So we moved slowly through the vegetation, but apart from a jungle fowl that slipped out from beneath a shrub and a few grey-bearded langurs, nothing stirred.

'He can't have got away,' exclaimed Sheena.

Indeed, there were no tracks coming off the island, but where the devil was the monster? He had simply disappeared.

'Let's sweep it once more,' I said, and we plodded into the greenery, eyes searching every patch of shadow.

We had just stepped over a fallen tree when Honey Blossom halted and seemed to vibrate. Something was up. Suddenly there was a great disturbance and barely forty feet from us the gigantic tusker stood up in a cloud of dust. He had been lying down for a brief sleep – elephants' internal organs risk damage if they lie down for long periods. We must have walked right past him and we were far too close for comfort.

Standing sideways to us, his nearest eye met Honey Blossom's. Then I saw something that made the hair on the back of my neck rise. A thin stream of yellow fluid was seeping from a gland behind his eye. 'My God, he's in musth,' I said to myself. There was no need to repeat it aloud. Pradeep, Man Dhoj and, I presume, Honey Blossom would have seen it and been aware of the implications. With a slight movement of his fingers, Pradeep waved the other elephants back. Restricted by the dense foliage, it was extremely difficult to turn around at this point or even to back up over the tree trunks. The only way out was forward and closer to the bull.

Male elephants, like men, go through several stages of sexual development. As teenagers they tend to flirt and indeed will mate any time with a cow on heat. However, when he is in musth all the most savage and violent instincts come to the fore. Up to the age of about thirty-five the discharge from the musth gland may last a fortnight or more, during which time he will be moody and aggressive. Between the ages of thirty-five and forty-five this mucus flows freely, often running into his mouth, aggravating

and annoying him to the point of distraction. A domestic tusker
in this condition must be securely chained to prevent him attacking his handlers and other elephants, for he will cease to obey
orders and can behave with terrifying madness, seeking only to
kill or mate. In later life the musth subsides and eventually dies
away, but the leading expert, Bill Williams, reckoned no elephant
in musth was safe until over sixty.

Raja Gaj was in the prime of life. Inside him burned a fearful
passion and his head must hurt like hell. We'd disturbed his rest
and were sitting only yards away on the lady he clearly fancied.
If he came at us, we would have as much chance as trying to
dodge an express train on a level crossing. Eighteen inches in
front of me, Man Dhoj sat astride Honey Blossom's neck, as still
as a statue, not a muscle moving in his body. There was nothing
we could do. I felt a stream of sweat running down inside my
shirt. My heart was pounding so loudly that even Raja Gaj must
hear it. I was scared stiff.

Then from deep in her throat came Honey Blossom's purr. The
monstrous bull towering alongside us swayed his head, side to
side, side to side. His rumbles were deeper and longer. If only we
knew what these two huge creatures were saying.

'Sorry about your head, Raja Gaj. Wretched business! I suggest
a good bath in the river to cool off.'

'It's all right for you, Madu Mala Kali, you haven't got this
problem . . . now why don't you push off and let me have a nap.
Maybe we can meet up for a drink later.'

For thirty long minutes we remained there, unwilling to move
lest we disturb the uneasy peace. Both elephants were now taking
titbits from the bushes and Raja Gaj moved a pace to his right.
By now I knew every scar and wrinkle on his body. I risked
raising my camera. The click made his ear twitch, but he went
on munching. With hardly a ripple of her black skin, Honey
Blossom took a pace to her left. So step by step we parted, finally
emerging on the other side of the island where our comrades
anxiously awaited us. My shirt was wringing wet and Pradeep
silently dismounted and sat quietly by himself in the shade. Man
Dhoj stood by his mount, talking in whispers to her.

An hour later we returned to the island and spotted the King
striding away purposefully and alone across the open flood banks.

It was a great opportunity for a photograph. 'Let's catch him up,' I urged, but try as we might, he left even the most nimble of our ladies standing.

'So much for the theory that if there is trouble we can outstrip the bulls,' said Big John as we halted.

Working south-east from the camp, we were searching for Kancha in an area of thick forest and tall ferns when Sakali saw a kill. Two spotted deer lay together, their necks slashed open as cleanly as if by a knife. 'Tiger,' said Pradeep under his breath, climbing down Honey Blossom's tail to investigate. 'These are fresh and as there are two kills, it is likely to be a female with cubs,' he said. 'We must watch out for she will not be far away.'

Suddenly a heavy pungent scent reached my nostrils. I looked up and found myself staring straight at a forked tree trunk thirty yards away. Resting in it was the head of a very large tiger. The orange, black and white of the face made perfect camouflage, but before I could even get my camera up, the great cat bounded out. At once our elephants started trumpeting as their drivers urged them to form a ring, in the time-honoured fashion, around the beast.

It was quickly surrounded and the ferns waved as it ran this way and that, trying to break out, but each time it approached, the trumpeting and stamping drove it back. Eventually, as if it had tired of the game, the tiger simply strolled past us and away. In a situation like this, one can never be sure what will happen next. Only a few days before, when a tiger with its kill was surrounded, it charged an elephant, clawing its way up the trunk until it was beaten off by a quick-thinking phanit armed only with his ankush.

The domestic elephants used in Nepal are trained in India, and the ensuing language differences can give rise to confusion. (Even the terminology used for the elephant handlers is different: in India an elephant driver is referred to as the mahout and the attendant is known as the phanit, whereas in Nepal the meanings are reversed.) In times of crisis, Hindi words of command have been known to cause problems for the Nepalese drivers. Pradeep tells how, on a training trip with a young elephant newly arrived in Bardia, they were charged by a tiger. The phanit gave what he thought was the command to back off, whereupon the elephant promptly sat down. The tiger, clearly taken aback by such extraordinary behaviour, stalked off in disgust.

The afternoon was well advanced as we reached the phanta and Honey Blossom was dying for a drink. In the clear water small brown fish flashed away from her massive feet as we entered the pool. Elephants won't be hurried as they suck up the precious liquid in their trunks and blow it into their mouths. It was at such a moment that the rhinoceros appeared. She had spent the hottest part of the day grazing in the cuckoo grass nearby and now she too wanted a drink. So did her calf, who lurked at the edge of the grass, but our presence was a worry. Rhino like privacy. At that moment Champa Kali appeared at the other end of the pool and we could hear more elephants approaching on both sides. Unintentionally we had surrounded the mother and baby. The ponderous, armour-plated beast tossed her head, the calf nuzzling against her for protection. Then, with a series of short snorts she was off, splashing through the shallows, but as she reached the edge, Sundar Kali appeared. Mrs Rhino turned and came trotting straight at us, then stopped to stare at Honey Blossom. These lumbering creatures are most unpredictable and, because of their shortness of sight, can charge without provocation. A fully grown rhino can do a lot of damage to an elephant. The mother's little tufted ears flickered, picking up every sound, for their hearing is as good as their sight is poor. No one spoke; Honey Blossom was nervous. We kept still and waited. 'Give her all the time she needs,' I wanted to say.

On an earlier visit to Chitwan I had gone out with my elder daughter, Emma, then only eleven, to try to film rhino. The first meeting was pretty dramatic. We were mounted on a frisky young bull elephant and moving through long grass when, without warning, a monster appeared only fifteen yards away. The first shock of a close-up view of one of these prehistoric-looking brutes is never to be forgotten. Standing almost six feet tall, it looked like something out of *Jurassic Park* and it took a few seconds to collect my wits and start filming. Suddenly the great grey lump shook its head and came straight at us in a trundling charge. Luckily our elephant side-stepped at the last minute and then, to my astonishment, turned and charged the rhino! 'Isn't it fun,

Daddy?' hooted Emma, but by this time my adrenaline was pumping around pretty fast and I was extremely relieved when the rhino eventually gave way. Back at camp I regaled all with this amazing tale. 'Don't worry, John,' said my host, Jim Edwards, 'that was George – he and that elephant perform that trick every day for our visitors.'

Now, sixteen years later, facing this agitated mother, I knew that if she attacked it would be no trick performance. We waited, giving her all the time she wanted. Looking at the monstrous creature it was not difficult to understand why it is regarded as possessing special powers. Indeed, if the Tharu find lumps of dried blood left by a rhino after a fight, they will collect it and mix it with water to make a cure for excessive bleeding. Sometimes this is used after childbirth. The people also believe that such ailments as asthma, stomachaches and TB can be treated with the beast's urine. Even the most rotten flesh of a dead rhinoceros is eaten to promote bodily fitness and vitality.

In the Middle Ages drinking cups carved from rhinoceros horn were believed to react if poison was poured in, causing the drink to foam. Thus the price of this rock-hard matted hair remained high. Contrary to popular belief, the Chinese do not use powdered horn as an aphrodisiac but more usually as a fever-depressant. However, in parts of India it's regarded as a stimulant for tired lovers. In the Yemen, dagger handles made of rhino horn fetch a small fortune, sometimes costing $15,000 a piece. With such demand on its body, the rhino doesn't have much of a chance.

A couple of mynah birds landed on the back of this enormous animal and began looking for bugs, but she faced us squarely, her nostrils quivering. Pradeep began to make a low clucking sound. The ears swivelled towards us, then she raised her head as if to say 'Come on, my baby, let's go home,' and she and the calf sauntered past and were swallowed up in the cuckoo grass. We watched the stalks waving as she cleared a passage through, and then breathed a sigh of relief. Honey Blossom gave a short trumpet of triumph and off we went with the usual 'pompity pom' rhythmic movement, her shoulders rising and falling like huge pistons. 'She really does feel like an old car with a broken shock absorber,' I thought.

\* \* \*

The moon had risen and its gentle light was filtering through the trees around the elephant lines when Dhuki Ram Tharu glanced up from the fire. Something was wrong; the ladies had stopped eating. Then he realized that standing in the midst of the tethered herd was a sixth elephant, a huge beast with great tusks. It was Raja Gaj. The phanit reached over to his nearest colleague who was chatting to another, and without a sound they retreated.

The bull moved soundlessly over the soft earth to his lady love and, reaching out, touched her with his trunk. Honey Blossom stiffened but did not move. Placing his massive foot on her chain, he picked it up with his trunk, and with one firm pull snapped the links. Together they walked slowly away into the forest.

As the BBC news came to an end I turned off my radio, blew out the candle and shut my eyes. But before I could drop off there was a violent beating on my tent. It was Pradeep. 'Come quickly,' he hissed. 'Raja Gaj is here and he has taken Madu Mala Kali.'

Hardly able to believe what I had heard, I stumbled out of my sleeping bag, wrapped a sarong round my waist and grabbed a torch. Fifty yards away in the elephant lines I saw that my riding elephant's leg chains had been broken. I knew she could not have done that alone.

'Raja Gaj taken Madu Mala Kali,' cried the phanits.

'How on earth could a seven-ton kidnapper walk undetected into a camp of forty people?' I asked myself as we followed her footprints into the jungle.

Mating between wild elephants is a very private matter. The female usually slips away from the herd at dusk, meets her chosen mate at a predetermined place and returns by dawn. The whole business is usually conducted very quietly; only in the event of a rival bull appearing on the scene would there be uproar, with a fight to the death the possible outcome. Affairs between wild tuskers and domestic cows are less discreet; because the ladies are chained at night, the male must first enter the camp to free her.

Entering the forest, my torch lit on a grey mass and I called softly, 'Come along, Honey Blossom, stop being a silly old woman, it's time you came home.'

The shape turned and two enormous curved tusks swung at

me. Thirty feet away Raja Gaj's piggy eyes reflected the light, then, ears forward and trunk tucked back, he came shambling at me in a deliberate charge. 'This is ridiculous,' I thought, running to one side. 'Here I am dressed only in a sarong, being pursued around the jungle by a colossal and very randy elephant.' As I switched off the torch he halted. Elephants have poor sight and the wind was coming from behind him. At this point Rod Barnes, who had followed me into the trees, pushed the image intensifier into my shaking hands. Now I could see in the dark. We stood silently watching the monster in the pale green electronic light whilst he tried to locate us with his thick trunk. As he sniffed the air, I could see Honey Blossom just beyond. 'Get our people among the boulders by the river for safety,' I whispered to Rod as the boys appeared with torches of burning grass. The tusker stood very still and I thought he was about to charge again, but thankfully he feared fire and with an angry snort he wheeled, pushing down a two-foot-thick sal tree as if it were a matchstick and the darkness swallowed him up. Before Honey Blossom could join him, her phanit shinned up on to her shoulders and, scolding loudly, drove her back to the lines. 'A disappointed lady and a brave man,' said Rod as we returned to camp, where we quickly emptied a bottle of J&B.

Suddenly someone remembered Sundar, the helmsman, who had stayed on with us after the other rafters had departed. He had been by the fire when the tusker arrived.

'He wasn't down on the beach,' said John Cochrane. 'I checked everyone.'

'I am here,' came a small voice from the sky. There, fifteen feet up a straight, almost bare tree was Sundar, who had shinned up the trunk the moment the monster appeared. It took us some time to convince him that it was safe to come down.

In spite of all these close calls, we seemed a pretty healthy bunch and Doc John had not had to treat many of us humans – most of his patients were animals. The phanits were fastidious in the extreme about the health of their mounts. 'No elephant, no work,' as Pradeep said. Sores on the back caused by a badly fitted howdah could put an elephant out of action for weeks, but the most common problem was with their feet.

When treating animals, a doctor's medical kit does not necessarily contain the most appropriate implements, as Doc John discovered when presented with the problem of removing a large splinter of bamboo from poor Chan Chan's foot. We had noticed that she was reluctant to put her weight on the foot, which she held up off the ground as a dog lifts a sore paw, and her phanit soon found the cause of the problem, but how to remove a spike so deeply buried? Forceps were useless and without machinery of any sort to maintain, we had no ordinary pliers with us. But my most essential item of kit, the Swiss Army penknife I always carry on expedition, includes a small pair and with these he set to work.

It was heartrending to see the great beast lying on the ground, trustingly allowing this stranger to poke about in her hideously painful foot whilst her handler whispered soothing words in her ear. And John showed no fear as he struggled to wrench the splinter out, crouched only inches away from Chan Chan's powerful trunk. It was obvious to us all just how painful the operation was as the elephant silently wept with pain, the tears running down her cheeks. When it was all over, John sat back on his haunches, valiantly displaying the four-inch spike, and cleaned off the pliers. We all watched as the patient got to her feet, gingerly tested the injured foot, and then put out her trunk and gently stroked Doc John in gratitude.

'A big snake,' shouted Sakali. 'Quickly, Mark, it is some way away. We'll go by elephant.'

Seizing snake sticks and canvas bag, and clad only in a pair of shorts and his battered bush hat, the 'mad Irish snake expert', as I'd come to call him, shinned up Chan Chan Kali's tail. Chris and Ian joined him and off they trundled into the forest.

Alarmed langurs scattered and rhesus monkeys scampered away as the two lumbering jumbos, ignoring all in their path, made best speed to the spot where elephant boys cutting fodder had spotted a large brown and cream reptile.

The serpent was still there when the hunters arrived and in a trice Mark was disentangling a rather stroppy python from a tree root. They marched home in triumph. Elephants don't seem the least bit worried by snakes, although it is said a small calf can die of snakebite. In any case, Mark's python was not poisonous.

'A ten-footer, but it's injured,' he reported as he tipped it out of the bag. Examining a deep wound mid-way down its muscular body, the herpetologist said, 'Looks like a leopard has chewed him. Better get Doc John and see what he can do for the poor chap.'

So our hard-worked medical officer found himself stitching up a python, mumbling, 'I'm not a vet, you know.'

Mark wasn't listening; his head was buried in one of his heavy manuals. 'Quite remarkable,' he said, after reading several pages. 'This is a Burmese python. It's well outside its normal range and I doubt if any of these have been recorded here.'

'Another first for science,' grinned Chris, sucking on his empty pipe.

Whether one likes snakes or not, it is impossible not to be fascinated by them: their colourful, intricate patterns, the deadly unblinking eyes and the flickering forked tongue. Soon even the most apprehensive members of the team were touching the beautiful creature as John finished the stitching.

A day later, the reptile team was called out again and this time found a real monster. A python, coincidentally another Burmese, was coiled up inside a hollow tree, completely filling the trunk. Pouncing like a mongoose, the scientist seized it behind the head, dragging it upward out of the tree trunk. But this was no sick, docile fellow. Instead Mark found himself struggling with an agitated sixteen feet of writhing constrictor. 'For Christ's sake, get a bigger bag,' he yelled, for it was obvious that the canvas sack wouldn't accommodate this chap. Chris found a sleeping bag and whilst he and Ian sat on the nine-inch-thick body, Mark struggled to push it in head first. In time, the captive quietened down and became extraordinarily easy to handle. The subject of numerous photographs, he was usually draped around our shoulders.

By now Mark was in seventh heaven, for, attracted by the rewards, local people poured in with reports of snakes and the team was hard put to it to keep up with catching, recording, scale-counting and photographing them.

'Anything you haven't seen yet?' I asked as we downed a cool beer at sunset.

'Well, I'd have expected to find a cobra,' replied Mark. 'Aberdeen University are doing a study of all the cobras and their DNA and venom samples, and they have no information on any from Nepal. I'd like to get them a DNA sample.'

Next day he was rewarded when villagers saw a black tail disappearing into a hole in a river cliff. After struggling to reach the spot, Mark felt unwilling to push his hands up unknown tunnels, so he lit some grass at the bottom to watch for smoke emerging and thus see how many entrances existed. Having established the layout, he began to dig from the top and soon came on the shining coils of a black cobra wedged in very firmly.

In a lower hole he could just see the snake's head. To be certain that all the coils belonged to the same head, Mark gingerly poked each in turn to see if the head flinched, just in case there were two cobras. The serpent wriggled and he reckoned it was safe to start feeling along the coils. So, placing his hand about the polished ebony scales, he gently eased his fingers forward over the pulsating body until he reached the neck. I hoped he wouldn't overshoot. Gripping it securely in both hands, he then pulled the snake slowly away from the hole and we breathed a sigh of relief. The Nepalese, with a traditional fear of all snakes, were wide-eyed with amazement. Never had they seen such courage.

So Mark got his cobra and also a useful quantity of venom which he milked out for Aberdeen University and the Liverpool School of Tropical Diseases. After their expert treatment of his bite by one of the West Midland Safari Park's rattlesnakes, Mark reckoned he owed them something. Before our reptile collection was eventually released unharmed to slide back into the wild, they served the cause of science and, furthermore, the wounded python was healing well.

John Edwards arrived in the evening. 'Caught this today,' he announced, handing us a thirty-five-pound mahseer for supper. Our eyes popped out. He also brought news of a large elephant seen near the army post at Danwathal. Later investigation revealed twenty-two-inch prints, but no sign of the owner.

Meanwhile, David Warren's group came home with tales of high adventure in the Babai Valley. They'd almost walked into a large tiger in high grass and had bumped several rhino that had 'treed' their guide. They also found some very large gharial. 'You feel very naked when you're on foot and only armed with a sheath knife amongst this lot,' confided Malcolm. 'Sally almost trod on a mugger and there were rhino tracks right round my tent,' he cried as they recounted their war stories.

Before our return to the UK we had time for one last trip and decided to pay a quick visit to Gola. At the village our worst fears were confirmed; the giants were getting bolder. The house raided for salt in 1991 had been revisited by the tuskers who had totally destroyed the building.

Gola was not the only settlement to suffer. Pradeep told of raids on the road construction camp near Chisapani. The cooks had used tent number thirteen as a food store and, scenting a free meal, our friends had crept in at night, ripped a hole in the fabric and looted the rations. Some time later, Pradeep had visited the camp and slept in tent thirteen, which was no longer a food store. He awoke to hear the canvas tearing and, switching on his torch, saw a gleaming tusk come straight through. Outside stood a hungry Kancha. Pradeep fled. Elephants really do have good memories.

To speed up our return, we would fly from Nepalganj direct to Kathmandu. The little airport had few facilities and it was advisable to wear wellington boots when using the loo. To avoid the overpowering pong of the place, most passengers stayed well away from the buildings until it was almost time to depart and then made a dash for the gate. However, on this day the plane was late so we amused ourselves with rickshaw races around the car park, and passing out our unwanted sandwiches to a pack of mangy dogs and snotty-nosed but lovable children.

Back in the capital, I found my old pals from Kenya days, elephant experts Iain and Oria Douglas-Hamilton, visiting Lisa Choegyal. They were on their way back to Kenya after attending the Tokyo CITES conference, at which the contentious question of the sale of ivory had featured, but excited by our news they went at once to Bardia. Unfortunately they were to see only dung and footprints; the enormous grey ghosts had disappeared again into the vast forest. But we had to do something to preserve these unique creatures before some ivory-hungry poacher killed them.

Thus, when I returned to Britain, I set about persuading my friends to support a programme to protect them.

The fax machine beside my desk hummed and I looked up from a mound of letters I was writing to raise money to help less-privileged youngsters in Liverpool. As the printout emerged, I saw it was from Peter Byrne and it brought grim news.

On a warm April night, Tula Hatti, the big tusker in which Peter had taken a special interest, ambled into his home territory in Sukla Phanta. It had been a long walk through the dusty fields of northern India. His head throbbed, his mouth was dry, but deep inside he felt a growing excitement and the need to dominate. Totally fearless and more aggressive than usual, he sought his females.

Even humans would have smelt the pungent odour that wafted from the thick yellow discharge running from his temporal glands. The great bull was in musth and, did he but know it, the level of testosterone in his blood was rising dramatically. At such a time male elephants, even tame ones, will attack anything.

Now that their ancient migration routes through the forest had been cut by the resettled hill people, the herd had moved earlier than usual and to a new area westwards. Like most great bulls, Tula Hatti led a solitary life away from the herd, only meeting his cows for mating. Now he had been left behind and there were no females to satisfy his raging desire.

As the first light of dawn tinged the eastern sky, Tula Hatti was still seeking his cows in the sal forest. Suddenly the trees ended and to his surprise he found himself in open fields where he remembered thick forest. In his absence the area had been cleared for cultivation. Fires flickered in the houses as women prepared food, whilst mangy dogs strolled and stretched, hoping for scraps. Into this densely populated area came six tons of confused, frustrated and short-tempered tusker. The hill people, unlike the Tharu of the plains, are unused to elephants and so they panicked. A pack of barking pariah curs, snarling and snapping, rushed at him as men and women screamed and shouted.

His first victim died as he slept, stamped into the ground by the frightened monster. Travelling north, the dogs still at his heels, Tula Hatti flattened a woman in a wheat field, killing her instantly. A third person was trampled to death as he slept. Then the maddened bull turned west, maiming another villager on the way.

Running amok, he encountered a large domestic buffalo and, swinging his massive head, speared it with his gleaming tusks, running it through from back to chest before hurling the writhing beast fifty feet. A few yards further on he repeated the act, executing a second buffalo. Now, his head covered in blood and gore and trumpeting with fury, he headed for the only shelter, a jungle-covered island in the Mahakali River which marks the border with India. Sore and tired, he stayed all day in the deep shade. The dried buffalo blood drew the flies in thousands, but the old bull kept still, moving only occasionally to pull a few stalks of grass. With the cool of evening his composure and confidence returned, and as the moon rose he paddled across the shallows to the Indian bank. Out of the darkness loomed a couple of menacing grey shapes. Alarmed once more and with renewed fury, he seized the first with his thick trunk and hurled it away into the night. Rushing on, he kicked its colleague aside with an awful blow. In twenty-four hours he had killed three people, severely wounded another, tusked two buffaloes to death and destroyed two concrete mixers.

Hikmat Bisht, after being called by the Park Warden at 7 a.m., had rushed out with his boys, but by the time he reached the scene Tula Hatti had gone. All the Colonel could do was to follow the killer's trail, sympathize with the grieving relatives and make a detailed report which he faxed to Peter. Of course it was a great tragedy. Tharu villagers would probably have restrained the dogs and let the tusker pass unhindered, but the Paharia hill people could not be blamed. They were as ignorant of big game as would be a villager in Dorset. It was simply an awful accident, not uncommon as man and animals compete for the diminishing forest. It would certainly happen again and, not surprisingly, the people wanted their attacker shot.

*Chapter Six*

# CLOSE
# ENCOUNTERS

THE ballroom of the Waldorf Astoria was packed for the 1992 Explorers Club annual dinner. From all over the globe astronauts, aquanauts, balloonists, mountaineers, sailors and scientists had made the pilgrimage to New York. This, the greatest gathering of modern explorers, is the climax of several days of workshops and lectures, when those driven by curiosity to seek what lies beyond the horizon meet to debate and swap tales, or simply to see old friends.

During dinner a number of presentations are given, and, thanks to ABC TV, I had managed to get John Hunt's footage of Raja Gaj and Kancha edited. So, in between mouthfuls of rare beef, my colleagues gazed in surprise as the two giants appeared on the vast video screen.

CNN had also heard of the discovery and broadcast the news world-wide. Thus in Kathmandu many Nepalese got their first glimpse of the massive creatures that live in their remote western forest.

The American Museum of Natural History was extremely interested. They put us on to Dr 'Hezy' Shoshani, a leading authority on elephants, and he and various knowledgeable folk examined our photographs. The general opinion was that we needed to get an experienced mammologist to study the giants, so I called Iain Douglas-Hamilton in Kenya. Enthusiastic as ever, he said he would do his utmost to come with us the following year, and if he couldn't make it he would find someone suitable. Thus we began recruiting for the Raja Gaj Expedition that would go back to Nepal in January 1993.

\*     \*     \*

I wanted to spend more time on the Karnali River, for I was not convinced that we had really covered the valley thoroughly, and some cow elephants might be lurking there. We would take two outboards, plus brackets and adhesive to fit them to the sterns of our Avon raft. Porters would carry the motors, plus fuel, from Chisapani to the Seti River junction so that after the major rapids had been navigated we would have engines to get us downstream between study areas more quickly. Pradeep assured me the grass cutters, who were permitted to enter the reserve to gather thatch and firewood once a year, would have completed their work by mid-January, and the river might be a little higher, which would enable us to use the engines. Mash and I finalized details by fax and the recruiting of the personnel began.

The *Mail on Sunday*'s *You* Magazine had published a full-length article on the previous expedition, plus an appeal for donations for the elephant fund set up by the Scientific Exploration Society. Yorkshire TV also did a good piece and the discovery had received widespread publicity, so plenty of people were interested.

The benefits of the expedition to the participants were a useful advertisement. To date, several had been promoted in their jobs and one personnel director was so impressed by the transformation in the executive he had sent along that he signed up another. One financier's wife who I met some weeks after our return said of her husband, 'You took six inches off his tummy and at dinner parties he now talks about elephants instead of the Nikkei index.' Susan Procter claimed it was three weeks before she allowed Malcolm to sleep in the house. 'I started at the bottom of the garden in a tent, gradually getting nearer to a sanitized existence as I stopped setting off to the trees with a spade, loo roll and a mug of boiled water for teeth cleaning,' he wrote.

Unfortunately, as the recession bit deep into the world economy, few companies could afford to send executives with us for management development or regeneration; however, places were taken up by adventurous people who simply wanted to tackle something worthwhile and different.

There was the usual briefing weekend when we camped out and cooked rabbits in the 'jungle'. Henning Caesar, a German industrial chemist with ICI, had heard me telling John Dunn about the jumbos on the BBC. Before he retired, he wanted to be part of a successful team tackling something challenging, interesting and of which he could be proud. He would do the video filming. An energetic engineering consultant from Yorkshire, Colin Gutteridge, was eager to try his hand at an activity hitherto reserved for the young, and was just the sort of practical, self-reliant person who fits in well on an expedition. I reckoned he would be good at anything and asked him to handle moss collection and insects. Libby Smith, the guide-dog walker who had been with us on the first expedition in 1991 and also with me in Mongolia in 1992, couldn't resist the opportunity to come back and actually see Raja Gaj.

Elephants are one of the most beloved of animals and some people, including myself, are crazy about them. Thus I was not surprised to read the application from Sue Hilliard, a fingerprint officer with the Merseyside police. Quite simply, Sue adored elephants and spent much time visiting those in Chester Zoo. I felt she could be useful in tracking the bulls by identifying the different foot impressions.

An adventurous doctor from Chalfont St Giles, John Cosgrove, had travelled widely and was also a good golfer, which was to prove useful for estimating distance on the river survey. His infectious sense of humour endeared him to me from the start. I felt that if an elephant sat on anyone, it would be helpful to be treated by someone who could bring a smile to their lips.

Les Dingle had been the Managing Director of Singer Europe. A strong, charming and practical man, he would be a good person in a tight spot if we had one. He was to bring with him one of the most useful items I've had on any expedition: a small hand-operated sewing machine.

When someone says they've been studying philosophy I wonder what they expect to get from an expedition, but Brigid Medlam, a humorous Irish lass with a great zest for life, was a joy to have in the team and good at bonding others together. Perhaps that's what philosophy is all about.

Ruth Stone, a quiet and thoughtful lady, loved the wildlife and much of her spare time was devoted to conservation. She was ideally suited to the project.

A well-travelled solicitor from Grimsby who had ridden camels, didn't mention his boat-handling expertise when I first met him. However, Denis Jebb was to demonstrate his skills on the Karnali.

My old pal Harvey Mann, picture editor of *You*, had been keen to come, but in December called to say he couldn't make it. 'What on earth am I to do about the essential photographic record?' I wondered, opening the door to our guests at the office Christmas party. Nick Brown was the photographer for our local 'freebie': the *Blackmore Vale Magazine*. He had been helping us in his spare time and I had admired his pictures of steeplechasers. After the second glass of mulled wine I said, 'Why don't you come to Nepal and photograph giant elephants?' He almost collapsed and next morning rang to ask if I'd been serious. Thus ended his career with the *Blackmore Vale* and began his life as a most successful freelancer.

Iain Douglas-Hamilton called from Nairobi to say he couldn't accompany us. That was a blow, but true to his word he had come up with a replacement. I had read how, in October 1990, Dr Chris Thouless, a courageous zoologist with the Kenya Wildlife Service, had been taking part in a darting operation on Kenya's Lake Laikipia plateau. The Zoological Society of London were funding the project and had sent out Miss Alexandra Dixon to assist Chris in fitting a radio collar to a suitable elephant. Guided by a spotter plane, the scientists left their vehicles and approached a herd on foot. They had gone about seven hundred yards when Chris saw small babies with the adults so the party retreated quietly, but a thunderstorm was approaching and as they backed away the wind changed and the herd picked up their scent. The elephants immediately became highly agitated. The team, still three hundred yards from their trucks, realized the imminent danger and ran for cover. At this point the massive matriarch charged and, singling out Miss Dixon, began to gain ground on the fleeing woman. Screaming with fury the beast came on at a frightening speed, its trunk waving. When the matriarch was almost on top of her, Alexandra swerved sideways, but in doing so slid on the slippery earth and fell. In a second the elephant was over her, and before she could struggle up it tried to kneel on her. Rolling into a ball she spun this way and that, desperately trying to avoid the raging creature. Chris had done his best to distract the animal by shouting and waving his arms, but it was no good, and to his horror he saw the matriarch kneel down to get at Alexandra. There was a sickening crunch as one great tusk went into her hip and another struck her calf. Then the monster seized the stricken woman in its trunk, and held her aloft before dashing her to the ground. As the helpless victim struck the earth, the beast lowered its massive forehead and attempted to crush her to death. Bellowing and trumpeting, the rest of the herd closed in.

Chris thought Alexandra must be dead, but then he heard her screams as the trunk entwined her and, ignoring the risk to himself, rushed forward, yelling like a banshee to distract the killer. It had no effect. His only weapons were his fists and with these the zoologist hammered the elephant's head, striking with frenzied might. 'I hit it with my fist between the eyes to try and grab its attention. Of course I was scared, but it was all I could think of doing,' Chris was reported as saying. At that moment a game ranger fired his rifle over the enraged animal. This did the trick and as the elephant backed off, Chris picked up the shattered woman and bore her to safety. Amazingly Alexandra survived. Iain Douglas-Hamilton reckoned it was one of the bravest acts he had ever known. Chris had saved her life, and for his selfless determination and conspicuous courage he was awarded the Queen's Gallantry Medal. He sounded like a useful person to have with us.

It is very tempting to regard all pachyderms as large, lovable, friendly creatures, but one has to remember that, if annoyed, they can become terrible killers – although the only injury I ever suffered was no fault of Honey Blossom's. As cameraman, I was sitting directly behind the phanit, which necessitated holding on to the corner posts of the howdah as it swayed from side to side. At times, the movement is pretty violent and one has to grip hard. By the end of the previous expedition, I had lost the feeling in the end of a finger on my right hand and could hardly feel the camera button. John Davies had a look and pronounced, '. . . carpal tunnel syndrome. Bricklayers get it and if it doesn't get better you'll need to have an operation to free the trapped nerve.' Back in Britain I explained to a surprised surgeon that I had done it riding an elephant and, as I submitted myself to his knife under local anaesthetic, he sliced my palm open. With my arm in a sling it made a great story at dinner parties.

We had almost finished selecting team members when a letter arrived from a lady who had been in the army for twenty-two years and described herself as being 'very fit and keen to go to Nepal'. Over the phone, she told me of her love for cats and how she longed to see a tiger. I was to lecture at a boys' school near Blackpool the next week and we agreed to meet. Arriving a little later than planned, I found the audience already seated. As the headmaster made the introductory remarks, I scanned the serried ranks of rosy-cheeked lads. Amongst them was a slightly built lady with silver hair, clutching a large bag. It had to be Miss 'Bimbo' Coleman.

'What branch of the Army were you in?' I asked over tea after the talk.

'The Royal Military Police,' came the proud reply.

'What is the most frightening thing that has ever happened to you?' I enquired.

'When my D-ring stuck at three thousand feet,' said Bimbo without batting an eyelid.

I gasped, 'You mean you are a freefall parachutist?'

She smiled and produced her certificates. 'And an Outward Bound instructor, canoeist, skier ... Until my mother died recently at ninety, we used to go camping together at weekends.'

Recovering my composure, I asked what job she had done since leaving the forces. Apparently Bimbo had been the gritter driver for the local council. She could see that I was finding it difficult to accept this. 'I thought that you might like to speak to my old commanding officers,' she smiled, passing me a list of names and addresses. Judith, my wife, had also been in the Women's Royal Army Corps, so she called her former colleagues. They confirmed all this remarkable lady had told me, adding, 'She's a terrible practical joker – beware!' So, in accepting this grand character, I made her promise 'No practical jokes – at least not with tigers.' We made her the expedition quartermaster.

At Gatwick, Royal Nepal Airlines could not have been more help-ful and reacted to a couple of outboard engines in our baggage as if no one travelled without them these days. The flight went smoothly and customs at Kathmandu waved us and our motors through. 'This is going too well,' I muttered to my son-in-law Julian Matthews, who had come as my deputy and was delighted to be away from the day to day running of Discovery Expeditions. But our luck continued and the team had a superb view of Everest and the adjoining peaks on the next day's mountain flight, whilst I rushed around meeting various officials and seeing Colonel Karki of the Nepalese Army, whose soldiers were on anti-poaching patrol in Bardia. In the afternoon, the team spent a few hours sightseeing and Henning, ever one for detail, recorded his visit to an area named Pashupathinat:

> By the holy Bagmati River and the burning ghats, we try to grasp the difference between ritual purity and cleanliness, which have nothing to do with each other. Here is a corpse smouldering on a pyre, next to him the remnants are brushed into the river where a woman is scrubbing her pots and pans and bathers immerse themselves. A young saddu, holy man or fakir, offers to show us his powers, acquired through prayer and meditation, by lifting a fifty-pound stone with his male member . . . Monkeys swarm over everything and sacred cows amble through the lanes, trying to sneak a mouthful of fruit or vegetables.

The road beside the Trisuli had been widened, and our journey southward went well until the bus blew a big end. We all piled into the raft crew's minibus and kept going. Dining and dancing at the Tharu Lodge that night raised morale and at dawn a new bus took us west. It was a long haul, some two hundred and ninety miles, to Birendranagar. Delayed by the exhaust pipe falling off and the universal joint breaking, we reached the campsite at dusk. Dinner and rum awaited, tents were up and in no time our snores echoed up to the clear starlit sky that heralded frost.

Marching north, we started our steady climb into the terraced foothills. The going seemed a little tougher than usual and we were all thankful to reach the campsite seven hours later. At five thousand feet it was noticeably colder, but we warmed ourselves around the fire. Les's compact portable sewing machine came in handy, mending split pants and sleeping bags. Then Henning produced *The Ascent of Rum Doodle*, which had been give to him by his British wife to read on the expedition. This story of the conquest of Mount Rum Doodle, the world's highest at forty thousand and a half feet, is an epic and it has to be one of the funniest books ever written. Henning tried to read it aloud, but collapsed in near hysterics; the more he laughed the more we laughed until the entire expedition was crying with mirth. John Cosgrove managed to carry on, but with little more success and thereafter we had to pass it around, each reading a short section. It reminded us vividly not only of the idiosyncrasies of the members of our own team, engaged in an almost equally perilous undertaking, but also of the qualities and strength of our guides and porters, without whom we could not have succeeded. *Rum Doodle* was to keep us laughing until the last night.

Climbing up the steep trail to Ranaikana, we met a herd of pack goats and sheep. Each beast was laden with about twenty pounds of salt bound for Tibet. The hardy men and women who drive them think nothing of their long hauls up and down the Himalayas. 'God, how do they do it?' muttered Sue, sinking on to the grass for a welcome breather.

'Namaste,' a farmer greeted us, his hands clasped together as if in prayer. He wore a woollen balaclava, wool muffler, shirt, pullover, the jacket of a suit, shorts, and flip-flops on his naked feet. He seemed faintly amused by these strange foreigners in T-shirts, shorts and boots.

'Tree bark for antiseptic, dried porcupine for stomach pains and asthma, cactus roots for diarrhoea and fox blood for VD,' noted Ruth, who was studying the traditional medicine of the region, as well as compiling a bird list. Determined that we should not be accused of passing through without discovering anything of the locality, I had given each person a task and, apart from encouraging the spirit of exploration, it made the march much more interesting. 'An explorer must bring out knowledge,' muttered Colin, slipping another moss sample into his day pack.

The long descent to the Swat Khola River turned our knees to rubber and again it was a weary group that hooted with laughter at the nightly reading of *Rum Doodle*. However, we were in good spirits and only the Doc was unwell with a tummy bug.

A jackal sniffing around the tents woke me at 1 a.m. In spite of my legendary snoring, I am a light sleeper and in a flash my hand was on my razor-sharp kukri, but Megh got to the beast first with a well-aimed rock. The troops slumbered on and in some cases snored. For those unused to sleeping with strangers, it can be an interesting experience as Henning recorded in his diary:

> It is odd to have to share your bedroom or tent with a man, a basically unknown person with different dressing or undressing habits, different toilet customs and definitely different sleeping noises compared with the wife. When she snores, I gently turn her on her side. I do not dare to touch another man in the night, gently or firmly, in case of misunderstandings. The answer is very good earplugs. The exception is JBS who is banned from the vicinity of all people who cherish their rest, and sleeps alone fifty yards downwind.

As the tail end of our column breasted the final crest, a crowd of children greeted us. They'd been drawn to Julian, who was painting the view. 'Their faces are a picture,' said Bimbo, who had shot up the slope with hardly a murmur. She was very fit.

The porters had easily beaten us to the river and the camp was ready and boats fitted for launching. Megh, who was to command the fleet, stood barefoot on the silver beach. His shock of black hair flecked with sand made him look like a friendly pirate.

'Good walk, John?' he said, pressing a mug of steaming tea into my hand.

'Best drink in the world,' panted Nick, putting down his heavy camera case.

Once again we were beside the turquoise-blue Karnali. It looked deceptively tranquil.

'The river's down a little,' said Megh, interpreting my thoughts. 'Maybe we run the House of God?'

\*     \*     \*

'Bearing 260°,' I cried.

'Range four hundred,' called back John Cosgrove, estimating the distance to the marker with uncanny accuracy.

'Jailhouse Rock coming up,' said Megh, turning the bulbous craft into the bank.

Whilst the skippers went forward on foot, Libby and I checked the navigation record in her waterproof notebook. High up a tree a grey langur groomed himself thoughtfully. The rumble of a rapid was clearly audible, but Megh came bouncing over the rocks, 'No problem, it's a four plus.'

'Should be good for action,' enthused Nick, setting off to find a camera position.

The boats raced through in fine style. The lower water level made it much easier. We knew that the really big one lay ahead, but the conquest of Jailhouse Rock had given us great confidence and no one lost much sleep that night.

I had memorized my sketch of the route through the cataract, and as we hit the first waves I glanced back at the waiting craft. As usual we would go through one at a time. Beneath our hull, the current quickened. 'Hold on tight,' sang Megh, pulling the brim of his cap down to shade his eyes. Looking forward, I felt my stomach muscles tighten with a pang of fear: ahead the sun was glinting off a fan of spray that sprang from a massive black boulder right in the middle of the river. Somehow we had to go left of that, then quickly right and hard left again. Megh leaned back on his oars. His biceps bulged as he fought the power of the Karnali. Without warning our velocity had increased and now the oars hardly needed to touch the surface to swing the raft. It was only by watching the bank racing past that one got an impression of speed. The angry roar of compressed water drowned all commands as we rocketed down a chute of grey glacier melt; gone was the turquoise. A wall of rock flashed past, the neoprene groaned as it rubbed the side and the stern came round, 'God, we're going broadside,' I thought, clutching the lifeline. But we met the curling stopper wave bow on. White water cascaded over us and through it I saw the great basalt rock, dead ahead. The surface bulged and I found myself peering over the bow, down into a deep green hole. By some miracle the dreaded boulder was to our right. Again the fabric complained as we touched and I heard an oar rasp on rock; then we were over the lip and riding a foaming torrent into the lines of standing waves. Water was pouring down Megh's swarthy face and running off the ends of his moustache. 'That was God's House,' he laughed, turning the bucking craft so that we might watch our colleagues come through.

The last to pass was the stores boat with Bimbo perched like some imperial princess on top of the cooking gear. She looked quite unconcerned.

As we came out of the Red Gorge, I saw a familiar figure waving from the beach. It was Mongol, another boatman, who had marched in with the outboards. It had only taken eight porters a couple of days to carry the two 9-horsepower engines, brackets, spares, tools and 120 litres of fuel over the hills from Chisapani. Not bad for a journey of at least twenty-two miles, and they hadn't spilled a drop of petrol. Denis Jebb's eyes lit up and he set to work with a will. To our astonishment the motors started at first pull – quite an advert for their makers, Mariner.

Having time in hand, we could now examine the Seti Valley and look further downstream for evidence of elephants and the Raji people. Above the confluence, a sheer cliff blocked the route on the west bank of the Seti and after a hairy attempt to climb it, we were forced back. So we carried one of the Avons a little distance upriver and, watched by a circling osprey, we crossed to the east bank. Here a well-worn track led north. Terraced fields appeared and red-beaked pochard swam in the shallows. The sun was well up when we tramped into a small hamlet called Banga. The people seemed hesitant and Megh explained we were the first white visitors. They had an interesting farm with fruit like durians and lemons from which they pressed juice, corn on the cob, wheat and bayleaf. Overcoming their surprise at meeting us, the villagers went about their work of making buckets and baskets from sal leaves smeared with mud.

The gorge was too narrow for elephants. As the villagers displayed their water-gauge and cable-car, we were told the river could rise thirty feet in the wet season. 'Do you know of the Raji?' I asked, and they pointed west. There was clearly no need to go further up the Seti River.

*       *       *

Expedition base camp at Bardia.

*Above:* Climbing the final slope before descending into the Karnali Gorge. (*L to r:* Bimbo Coleman, Megh Ale, Les Dingle, Dr John Cosgrove, Libby Smith, Patti, JBS.) (*Nick Brown*)

*Left:* Near the hidden lake on the Bheri River we met hunters with ancient muzzle loaders. They spoke of monsters 'to the south'.

*Above:* Crossing the deep waters of the Karnali by elephant for the first time.

*Left:* JBS measuring the height of the giant elephants in Bardia with the aid of a Polaroid photo. *(Nick Brown)*

Pradeep Rana (*left*) and John Hunt measuring Raja Gaj's footprints after his discovery in 1992.

*Above left:* Mark O'Shea faces an angry Indian cobra. *(Mark O'Shea)*

*Above right:* Anna Lubienska and her sister Rula Lenska during a lunch break on the track to the Kali Gandaki.

*Right:* Phanit Indra and Dr Adrian Lister taking shoulder heights from a mark on a tree.

*Above:* The ruined Rani Mahal palace towers above the expedition's Avons on the Kali Gandaki River. *(Rula Lenska)*

*Left:* The Karnali Gorge. *(Mark O'Shea)*

*Below:* Major Pat Troy and Brook Hanson giving out gifts for the local school near the Tiger Tops' Karnali Lodge.

*Above:* Emergency operation to remove a bamboo splinter from Sundar Kali. *(Jack Picone)*

*Right:* Rafting on the Kali Gandaki. (*L to r:* Judith Blashford-Snell, Sue Hilliard, Dr Garry Savin, Brook Hanson, Ase Ale)

*Above:* Rula bids farewell to Chan Chan Kali at the end of the 1994 expedition. *(Sunday Mirror)*

*Right:* Dhan Bahadur, Wendy Bentall, Rula and Anne Cooke on Chan Chan Kali near our base camp at Bardia. *(Sandy Crivello)*

*Above:* Dr Adrian Lister and Dhuki Ram collecting dung for DNA sampling.

*Right:* The first sight of the giant elephants: Raja Gaj (*left*) and Kancha emerge from the forest.

*Above:* A young wild bull scenting Honey Blossom.

*Right:* Moving slowly and silently, Raja Gaj suddenly appears from the cuckoo grass right beside us – too close for comfort.

*Right:* Raja Gaj displays his incredible domed head as he lifts his heavy trunk to feed. *(Rula Lenska)*

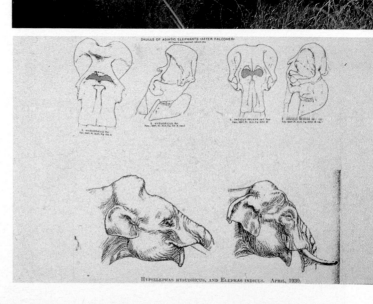

*Right: Elephas Hysudricus* with its domed head is pictured bottom left. Could this prehistoric elephant be the ancestor of Raja Gaj?

Spotted deer in Bardia, known locally as 'tiger food'.

Bimbo's tiger, photographed by Dr John Cosgrove the moment before it charged. *(John Cosgrove)*

Rhino bathing in a side channel of the Karnali at sundown.

Back at camp, Colin had news. Heading downriver, he had found a group of Raji, and when questioned about the jungle monsters, they had simply pointed south.

'Well, we'd better move on,' said Libby, scratching her sandfly bites. 'Can't get a thing in my insect trap, but this beach is alive.'

Indeed it was and most of us were suffering from itching bumps that oozed yellow fluid.

'It's the blood creating serum to reject the antibodies injected by the sandflies,' explained John Cosgrove.

'That's a great comfort,' moaned Les.

Megh had found a pool at the river junction alive with mahseer between four and ten pounds in weight, and we could see them flickering in the deep still water. Soon we had enough for a tasty fish supper. Denis looked envious. 'I've always wanted to catch a fish,' he said wistfully.

'Here's the chance,' I replied. 'Take my rod in the morning.'

I heard the cry for help while I was still in my sleeping bag. 'Must be someone in trouble on the river,' I assumed, tumbling out of the igloo-shaped tent. By the fire our cook was standing, ladle in hand, peering towards the sunrise. Some two hundred yards distant, beside the turbulent meeting place of the rivers, a figure was gesticulating. It took a minute to reach Denis, and as we came panting up he pointed frantically at the water. 'A bloody great fish – it's on my line.' Two of the raft lads waded in as a massive, glittering shape broke the surface. With much care, Denis played the monster, edging it ever closer to the bank. At last it seemed exhausted and Mahendra seized it by the gills, flipping it ashore in one quick movement.

'The first fish I've caught,' gasped the solicitor.

He had good reason to be proud: the mahseer weighed at least thirty-five pounds.

'Sponsor photo,' cried Nick, trotting up with his cameras ready. So our kind sponsors Shakespeare and Farlow's got the pictures of their rod and tackle in action.

Brigid took a hand in the cooking of the monster and produced a mouth-watering dish few will forget. A day off in camp gave us time to catch up on reports and diaries. At the same time, Brigid and Sue set up a massage parlour which got the Nepali boat boys terribly excited, and Bimbo shampooed the hair of anyone willing to test some environmentally friendly preparation that Colin had obtained.

The two motorized boats each towed another and with the Mariners to propel us, we covered seven miles in ninety minutes before pausing for lunch. Waterfalls alive with miniature rainbows tumbled through gardens of vegetation hanging from the cliffs. Along the shore, water birds rose in profusion and parakeets flitted from tree to tree. The engines ran surprisingly quietly; their sound did not distract us and it was wonderful to relax and enjoy the scenery. Megh and Tej Rana took the helms like children with a new toy. 'Much better than rowing,' smiled Sundar, appreciating this rare opportunity of effortless progress. The only problem was to get our Nepalese friends to pull the tiller in the opposite direction to that which they wished the raft to take. We ran into several rocks before they mastered the art of steering.

Moving so quickly made it difficult for them to recognize features, and suddenly Megh said, 'Baba River coming up. It's a grade three, better lift the motor.'

'Why not try driving through?' suggested John Cosgrove, and so we did.

Clutching the lifelines as we pitched down the slope, I watched the polished river-bed stones race beneath our hull and prayed none would catch our propeller. Then the stopper waves slammed into our bow and, pressed forward by the thrust of the motor, the craft bent upwards like a banana. Some invisible force wrenched us astern and through the spray I saw the heavy stores boat that we had in tow, now firmly gripped by the flow, heading straight for a jagged wall of basalt.

'Look out,' yelled Libby.

'Hold on tight,' cried Megh, scrambling for his faithful oars.

The engines screamed as John twisted the throttle to full power. 'Ponk!' The inflatable's bow struck the rock face and ricocheted back into the stream. I waited for the hiss of escaping air, but the Avon was hardly scratched.

With a squeal of neoprene on stone, the stores raft rubbed along the cliff face. Cormorants scattered in alarm and pigeons exploded from their perches. Then the tow line went tight, the engines' revs dropped and we cruised in clear water. 'Better keep well to the inside of the bend next time,' muttered Denis from our sister craft that had just picked up Sue, who had been so intent on admiring the view that an unexpected stopper wave had catapulted her over the heads of the surprised crew and into the river. In the process of being pulled aboard by Sundar, the back of her pants had come adrift, which caused much mirth.

I was watching a water-snake seek refuge in a crevice when some fishermen arrived to mend their nets. The couple looked familiar. 'Raji?' I asked and they nodded. Tej interpreted my questions, and when they were asked about animals they stated that since the great flood of nine years previously, many more people had settled in the valley. The forest was disappearing fast. Now all the big game had 'gone south'. One old man remembered my previous visit and asked for the photographs we had taken last time. I did a Polaroid shot of him at once and that made him happy.

Back at camp, the Doc did his best to ease our itching bites and stuck a crown back on my tooth with Superglue.

As the full moon rose in all its tropical glory, we sat around the fire attempting to dodge the swirling smoke and trying to sing, but no one could remember many verses of popular songs and the conversation turned back to the Raji. The verdict from all those we had met was the same – all large beasts, except possibly a leopard, had left the Karnali Valley. I felt rather sad and disappointed.

Resting his back against a rock, Henning was writing in his log with an earnest expression. High science I assumed, until he showed me his latest observations:

'Kaha charpi chaa?' Where is the loo? A constant concern while in built-up areas, but once in the country I grasp a garden trowel brought for just this purpose, allow myself a carefully rationed amount of paper, and disappear. Freezing nights in the mountains pose other problems: a) I do not want to get out of the warm sleeping bag, b) If I did I would definitely wake Colin which would be unfair, c) Outside is pitch-dark and tent ropes stretch everywhere, d) By the time I am back I am wide awake, e) Opening the tent again and climbing in would wake Colin once more. I am therefore hoarding a wide-mouthed

Sainsbury juice bottle with screw lid, which I can use in the sleeping bag, close firmly and place outside the tent flap. How nice it is to be a man! On the river banks we dug deep privies in the sand, with two stones to squat on, surrounded them with a wind break and filled them in before moving off.

The enormous suspension bridge had almost spanned the river at Chisapani, and soon the rusty old ferry would be redundant, left to decay or, more likely, carted off to spend the last of its days on another Himalayan waterway that bore the ashes of the faithful down to Mother Ganges. The hot sun was still high as we sailed up to the campsite.

Mash and a tall man with an inquisitive smile stood at the top of the bank.

'Dr Chris Thouless, I presume?' I said pumping his large hand.

'Raja Gaj is very near. He knew you were coming,' grinned Pradeep. 'We haven't seen Kancha lately, but I expect he's out there somewhere.'

The bar did a roaring trade and a mouth-watering curry restored our spirits. After supper, I strolled down to the elephant lines. Bathed in moonlight, the ladies were munching contentedly. 'Namaste, Madu Mala Kali,' I said, walking over to Honey Blossom. She stopped eating and uncurled her trunk to touch my hand. Then she gave an affectionate rumble from somewhere deep in her throat and winked her long eyelashes at me before filling her mouth with leaves once again. I stayed with her for almost half an hour until I felt she remembered me, and slipped out a juicy apple from my pocket. With a little squeak of pleasure, she took it from my hand with the sensitive tip of her trunk and popped in on to her pink tongue. 'Please look after us when we meet your boyfriend,' I said, before returning to the campfire.

Dawn was just breaking as we advanced through the ten-foot cuckoo grass with only the swish, swish of the ladies' tails and the occasional slap of an ear breaking the silence. Walking elephants, seen from behind, look like overweight ladies in grey tights with enormous wobbling buttocks.

It was a perfect morning. Against the blue sky parakeets and forest babblers flitted from tree to tree, whilst wigeon and tern wheeled over the creeks. John Cosgrove had his field glasses out and was busily adding to our bird list. Our line moved steadily forward towards a clump of sal trees. A couple of Brown Fish Owls flapped silently off a high branch, leaving their baby staring rather wistfully down at us. Then in the deep shadow something stirred. Pradeep touched my shoulder, 'Raja Gaj,' he hissed, and Man Dhoj brought Honey Blossom to a halt.

The big fellow had already found a cool resting place to avoid the heat of the day. Clearly he had dined well in the night, for all around was the debris of his meal, broken branches and fallen trees. Julian slid out the BBC recorder and in hushed tones Chris and I talked into the microphone. Raja Gaj watched us with passing interest. Our other elephants took up different positions around the King and we kept an eye out for Kancha.

'He's certainly enormous,' agreed Chris, studying our quarry through his binoculars. 'I reckon he's around fifty.'

Nick and Sue were taking detailed photographs of the ears while Henning's video hummed away. Seen sideways, Raja Gaj's magnificent curved tusks were most impressive.

'Around sixty to seventy pounds each, I'd guess,' Chris muttered. 'He's in very good condition.'

Julian pressed my arm and pointed. A hundred yards away a bush was waving although there was no breeze – Kancha was feeding nearby, but he had our scent and a few steps at a time was working his way towards us. 'We're being stalked,' whispered Julian, keeping the tape running. Raja Gaj remained peaceful, but his escort was obviously in a more aggressive mood, although he seemed to be pretending to ignore us. At least ten years younger, he was so like Raja Gaj that we felt he must be a brother.

When he was thirty paces off, Pradeep signalled to the other elephants to move away and, with an unseen pressure of his toes, Man Dhoj turned Honey Blossom's head in the direction of the best line of retreat. The younger bull watched, but went on feeding. He was twenty paces away now. Knowing how elephants hate being disturbed whilst feeding, I became conscious of my own heartbeat. Suddenly up went his head and his trunk curled back into his mouth like a coiled spring. I felt the hair stiffen on my neck. 'Go, go, go,' urged Pradeep, and Honey Blossom took off. Behind, Kancha crashed after us, scattering twigs and leaves.

After a short distance he seemed to lose interest and having got rid of the intruders, returned to browsing. My motor drive had given me a series of splendid pictures of an angry jumbo, albeit too close for comfort.

Later we looked back and found the sly fellow was following us and closing up fairly quickly, so we increased speed. Pradeep ordered Man Dhoj to use Honey Blossom as the rearguard. When Kancha was only a hundred yards behind I began to worry, but then he stopped and, seizing a tree in his trunk, snapped it off and waved it at us like an old man shaking a stick at naughty children.

Measuring a wild elephant is no easy task and Chris suggested using our Polaroid camera. Finding the big tuskers on an island in the river, we managed to keep Kancha's attention occupied by Chan Chan and Champa Kali tiptoeing around to one side of him. Meanwhile the rest of us followed Raja Gaj until he stopped to feed on level ground. Behind him Luksmi and Sundar Kali kept their distance whilst, as quietly as possible, Honey Blossom moved parallel to him. We tried to behave as if we were simply a herd grazing together. My heart leapt as a hog deer, head down and going fast, suddenly crashed through the undergrowth.

Thirty yards from the bull, we stood beside a tree on the same level. Sideways on, he was perfectly placed and I quickly snapped off two Polaroid shots across his back. The noise of the film winding on spooked the King, but I had my photographs, so, placing a piece of tissue in the tree to mark the exact spot, we rolled after him.

Following in the giant's wake, we crossed a clearing, three girls following an old man. 'Like grandpa's footsteps,' said Nick. We were barely sixty feet behind. Raja Gaj looked like an enormous, round, grey boulder as he rocked from side to side. It was an incredible sight. Something, perhaps the dust or a piece of grass, tickled the triangular underlip of Honey Blossom's trunk and she gave a loud snorting sneeze. With incredible speed the bull spun round to face us, creating a small cloud of yellow dust. For the first time I really saw his body, the massive domed head and the great girth, at close range and right out in the open. The grass was short and we got fantastic pictures.

'Kancha's coming,' warned Pradeep, and we backed away.

Returning to our earlier vantage point, I repositioned myself with my eye alongside the tissue marker and got Henning to move his elephant into Raja Gaj's footprints. There he held a graduated bamboo pole and, using the Polaroid pictures, I sighted on the horizon. Henning then moved his hand up the pole until it coincided with the position of the top of the tusker's shoulder in the photo. After several readings we reckoned he was between eleven foot and half an inch and eleven foot six inches at this point. 'Eleven foot three inches seems a reasonable estimate,' recorded Sue.

A few days later we had another brush with Kancha, who chased us for half a mile, eventually stopping to push down an eighteen-inch-thick kapok tree before retiring. It was as if he had said, 'See what I can do.' We discussed his behaviour over supper. Pradeep and Chris agreed there were various degrees of aggression. It seems that when nervous, tuskers may lay their trunk across their tusks or seek reassurance by touching a colleague. Indeed, we had seen Raja Gaj and Kancha doing this. They had also exhibited signs of agitation by throwing earth and branches over themselves.

Pradeep pointed out that the first charge may simply be a short run forward with loud trumpeting, but if this does not have the desired effect the beast may launch a mock attack ending in an impressive demonstration close to the intruder. Kancha's felling of the kapok tree was just that. Generally, the larger the elephant, the less nervous it is and thus less likely to charge. So far, the only one to go for us had been Kancha, the younger of the two giants.

A serious attack by a bull or cow determined to destroy its enemy is far more dangerous, as Chris knew from his experience in Kenya. If one of our two monsters ever did this, explained Pradeep, we could expect the trunk to be coiled back out of harm's way and the ears flattened against the body. He would come at a frightening speed, possibly without any warning or sound. Reaching his target, the bull would extend his ears, uncoil the massive trunk and strike down anything in range with a blow that could kill even a buffalo. Some elephants will then kneel or stamp on their victims. After that, he'll turn away with head and tail up and move off at right angles so that he can keep watch on the scene. When it is all over the beast may vent his wrath on trees and bushes.

'What's the best thing to do if we are charged?' asked the ever practical Colin Gutteridge.

'Well, if you are mounted stay there, let the tame elephant protect you,' recommended Pradeep.

'I recall Elephant Bill says it is better to run downhill,' I interjected, 'or try to get across a ravine that can act like an anti-tank ditch.'

'It may be possible to stop him by shouting,' said Chris.

'Of course, in the forest it's best to get out of the line of sight,' suggested Sue, who had been reading Peter Byrne's book.*

In view of Kancha's behaviour, I felt it wise to find out what sort of speed our ladies could manage in an emergency. A hundred-yard course was marked out beside the camp and one of our fastest elephants, Sundar Kali, became the guinea pig. Taking an average of three runs, we found she did about 4 mph when walking normally but could manage 10.6 mph when urged to move faster. This was at a very fast walk. Elephants don't normally trot or gallop, but I knew Raman Sukumar, the Indian elephant expert, had clocked a wild female charging after his jeep at almost twenty miles per hour. Since our earlier meetings with the giants I had realized we could not outrun them, but I had not appreciated that the difference in speed would be great.

'If the bulls get aggressive the best tactic is to confuse them,' advised Pradeep. 'We must always work in groups.'

The mist was still lying in the phanta and a heavy dew hung on the cobwebs in the trees. Our days were entirely governed by sun and moon, and now both were peeping through the fog above us. This morning there were no bird calls, no monkeys, no deer . . . I shivered in the chill air, scanning the watercourse that was looming out of the gloom. There were ripples on the water and I swung my binoculars towards the spot in the shallows. Man Dhoj did not speak, he simply raised his right arm slowly and pointed with his ankush. No one uttered; we had all seen it.

* Peter Byrne, *Tula Hatti, The Last Great Elephant* (Faber and Faber, 1990)

Barely a hundred yards away was Bagh, a big male tiger, his stripes hardly visible in the early dawn. He would have heard us long before he saw us, but fearing little he continued to drink. I raised my camera, but even with 400 ASA it was no good; in this light one needed a much faster film. We kept quite still. The ladies seemed to know what was expected of them and stood like statues. Having filled his belly, the tiger stopped lapping and straightened up, staring right at us.

Through my binoculars I watched entranced. His orange-red coat was darker than usual. Crouching by the pool his black stripes had given him no camouflage, but once in the forest they would blend in with the shadows and become all concealing. The unblinking yellow eyes were like pools of gold. Above them, the white patches of fur were flecked with blood from last night's kill and droplets of water dripped from his whiskers. A peacock's alarm call broke the silence. The great cat turned and loped away, topping the ten-foot bank in a single bound. There he stood for a moment, watching us from the edge of the forest, before vanishing into the undergrowth. As if to say, 'Come on, let's get moving,' Honey Blossom tapped the end of her trunk on the packed earth. The trunk being hollow, this produced a strange, clear, fluting, almost metallic sound. Was it her way of saying good riddance?

'Magnificent,' said Julian. It was his first tiger.

Our expeditions have always relied on the help of many companies who kindly donate products. For the anti-poaching unit, Reebok had sent shoes and Berghaus had given rucksacks. The Scientific Exploration Society's Elephant Fund had purchased torches and Silva had donated compasses. There were other items that made life more comfortable and Barts spices were always appreciated.

To thank these generous firms we took photographs of their products in use in the field, and I suggested we get Honey Blossom to hold up a pot of Barts' garlic powder. With a little encouragement from Man Dhoj, she managed to pick it up in her trunk, but the lid came off and out poured the powder. The elephant started back and sneezed violently. Giving me a very disapproving look, she refused to repeat the performance so I used Chan Chan for the other photos. As I collected my gear together I glanced back at the matriarch. She was holding an elephant sandwich in her trunk and quite deliberately rolled it into the garlic powder before popping it into her mouth. 'How strange,' I thought. 'Obviously the old girl likes garlic. She'll probably smell to high heaven tomorrow.'

Before turning in I thought I should see if there had been any effect, so I strolled down to the lines to see her. The moon was bright as I picked my way through the herd. They were too busy munching at their piles of leaves to pay me any attention, but where was Honey Blossom? Her greater height made it easy to recognize her yet I could only see four beasts. Then, above the gentle crooning of the boys' singing to their elephants, I heard a soft burbling sound. There she was, lying sound asleep like an enormous smooth black rock with her trunk curled on to her feet, snoring gently. Elephants only lie down for short periods. I'd been lucky to see her like this. I wondered if it was due to the garlic.

There was always a chance that Raja Gaj's cows might be lurking on the eastern side of the reserve, so I took out a recce party.

'Are there any crocodile here?' asked Henning as we waded through the knee-deep Babai.

'Plenty,' I reassured him.

I'd quite forgotten the remark when Tulbahadur raised his hand for us to stop. The river was behind a reed bed and, signing us to wait, our guide slid forward through the stalks. Ten minutes later he was back, motioning us to bring cameras and come very quietly. Moving with the utmost caution, we reached the water's edge and saw two thick grey logs on the far bank – at least that was what they appeared to be until I focused my zoom lens. They were gharial, the fish-eating crocodile, but absolute whoppers. Motionless, they lay on the sand. The whirr of the video didn't disturb them and in the end Tulbahadur clapped his hands. With a flash and a splash they were gone, but a few minutes later one head emerged to look around. 'Must be at least fifteen feet,' said Colin as he concentrated on estimating their lengths. 'Thankfully, they are harmless.'

We were still discussing the gharial over tea in our night campsite when I heard a faint metallic click in the long grass. I looked up, straight into the barrel of a Sterling submachine-gun. Six camouflaged figures rose as one, their guns pointed directly at our navels. Although they wore no hats, they were too uniformly dressed for poachers and all carried kukris on their belts. As the submachine-gun's owner turned to give an order, I saw three stripes on his arm and breathed a sigh of relief. 'Namaste,' I said, putting my hands together in the traditional manner.

The soldier slung his weapon over his shoulder and replied, 'Please may I see your permits?'

Tulbahadur quickly produced them. 'It's an army anti-poaching patrol,' he explained.

'Chi?' I asked, pointing to the teapot.

'That's a very civil offer,' seemed to be the gist of his answer, and soon we were chatting like old friends over a cup of tea.

Henning, who was not happy when faced with armed men, stayed silent, but they allowed me to inspect their guns and I complimented them on having British weapons and keeping them so clean.

'Dan y bat, Colonel Sahib,' said the sergeant as they melted away into the forest. It was comforting to find the wildlife of Bardia so well protected.

The embers of our little fire glowed in the breeze as a distant tiger gave his mournful call. 'Ever met one on foot?' Nick asked Tulbahadur.

'Once at Chitwan, I almost rode into Bagh on my bicycle,' he admitted.

'What on earth did you do?' asked Henning.

'Oh! I just got off and stared at him for about three minutes, then he went away.'

On the trail next day, we met a couple of villagers and our guide fell into deep conversation with the elder of the two. Later he reported that the man had told him of a giant bull with huge tusks living in this forest five years ago, but he had gone west to Sukla Phanta taking all the cows with him. He left behind three big males which they named Jeta, Maila and Kancha. All had strange domed heads, but Maila had now gone too, leaving just Jeta and Kancha. 'So Jeta is Raja Gaj,' said Libby. 'Perhaps Peter Byrne's Tula Hatti was the one that led the herd away.'

A great storm struck us on 17 February, coming as before from the Chisapani gorge with incredible displays of lightning and gale force winds. All night the thunder rolled around the valley as the deluge lashed our camp. In spite of all the noise and blinding flashes, as before, the ladies showed little reaction; unlike dogs who are often terrorized by thunderstorms, elephants do not seem unduly concerned by bad weather. Perhaps they feel big enough to be able to ignore such events. Only if storms are so severe as to herald a flood do elephants become concerned. Even forest fires seem not to worry them. The fiercest grass fires, whether part of the annual burn or started by spontaneous combustion or lightning, are usually confined to the tall grass in the phantas around the river, where creeks and dry stream beds act as fire-breaks and provide means of escape. The slower-moving conflagrations that creep along the forest floor are no problem and tame elephants can be driven straight through. The thick soles of their feet will put out fire, and provided that they keep moving, their feet won't suffer. Using their intelligence and knowledge of the effect of wind on fire, I reckon wild elephants will avoid danger. Yet flaming torches had turned Raja Gaj away from our camp the previous year, possibly because of the scent of man attached.

At daybreak the marquee was a wreck and the distant mountains were coated with snow. It was our last full day. As we sipped steaming tea, Bimbo came over. 'I've only one complaint,' she said; 'I've not seen a tiger.'

She must have been the only one who had not so I said, 'OK, Bimbo, go on Champa today. She's fast and fearless and if we spot a big cat we'll divert to give you a view.'

Unfortunately, Champa's howdah was being repaired, so Bimbo, Libby and the Doc climbed up on a bare sackcloth saddle and held on to the girth rope.

I should have been alerted by the alarm call of the deer quickly taken up by a peacock, but my attention was focused on a film change. We were moving through five-foot ferns when, with a blood-curdling growl, a large tiger sprang from beneath Honey Blossom's feet. The old girl trumpeted and raged but stood her ground as the orange-and-black figure of a big male bounced away through the cover.

'He's carrying a kill,' said Chris.

Sure enough he had a spotted deer in his powerful jaws.

'It won't go far,' said Pradeep as we set off in pursuit.

As predicted, the tiger turned into a small copse and lay down, breathing heavily. With practised drill, the elephants formed a ring. Bimbo and her team were in the best position and for several minutes had a clear view of a truly magnificent Royal Bengal tiger at the edge of the trees. We felt very privileged, as many more humans are seen by tigers than ever glimpse them. Cameras clicked and from where I was placed I could just see its tail beginning to twitch from side to side.

'Looks agitated,' muttered Henning.

'Yes,' I said, 'we'd better leave him in . . .'

Before I could finish there was a shattering roar and I saw its back legs working like pistons as the predator hurled itself at Bimbo's elephant. Seeing the cat coming, Libby screamed. In the same instant, squealing and trumpeting, Champa turned to face the charge. Her trunk flailed as the tiger dodged and stopped its rush a few feet from the ex-gritter driver from Yorkshire. Then, still trumpeting, the young elephant turned and gave chase, almost tipping off the gallant trio. Our herd were in full cry as we rounded the wood.

'Are you all right, Bimbo?' I shouted.

'Yes, thank you,' she replied serenely, 'but that pussy should have a collar on it.'

Later I heard that the tiger's teeth had been a couple of feet from Bimbo's leg. It took several minutes for everyone to stop chattering like excited children and for the adrenaline to die down. 'There's not a lot of room here,' shouted John Cosgrove, from the howdah-less Champa, so I invited him to join me on Honey Blossom. Climbing aboard, he confided that the real reason for wanting to change mounts was that when the tiger had charged, Bimbo had grabbed his trousers and got so excited she'd almost pulled them off. 'I'm worried what might happen if we meet another one.'

On the way home we talked about the courageous way Champa Kali had behaved. Given a chance, tiger will kill a calf elephant and thus the females regard the cat as a threat. Over the years, domestic elephants have been used to hunt tiger. Naturally enough the quarry may object to being surrounded and will charge. Occasionally one will spring on to an elephant's back or claw its way up the trunk, which may account for a certain amount of inbred dislike for the large felines by jumbo.

It is not uncommon for tiger to charge elephants if they are feeding on a kill or, more likely, have cubs nearby. The fact that they roar shows that their intention is to frighten them away rather than to kill. However, it is not easy to convince anyone of this if they have been attacked.

Highly elated, we rode home under clear skies with the sun sinking fast and Venus already glowing in the west. In the mountains, lightning still flickered amongst the peaks. Back at camp a message awaited me. 'If you would like a two-week visit to Arunachal Pradesh in the far north-east of India, beyond the Brahmaputra, please call John Edwards a.s.a.p.'

So it was I found myself in one of the most remote, fascinating and least explored rainforests in the world.

## Chapter Seven

# INTO INDIA

WAVING their heads, the odious worm-like creatures looped towards us, seeking blood. Even as we walked they advanced. I had never seen leeches in such profusion, and in the virgin rainforests of Namdapha in north-east India where I had gone in April 1993, they were a real plague. The canvas anti-leech gaiters helped, liberally soaked with deet, but they could still drop on us as we moved through the moist dark corridors of jungle. Preferring warm-blooded animals, the leeches consider humans a delicacy. 'It's no good, I can't tackle the botany if my boots are full of blood,' said Judith Heath, a well-travelled New Zealander who was in our recce party. I noticed there was even one of the loathsome beasts crawling over her floppy sun-hat.

Back at camp, patching up our wounds, I asked if there were any elephants in the area.

'We have two and a half elephants,' replied the village headman.

'What is half an elephant?' I queried.

'A baby,' came the reply.

'That's the last thing we need,' groaned John Hunt. 'It will be untrained and ill-disciplined.'

'But you must take baby,' stated the chief. 'Mummy will not go without baby.'

'How about the other elephant?' asked Eric Niemi, our American zoologist.

'That is Auntie, she won't go without it, either.'

Next morning, breakfasting on the lawn of the picturesque little lodge, we heard the familiar cry of 'Aghit' and out of the trees appeared John Hunt seated confidently on the neck of a large female. Closely behind came another and then running to catch up was Lucky, a four-foot-tall four-year-old. John's training in Nepal had been put to good use. As expected, the baby was totally uncontrolled and with a squeal of delight Lucky headed straight for our loaf of bread.

We climbed on to our leech-proof mounts but, sure enough, the journey was much delayed. Whenever its mother plucked some choice snack, her offspring would dash in and try to steal it. The resultant slap from mama's trunk produced a scream of rage and the baby would go off to sulk in the undergrowth. A while later the mother would notice she was missing, so Auntie would be despatched to find her. The process was repeated frequently and our study of the ferns, orchids and airplants was seriously held up.

On the way home we had to cross a deep, wide and fast-flowing river. 'What about the baby?' asked Judith, as we pushed across the current. The adults seemed to have forgotten the young one and already I was having to pull up my feet to avoid the swirling water. Pivoting round, I expected to see a mournful Lucky on the bank, for she surely could never wade across, but there behind was a little trunk, happily snorkelling along in our wake.

In camp, we dismounted but the elephants' path to their quarters was blocked by a contractor's car. The big old ladies stood waiting for someone to move it. Lucky was not so patient, and without warning lowered her head and butted the wing hard, several times. As the metal buckled a demented driver appeared, calling down the wrath of all Hindu deities on baby elephants. They may be adorable, but they are also mischievous.

Whilst in north-east India, we showed our photographs of Raja Gaj and Kancha to anyone interested, in the hope that they might have seen some similar beasts. No one had, but it was suggested that large elephants were more common in the north-west of the country. 'Perhaps we should look in the reserves near the Nepalese borders,' suggested Julian, when we returned to my expedition base in Dorset to discuss plans for the next move in the investigation.

The BBC Natural History Programme had used our tape recordings, and consequently the publicity had spread. One of many

letters we received came from Clive Coy of the Royal Tyrrell
Museum of Palaeontology in Alberta, Canada, to whom I had
sent a photograph and a report:

> Thank you very much for the excellent black-and-white photo-
> graph of Raja Gaj, truly a magnificent animal. I was very pleased
> to see that the elephants really exist as some sceptics here felt
> it was another 'sasquatch' story. Dr Thouless' report was very
> informative and put the situation into clear perspective.
> Canada's vast wild areas are also under constant threat of deve-
> lopment and destruction.
>
> Asian elephants of this proportion have not been previously
> reported in the literature. While it is possible that their size is
> due to a 'wild' environment, certain morphological features beg
> further investigation ... Were any skeletal elements found in
> the surrounding area? A single cheek tooth could be very
> instructive.
>
> Recently a student from Nepal, Gopal Dungal, recovered the
> first mammoth remains from Nepal. These animals were pre-
> viously unknown in this part of Asia and opened up the range
> of mammoth habits.
>
> We at the Royal Tyrrell Museum wish you and your Society
> members the very best in future endeavors. If I or the Institution
> can be of help to you, please feel free to contact us.

Encouraged by this, we felt it would be useful to see if any
bones could be found. Elephant graveyards are something of a
myth. Most of the great beasts choose to die near water and
their remains are washed away by the monsoon. However, a
sharp-eyed phanit might have seen something in Chitwan or
Bardia, so I phoned John Edwards.

'K. K. Gurung found a molar near the Indian border some years
ago,' he said. 'I'll see if I can locate it.'

As KK was now working in London, I sought him out. 'It was
in the late Seventies,' he recalled, 'I was following the Kama
Mana Khola, a river on the western edge of the park. We'd been
on an expedition along the Narayani and my thoughts were really
only of getting home. Passing by a small stream, I saw something
strange jutting out of the sand. At first I thought it was an oddly

patterned rock, but when I picked it up I found it to be an old tooth of an elephant. Although it was quite heavy I popped it in my rucksack and we used it as a paperweight in my office.' It was there that John Edwards found it. Now we needed a palaeontologist.

Andrew Mitchell, zoologist, TV producer and deputy director of Earthwatch, had worked with me on many projects and I put the problem to him. 'Adrian Lister is the man you need,' he replied to my letter. 'He did an excellent job when we excavated the mammoths in Shropshire.' I remembered reading of Dr Lister's work in the press after a mass of fossil bones had come to light in a quarry and immediately phoned him at University College, London, to arrange a meeting.

The construction of the King Mahendra Highway running east to west through the foothills had destroyed the corridor along which wild elephant moved between sanctuaries and, although those in Sukla Phanta could go west to India, Chris Thouless reckoned our two bulls in Bardia were isolated from other elephants. The corridor to the Dudhwa reserve in India had also disappeared. However, in his report Chris had mentioned that it was not yet impossible for elephants to leave Bardia. 'They are able to cover considerable distances in the course of a single night and have been known to move across substantial tracts of arable country,' he wrote. 'Much would depend on their motivation for leaving, their ability to remember a route that has been changed through human influence and avoiding harassment by people.'

However, assuming that the tuskers were isolated, Chris went on to consider the desirability of bringing in cow elephants to Bardia. There were already problems of crop-raiding, for all that this was not entirely due to elephants (in fact, rhino were said to be far greater culprits). Chris felt that although the problem might be exaggerated, it was real and he found it particularly galling when the people did not get compensation, or benefit financially, from the presence of the park, except by being allowed to carry out grass cutting there once a year. He wrote: 'While people may be sanguine about crop raiding by animals already existing in the park, since this is a natural process, they are likely to blame any additional problems caused by introduced animals on the people who carried out the reintroduction. During a period of political change where a greater element of democracy is being introduced in Nepal, these issues are likely to become aired more publicly. It is important not to give additional ammunition to those who would like to see the park abolished and the areas turned over to agricultural land for Nepal's ever-increasing population.'

Chris recounted that another argument for reintroducing cow elephants to Bardia would be to preserve the genetic resource of the large elephant. 'It has been argued that they are unusual morphologically and may represent a distinct type. The particular features that have led people to this conclusion are the large body size, the considerable girth and pronounced domed forehead. However, it seems likely that these are just extremes of the normal range of variation and people are unused to seeing large wild male elephants since they are rare and shy, particularly as a result of poaching pressure on big tuskers throughout Asia.'

He went on to state that 'the ecological role of elephants in maintaining eco-systems at pre-climax state is of potential significance, especially since in Bardia the most diverse and rich wildlife habitats are the intermediate successional states of grassland and savannah, rather than the climax sal forest. At present these sub-climax habitats are maintained by seasonal inundation and changes in the course of tributaries of the Karnali River. If the proposed dam is built upstream, these effects may be reduced and, with them, habitat diversity. Rhinos are also of importance for this. Further study is needed.'

Finally he concluded that 'in view of the public relations at a time of political change, cows should not be introduced.'

Strangely the elephants managed to solve both problems. In November 1993 I received word from John Edwards that four or five additional wild elephants had been seen in the Bardia reserve. They were all thought to be bulls. Where on earth had they come from? My guess was Dudhwa, the park in India nearest to Bardia. It was also the home of the legendary conservationist Billy Arjan Singh. In fact Chris Thouless had reported that a herd of over thirty had spent nearly ten years there in the 1960s and 1970s. They were thought to have come south from Nepal following massive destruction of their habitat. The herd bull was described as 'a magnificent animal, more than eleven feet tall at the shoulder'. Perhaps this was Raja Gaj.

Adrian Lister's office was at the top of many flights of stairs, and as I climbed I wondered how he got his larger specimens to this height. In his garret, fossils were laid out neatly on the shelves, and books covering every aspect of mammoths were spread throughout the room.

'It's a sub-fossil,' he smiled, 'an unerupted tooth, I'd say.' Handling the molar K. K. Gurung had found, which had now been brought in from the Tiger Tops office, he went on, 'Probably hundreds rather than thousands of years old.' Clearly his interest was aroused. 'If we could find the site, there might well be more undiscovered material.'

Over lunch in the UCL dining room, we talked of Raja Gaj and Kancha. Adrian, who had just completed a five-year study of mammoths, had never been to the Indian sub-continent. Whether it was Clive Coy's remarks about the Nepalese finding the remains of a mammoth or just the need for a change of scenery I'm not sure, but by the time the coffee arrived, he had agreed to come with us.

To have one of the world's leading authorities on the evolution and natural history of mammoths in the team would certainly help to solve the mystery of the origins of our big bulls. I promised to contact KK straight away to see if he could remember the site well enough to give directions. So the next phase was planned. We would send Adrian ahead with John Edwards to search for the fossil bed at Chitwan, whilst I brought up the rest of the team through India. We would pause to seek information at Corbett National Park, and then spend a few days with Billy at Dudhwa to get his opinion on the giant elephants, before finally meeting up with Adrian at Bardia.

Since our previous expedition I had lost a key member of our team: Sally Cox, my PA for much of the time since 1987, had married Megh Ale, the outstanding Nepalese rafter. Sally had always said she didn't like boats so this caught me by surprise. However, I had been lucky enough to find a super replacement,

Carol Turner, and it was she who bore the brunt of organizing the new expedition.

Sandy Crivello, an enthusiastic computer expert and an excellent photographer from Arizona, had been with the Discovery Expedition in Guyana the previous year and was the first to volunteer. My good friends Robert and Faanya Rose were also keen to come. Robert, a tall, slim American living in London, was in his early seventies, extremely fit and great company on a trip. He had been with me to both the Kalahari and Gobi deserts. Faanya, whom he had recently married, was a most astute businesswoman and the Treasurer of BAA plc. Originally from Zimbabwe, she was far tougher than her slim build suggested. From Canada came a pal of Robert Rose's: Ray Lowes was the toughest octogenarian I had ever met and had a good sense of humour. He was a passionate conservationist and had done much good work in his native land.

In Jersey I recruited Pat Troy, formerly a major in the Royal Marines, who had served in the Special Boat Service. I had known Pat for over thirty years, a good man in a tight spot. Now sporting an impressive grey beard, he looked more piratical than ever. Also from Jersey was Graham King, a retired traffic warden who had been brought up in India and could speak some Hindi.

I had met Wendy Stephens at a dinner in Devon. Her interest in birds would be extremely useful. Anne Cooke had been helping me in the office. She was an accomplished artist, a great traveller and a very effective local magistrate. Michael St George Wilson was an adventurous doctor with a practice in Chelsea, whilst Wendy Bentall was a most amusing lady with a deep interest in plants. My colleague of many expeditions, Paula Urschel from California, came as the nurse and was to prove her worth in no uncertain way.

It was Christmas when the actor Dennis Waterman called. 'I want to give Rula a very special wedding anniversary present,' said the star of stage and screen, whom I'd known since Operation Raleigh's time in Australia. 'She is crazy about elephants. Could you take her on your next trip?' Rula Lenska, his stunningly attractive actress wife, was noted for her very genuine efforts to protect wildlife. She had done much to help me during my days with Raleigh and I had no hesitation in accepting her on the spot.

'Keep it quiet, John,' asked Dennis, 'I want to surprise her.'

So the team was made up and, when news of Rula's involvement broke, the press took an immediate interest and wanted to come too. In the end we settled for *Hello* magazine and took along Jack Picone, a charming Australian photographer.

Those who did not know the fiery redhead of Polish origin might have thought her just another actress out for publicity, but as our group soon discovered, she was a dedicated conservationist and completely genuine in her love of animals. Rula was also an accomplished photographer and an able writer. Her reaction to Dennis's surprise gift is best summed up in a letter she wrote to a friend:

Dennis has always been not only generous but extremely innovative with presents and never more so than with anniversaries. January 4 was our seventh and my whole family had been hinting for weeks about the incredibility of this one. Hints and secret smiles, particularly from my daughter and younger sister – remarks like 'You are so lucky,' and 'You will never guess, even in your wildest dreams.' I was intrigued and very excited.

Finally the morning arrived and we were brought a delicious breakfast in bed by my daughter. On the tray was a bulging envelope with the words 'To my lady' written on the front. Nervously I opened it and took out a thick sheaf of folded papers. The first thing I saw was 'Discovery Expeditions' Giant Elephant Quest'. I couldn't believe my eyes. I think my first verbal reaction was, 'I don't believe it.' There was the brochure, the itinerary and a letter from John whom, of course, I had got to know very well since I had been an Honorary President of Operation Raleigh for several years.

I was completely overwhelmed as I read through the itinerary: from Heathrow to Delhi to Corbett, on to Dudhwa and finally to Bardia. An Asian safari. A dream come true and, most magical of all, on elephant back! Tears of gratitude streamed down my face and I hugged my generous husband. I still had six weeks to go – at that moment I never thought I would be able to wait that long. Surely the most wonderful present I'd ever had.

From that day to the day of our departure, every moment was filled with excitement and planning. The preparation list was long: hundreds of injections, special kit, many books to read, camera and video gear to prepare, visas, briefings and dreams – dreams of elephant and tiger and sitting round campfires in the jungles and spending three weeks discovering, learning and exploring. I had always known that anticipation holds at least a quarter of the joy of the actuality, but the actuality was more than I ever dreamed of. Thank you, Dennis!

On expeditions long and common names can cause confusion. We had a great many Johns, several Wendys, and Blashford-Snell is far too much of a mouthful over a bush radio. Since my earliest expeditions I had given those who were referred to most frequently a nickname for use on radio or telex. 'Choose a four-letter word that describes you,' I'd say. 'Don't use colours, place names or anything unpronounceable.' I had long been Lion and now Rula was aptly called Tigress – a bit long but it was easy to use. She promptly produced a marvellous orange sweater with a huge tiger's head on it. It matched her hair perfectly!

In addition to studying the giant elephants, we had agreed to find out as much as possible about the tiger population in the various reserves. Once again, the great cat's very existence was threatened by poachers supplying the insatiable demand for almost every part of the tiger's body. There were also botanical and cultural studies to be made and, as always, a survey of traditional medicine. Everyone in the team had a job.

Equipment for the expedition included our faithful image intensifier, kindly loaned by Pilkingtons, and a couple of global positioning system receivers (GPS) from the Scientific Exploration Society. In order to steady my camera whilst photographing from the swaying howdah I searched for a mount like a rifle butt. Eventually I found one at Jessops in Liverpool. This would enable me to operate my Nikon single-handed.

A smooth overnight flight to Delhi was even more comfortable thanks to British Airways upgrading all fifteen of us to Club Class. The gods were smiling. Yatish from Tiger Mountain was at the airport to meet us as we emerged into the blinding sunlight. With little delay, we clambered aboard our bus which, curiously, had carpet on its ceiling. 'Perhaps it is in case we turn over,' suggested Wendy Bentall. The shock absorbers had long since given up, and the brakes squealed in protest as pedestrians and animals hurled themselves across our path. The only item that worked well was the horn, which blared incessantly.

The journey to Corbett took ten hours, passing the Viceroy's fascinating palace. '. . . each section a frame of life, people and animals living on the edge of the road, lorries and cars always hooting, people shouting, making, mending, cooking, washing, selling or simply sleeping and talking. Occasionally we crossed wide, almost dry river beds. Sometimes we went through large towns which took twenty minutes to traverse. We saw a steam train, buffalo carts, ancient cars from the Fifties, rickshaws and ladies carrying wood and straw on their heads. We passed our first road death: a man with his head sliced in half following an accident,' wrote Mrs Bentall in her diary.

Having travelled for several hours we came upon an open area with fields and a lake, where Wendy spotted a group of three or four enormous man-size storks standing on the edge of the water. 'Stop the bus,' she shouted, and we screeched to a halt. Grateful for a chance to stretch, we piled out. Almost immediately, out of nowhere it seemed, we were surrounded by a group of wide-eyed Indians, who could hardly believe what they were seeing, especially Rula in her leopard-print leggings. The men appeared to be wearing giant nappies and flip-flops but the women looked graceful in bright saris. One man arrived carrying a tray of freshly cooked hot spicy chickpeas which some gobbled up with relish. I hoped the effect on European stomachs, which can suffer terribly from Indian food, would not be too dramatic.

Even though it was 9.40 p.m. when we reached the Quality Inn Lodge set in green hills near Corbett, a filling curry awaited. We needed it because the temperature was dropping rapidly and we blessed the fires in our rooms. As I briefed the team, Wendy, being of the opinion that no right-minded traveller should proceed without a bottle of Grand Marnier, warmed our hearts with some of this very welcome grog. We slept soundly but the night was all too short; dawn was chilly and damp.

It may seem strange that India's foremost national park should be named after a legendary hunter. Between 1907 and 1939 Jim Corbett tracked down and despatched a large number of man-eaters that had slaughtered a total of 1,300 people. Two of his most notable successes were the Champaw tigress, said to have accounted for 436 victims, and the Panar leopard, who had killed 400. But Jim was also a naturalist and one of the first shikari to turn to conservation. In the 1920s he laid down his gun and started shooting game with a camera, turning his sights to the preservation of wildlife.

Much concerned about the growing independence movement in the 1930s, Jim feared what the end of European administration would mean for the forest and wilderness areas of India. Foreseeing corruption and mismanagement, he prophesied their decline. Tiger were already decreasing and, if the continent's animals were to be saved, a large well-run reserve must be created. Jim had often fished and hunted with Sir Malcolm Hailey, Governor of the province. One of their favourite spots for mahseer and trout was the Ramganga River, south of Kanda. Corbett had once shot a man-eating tiger there and he knew the area well. The forests were still intact, leopard and tiger were plentiful, and there was a large population of deer. Winding through the low hills, the fast-flowing river contained mugger crocodile and otters. Bird life was prolific.

Thus it was that Hailey, persuaded by Corbett and his forest officers, recommended the establishment of a sanctuary in which there would be no hunting or logging. So in 1936 India's first national park was established. It was hoped that, free from human interference, tiger would multiply. Indeed, Sir Malcolm hoped this would enable other hunting areas of the country to be restocked with tiger. Whilst Jim might not have fully supported the restocking for hunting policy, he realized this was a step in the right direction as far as conservation of wildlife was concerned. However, the idea of a reserve area was not all Jim's. His friend E. A. Smythies, a forest officer, had put forward a proposal in 1916 but it had been rejected. Other shikari also recognized the need.

All these men were hunters and, in many cases, so were their wives. Mrs Smythies had the rare distinction to have been attacked in a tree by a tiger. While sitting in a high machan (shooting platform) near Tanakpur, she was spotted by an extremely aggressive cat. Seeing her in her lofty perch, the snarling beast had clawed its way up the trunk and was about to seize her feet when the good lady promptly put the rifle between her legs and fired into the gaping mouth. Blood squirted over her as both she and the tiger plummeted to the ground. Luckily her husband, who was nearby, finished off the attacker. Today the place of this unusual battle is marked by a small obelisk. It was because of such people, Europeans and Indians who knew and respected wildlife, that the reserves were set up all over India.

Corbett National Park is currently managed by the state government and Project Tiger. Being 530 square miles it is one of the few places where tiger live wild in their natural environment. Movement is largely by elephant, for thankfully there are few motor tracks in the park.

Reveille came at 4 a.m., causing some of our number to regret the Grand Marnier session. An hour before dawn the jeeps awaited us, their drivers swathed in heavy woollens, their exhausts puffing clouds of steam into the cold, still air. Gulping strong tea, we clambered aboard, our eyes still heavy with sleep, and bounced over the rough track towards the park gate, for Corbett, unlike the reserves of Nepal, opens and closes at set times and visitors must therefore sleep outside the reserve. Looking around our gallant band in the cold grey dawn, I saw that the effects of Wendy's sweet, sticky liqueur, the spicy curry and the short night had not been relieved by hot tea.

To make matters worse, this was to be our first disappointment, for by the time we had queued for admission at the entrance, we had lost half an hour of the best game-viewing time. With us had come two experienced Nepalese naturalists, Dhan Bahadur and Ram Din Mahato. Both spoke good English, but in India they were very quiet. 'They do not like us here,' confided Dhan. Possibly because of their expert knowledge of wildlife there was some jealousy. I watched with interest as they manipulated the Indian guides with diplomacy that would have befitted an ambassadorial post. In fact, I think they felt themselves to be ambassadors for their country. Certainly their smartness, tact, manners and wisdom suited them perfectly for the self-appointed role. Even if the local guides resented Dhan and Ram, we loved them.

Although eager to see the big cat, our task was primarily to gather more information on elephants. It was thought that we might find more giant bulls with great domed heads and enormous bodies here and perhaps learn of some migratory pattern that would link Corbett to Bardia.

With the agility of a much younger man, Ray Lowes led us into the howdahs and, mounted on our jumbos, we set off at a steady pace. From the start it became obvious that the mahouts, as phanits are called in India, only took tourists on sedate game walks. No amount of pleading could persuade them to divert from well-worn routes through the stately sal forests and along the dry creeks. Even the elephants seemed bored and, compared with the ladies of Bardia, this lot was a timid, unenterprising bunch, interested only in doing as little work as possible. I hoped we wouldn't meet an irritable tiger. A sambar bellowed and chital called, but we were not likely to see either wild elephant or tiger with these drivers.

'There,' whispered Paula as she caught a glimpse of a large grey brown stag. Its short, sharp alarm call, 'Pook!', echoed through the forest. The sambar stamped his foot, then with ears pricked and tail raised, trotted off into the shadows. Wild boar scuttled through the grass and pausing by a pool we watched an iridescent kingfisher diving for minnows. The skeleton of a big python gleamed white in the grass and, as the ubiquitous langurs leapt from tree to tree, a muntjac scampered for cover, but all we saw of tiger was a fairly fresh pug mark. 'The big animals are all in the core area,' explained the warden. 'It is not permitted to go there.'

The park gates closed at 5 p.m., just as the game started to move, and we had to leave. 'A frustrating day,' I wrote in my log.

The only one of us who had any real success was Wendy Bentall, our botanist, whose findings already filled a large notebook. Perched on an elephant's back, she had every opportunity to study the flora and had soon discovered Bengal quince (*Aegle marmelos*), whose fruit is used for many purposes including making glue and laxatives. The young bombax (or kapok tree) is covered in protective spikes resembling limpets, its branches grow out in regular whorls and the leaves digitate like a chestnut. On this spring day, its beautiful red-orange flowers, rather like magnolia, had made a splendid sight against the deep blue sky. Rhesus monkeys were feasting on the pods as we tramped past. The white cotton fibre that bursts from the seeds is used to fill life jackets, and the flowers also have medicinal properties.

Like a mobile encyclopaedia, Wendy gave us a running commentary on her finds. 'You can get a red gum from the freshly cut bark of this tree,' she enthused, pausing by a Bengal kino tree. 'A great cure for numerous complaints.' In her sun hat and long dress, she was the image of an elegant Victorian lady. 'There,' she cried, 'touch that and watch.' I reached out from the howdah to a small, sparse *Gardena turgida*, a touch-me-not tree, with its two-inch-long spikes. As I stroked it, the branches trembled. 'Must be your touch, John,' called Rula. Michael then had a go and it wriggled with joy. Wendy asked our guide to pluck a leaf, whereupon he pulled off a large twig – at which point the tree nearly had apoplexy, swaying all over the place. As game was scarce, it was a relief to find something of interest and the Doctor took note of some clumps of *Cannabis sativa* or hemp.

We were especially concerned by the presence of *Lantana camera*, also known as Cherry Pie or Cloth of Gold. A native of South America, it is slowly killing Corbett National Park. Of the ten square miles we visited, about seven were choked with this weed. The leaves are poisonous, causing animals to be sensitive to ultra-violet light, resulting in dermatitis and internal haemorrhage. In the National Park creatures such as deer and pig keep away from it, thus predators like tiger and leopard, finding no prey, are also absent.

In addition, *Lantana* swamps the local plants, smothering them and preventing regeneration of native species, denying grazing animals their food. Trees in the area are mostly fire resistant, so controlled burning is the first step towards a solution. When the weed starts to re-grow, the correct use of a translocated herbicide will finish it off once and for all. This would need to be done by an expert, but the chemical is safe to use since it is neutralized on contact with the ground and is not poisonous to animals.

Without treatment, Corbett National Park will be dead by the beginning of the next century.

Up before first light, we were sipping our morning tea in the lodge when Ray said, 'Just a moment, I'm going to get something,' and went across the darkened lawn to his room. We all heard the thump and a grunt. The poor chap had tripped over a low wall and fallen heavily, breaking his glasses. Michael had a quick look at him and prescribed rest. Although shaken, the rugged old Canadian seemed more concerned about missing a chance to see tiger.

The sun was scorching when we stopped at midday for lunch and, having dined on cold, soggy chips wrapped in newspaper, I fell asleep. Seizing the opportunity, Wendy recorded my snores whilst Rula did a wildlife voice-over. I was awoken by the arrival of A. S. Nagi, the Field Director of Project Tiger. He was a charming, charismatic, handsome man with steel blue eyes. 'I am very sorry you have not seen much,' he apologized, 'so I have brought something to show you.' He gestured to a game guard standing by a three-ton truck that accompanied him. As the tailgate dropped, we heard a rattling growl for there in a stout cage was crouched an extremely angry leopard.

'It was caught in the wire of a farmer's fence,' explained Nagi, 'I shall release him in the core area.'

'Could we watch?' questioned Faanya.

'I'm afraid it is not possible. For safety's sake the guards stay in the cab of the truck and open the door of the cage by remote control. A leopard can be most unpredictable.'

To illustrate his point, the snarling beast bared his teeth and struck at the bars. Unperturbed, Anne Cooke, our JP, closed in for a photograph. 'Just another juvenile delinquent,' muttered the magistrate.

Mr Nagi reckoned that there were between 110 and 130 tigers in Corbett and poaching was negligible. Then he turned his attention to the pictures of Raja Gaj and Kancha. For a while no one spoke, and he passed the photos to his colleagues.

'It is a strange fellow,' he said, shaking his head. 'We have not seen one like this here, but in Hindi we call dome-headed elephants Kumaria Bund.'

'Is there a migratory trail between Corbett and any of the Nepal-ese reserves?' asked Rula.

Nagi thought not, pointing out that the range of high hills lay in the way. 'The largest elephant here is a tusker called Lord Jim. He is ten foot three inches at the shoulder. I feel your odd giants may have come from Dudhwa. Perhaps Billy Arjan Singh can help.'

'That's just where we're going,' smiled Rula.

## Chapter Eight

# ON THROUGH
# TIGER HAVEN

AS the afternoon cooled, we drove in jeeps through wooded hills with little to see. When we paused to film a small herd of spotted deer, a couple of Europeans arrived behind us, glaring impatiently, and overtook in a cloud of dust, scattering the animals. 'Oh to be in Nepal,' sighed Ram.

At the lodge, Ray had taken a turn for the worse. Michael decided that the shoulder was fractured and there was no way he could continue. We all felt sad, for in his short time with us he had become very popular. 'I'll take him to Delhi,' volunteered Paula, ever the caring nurse, and we ordered the best taxi in the area.

That night a violent storm hit us, heralding a day of rain and thus problems on the roads. The food at the lodge was pretty dull, the visit to Corbett was not proving particularly productive and on the way home both Rula and the video camera had been thrown out of the jeep as we motored across a flooded section of road. Whilst Rula recovered quickly with the aid of a few expletives and a stiff drink, the camera did not. However, the next day we found a tame baby elephant being displayed at the entrance to a lodge. Its owners, Mr and Mrs Khatan, made us very welcome and the little fellow cheered us up.

So if the giants did not come from Corbett, perhaps, as Mr Nagi suggested, they had originated in Dudhwa. Billy Arjan Singh, a passionate conservationist, had devoted much of his life to protecting the wildlife of this particular area. Tiger Haven is at Dudhwa on the northern edge of the Indian Plains, five miles from the frontier with Nepal, where the rolling flat land gives way to the forest of the Terai, before rising into the foothills of the great Himalayas. Here Billy, in the face of many difficulties, had fought to set up a sanctuary to shelter one of the last great herds of swamp deer. He had made this place his home from which he could study the animals, and in particular the tiger. Like Jim Corbett, Billy had developed from hunter to farmer to conservationist and photographer. Years before, he had become famous for his pets: the unlikely combination of a dog, a leopard and a tigress all lived happily in Billy's home. Today few men knew more than Billy about tiger and I looked forward to hearing his views on their somewhat doubtful future. His opinion on Raja Gaj would also be very useful.

The journey should have taken seven hours, but either our bus driver did not know the way, or he took a longer road to avoid the mud. Graham endeavoured to keep him on the right track, but it was all to no avail. Darkness had already fallen by the time we neared our destination. Few foreigners came this way and the sight of Rula in her python-skin leggings and a tiger sweater, striding back from a comfort stop, almost caused a bullock driver to fall off his cart.

None of us knew the area and we arrived at Dudhwa much later than planned. After many stops to ask directions, we found a barely discernible sign pointing into the bush. It said TIGER HAVEN. Without hesitation, our driver plunged his vehicle off the tarmac and down a slippery dirt track. I was dead tired but thankfully not so dozy that I failed to see the gleam of water in the headlights' faint glow. The bloody idiot was driving straight into a river. 'Stop,' I bellowed, and we pulled up with our front wheels in the water. The flood stretched as far as we could see and when put in reverse the wheels simply dug deeper into the mud.

'Women and children first,' cried Wendy Bentall as we debussed into the moist, insect-ridden darkness. Pat Troy and I did a quick recce ahead. A nearby river had burst its banks.

'This vehicle is not going anywhere tonight,' pronounced Graham King, with a traffic warden's authority, pulling on his green sou'wester purposefully.

Rula recorded the rest of the drama in her diary:

*We disembarked from the bus, tired and slightly nervous. We were actually within the park boundaries and had been informed that tiger, elephant and rhino were abundant. Since we had seen so little in Corbett, my heart was crying out for an encounter, even a dangerous one. While the men tried to wedge grasses and twigs under the wheels of the bus to stop it sinking further, the two Wendys, Anne, Sandy and I gathered whatever was available to make several small fires. It was pitch black and even the torches strapped to our heads did little to illuminate the situation. Dhan announced that he was going to jog the half mile or so to the park gates to get help. I wanted to go with him but he felt he could get there faster on his own. Small faith in my female stamina!*

*Within a short time he was back with Mr Khan, the park warden, whose heavily perfumed betel nut breath wafted over us as he purred his greetings and invited us back to the lodge for the night. The luggage was transported first and then the human cargo. Jack, Dhan and I opted to walk to save the minibus another journey. I kept imagining sounds and seeing eyes, but we arrived safely and were shown our living quarters. All but Jack and the Colonel, who were the loudest snorers, were assigned to one dormitory: soiled, lumpy mattresses and old iron bedsteads, no sheets, all manner of dirt and bugs on the walls and floor, a leaking tap and two filthy toilets that didn't flush. Magic! We all bagged beds, ladies interspersed with men. Our trusty Dhan elected to sleep in his sleeping bag across the threshold – just in case. Within half an hour, having partaken of a mixture of whatever alcohol we had saved – Grand Marnier, Vodka, J&B – we were like a bunch of giggling school kids.*

*After a brief conversation with the slightly inebriated and highly perfumed Mr Khan, who assured me that we would see everything in large quantities in the morning, even a Rhino Project encampment with babies, we trooped in to a welcome supper. Further fuelled by some beer, we tumbled back to our dorm, huddled together, covered with every spare bit of clothing and whatever moth-eaten, raggedy blankets we could find. We finally dozed off dreaming of elephants, tigers and rhinos. I really believed the following morning's game ride would finally reveal the majestic beasts which had evaded us so far. Wishful thinking . . .*

During the night, Dhan had organized riding elephants and at first light we marched into the swirling mist. 'We're not going to see much in this,' muttered Sandy, loading the fastest film she had. True enough, only a barking deer and a lone, serpent-crested eagle, perched like a solitary sentinel on a branch, were there to greet us. Then I heard the most unusual noise: 'Chuff-chuff.'

'Sounds like a train,' remarked Wendy Stephens, who'd been listening for bird calls.

'Could it be a rhino?' I thought, 'they make a short snorting noise.'

The chuffing got louder and then out of the mist we saw a railway line and a train pulled by an ageing steam engine, chugging along to Dudhwa Junction.

Back at Park HQ, Billy Arjan Singh had arrived. A little more frail than when we had last met in London, he still had a twinkle in his eye. His soft-spoken manner concealed a fiery and determined character which fought obstinately for the animals of India. Also there was Mr M. G. Ghildial, Chief Conservator of Forests (Wildlife), from the State Wildlife Department at Lucknow. Over a good breakfast in the canteen we discussed the problems. The government servant and conservationist were perfectly civil to each other, but I sensed Mr Ghildial was wondering what Billy was up to. The presence of our group and the attendant publicity potential was not lost on him.

At this point Paula rejoined us, having seen Ray safely into hospital in Delhi where he was already mending. Her journey had been pretty dramatic and, having witnessed four terrible car crashes, she was glad to be back with friends.

I had sent out in advance copies of our photos for Billy to examine. 'A very large and similarly structured elephant has been raiding my sugar cane fields and my nightwatchman affirms that it is the same as in the photographs,' he had written. He went on to say, 'It is unfortunate that unbridled destruction of habitat, especially in Nepal, has turned these great mammals into wanderers as it has with tigers whose breeding grounds are no more.'

We discussed the idea of using Raja Gaj and Kancha as standard-bearers for Nepalese wildlife, rather as the panda has become a symbol in China. If the Nepalese Wildlife Department could be convinced of the value of these monstrous beasts in attracting tourists, it could mean increased revenue. Hopefully more could then be spent on protecting the creatures and assisting those living around the reserves who might suffer from the presence of large dangerous animals. It all sounded like common sense.

Rula kept a very detailed journal and in it she described our few days at Tiger Haven:

*After a cold and very uncomfortable night and perhaps the most disastrous safari so far – burly, uncommunicative mahouts, nothing at all to be seen, not even droppings – disillusioned, we lumbered slowly back to the park HQ. Where were all the beasts that Mr Khan had promised we would see? I was beginning to feel very despondent. A hot breakfast, however, worked wonders and soon after we were informed that a tractor and trailer had arrived from Tiger Haven. We assembled our luggage, climbed aboard and made our way back to where our poor, hapless bus was still axle-deep in the mud.*

*There were already signs of the water abating, however, and stripped to bare feet, leggings rolled above my knees, I squelched through the slimy mud to the waiting jeeps which would transport us the last mile or so to Tiger Haven. The sun was up, the sky was blue and ahead we could see a series of low, whitewashed buildings followed by the main house bathed in the bright sunshine. Billy, his brother Balaram and his wife Meera with their warm, smiling faces lined the road as we arrived dirty, dusty and muddy. There were drinks and delicious home-made cookies laid out on the veranda, and smiling boys cheerfully helped us to unload our bespattered luggage.*

*I shared a room with Anne which led straight off the veranda. We had already become close friends at Corbett and, having greeted our hosts and then knocked back a most welcome vodka and tonic, we went in to inspect our dear little room. Pristine with comfy beds, colourful rugs on the floor and a bathroom with an old-fashioned tin bath filled with piping hot water. What a treat! Anne and I tossed up to see who would go first. There was no shortage of hot water since the wonderful houseboys were boiling huge cauldrons right outside our bathroom door and as soon as one of us had finished, we were to knock on the door and the dirty water would be replaced for the next bather. What joy, what luxury! Even though it took some phenomenal bodily contortions to immerse oneself, clean hair, bodies and albeit slightly crumpled clothes made new ladies of us both. Three-quarters of an hour later we presented ourselves at the main house for a delicious home cooked curry. Drinks flowed and we were waited on hand and foot. Billy, Meera and Balaram were perfect hosts.*

*Dudhwa became famous mostly through Billy. He had hand-reared a tiger cub called Tara and a leopardess called Harriet, and successfully reintroduced them back into the wild. After dinner we watched a docu-*

*mentary about the latter called,* The Leopard That Changed Its Spots. *It was delightful and emotional and, as the lights came up, we were all unashamedly wiping tears from our eyes.*

*The room was warm and cosy with a roaring log fire and every available bit of wall space was covered with photographs of Billy with Tara or Harriet and/or Eelie, the dog. Billy, a die-hard conservationist, openly admits a preference for animals to people, a view I well understand. He told me many disturbing facts about wildlife management in India and Nepal. In Dudhwa itself, cultivation surrounds the forest and there is virtually no buffer zone. Billy said, 'The local streams are poisoned and devoid of fish. The gharial is extinct. The marsh crocodile is in very short supply and the otter has disappeared. The wild dog, hyena and leopard have all vanished as has the black buck.'*

*The rhino reintroduction programme has not been very successful. We all know this animal is in a very precarious position. Asian rhino horn has fetched as much as US$80,000 per kilo. The elephants only number between thirty and forty and, over the years, with the destruction and restrictions on their habitat and migration routes, they have taken to crop raiding. Whilst they might appear docile, the males in musth can prove to be a problem. Patrolling of the parks by well-informed, trained and dedicated wardens is an absolute necessity. Billy said that frequently wildlife assignments are regarded as punishment postings with little incentive and very poor pay.*

*The Dudhwa reserve is said to have approximately ninety tigers. Billy reckons that in reality it is probably more like twenty to thirty. He claimed that the tiger census during Project Tiger was a farce with untrained forest guards conducting pug-mark tracings, some of which had five toes instead of the tiger's four! All in all he believed that the point of no return has almost been reached. A black and depressing picture and I was inclined to believe him. Three days in Corbett and we had seen no big game and three days in Dudhwa, though I did not know it then, we would see nothing apart from birdlife and barasingha (swamp deer). I went to bed very depressed. A world with no elephants nor tigers, just because of man's greed. For thousands of years creatures and man had co-existed as God intended. Now, perhaps in my lifetime, my grandchildren might only know these animals from pictures. I want to do something, but what? How can one persuade the Chinese, who for thousands of years have believed that rhino horn and tiger penis have some magical aphrodisiac effect, that it is nonsense? As John Aspinall said, 'Man was not put on this earth to conquer but to share.'*

*I am already a member of most world conservation movements but none seem to be making any real difference. I drifted off into a troubled sleep, fighting with poachers and single-handedly trying to save animals like a sort of Francis of Assisi.*

The following morning Anne and I woke early to the sun streaming through our windows. I dressed and sat outside on the veranda, watching Billy's haven come alive. Opposite in a large tree sat a beautiful, lone peacock, tail spread, responding flirtingly to my useless bird noises. To my right was Billy's first-floor office where he still spent many hours tapping away on his ancient typewriter, colourful woollen hat on his head. A delicious breakfast followed and plans for the day were discussed. Meera led a bird safari on foot around the Haven and in the afternoon Dhan took us for a walk along the river banks to see mugger crocodile. In between, there was time to sit around in the sunshine and catch up on our journals.

Later that afternoon, Billy and Balaram drove some of us by jeep deeper into the Dudhwa reserve, hoping again to see big game. Once more we were disappointed but at least saw large herds of barasingha and the birdlife was indeed prolific and varied.

That evening another delicious dinner was followed by the film of Tara, the young tigress Billy had raised and then reintroduced into the wild, which was a moving insight into this man's true dedication. Early to bed as the next morning we were moving on to Bardia. At dawn we packed up and said our goodbyes, piling into a large truck reminiscent of the sort of vehicle used to take people to the guillotine during the French Revolution.

Our rescued bus should only take two hours to reach the border, but within about thirty minutes I realized that I had left my passport back at the Haven. There was a quick consultation with the Colonel (as I liked to call JBS) and it was agreed that Jack, Dhan and I would wait for a local bus going back towards Dudhwa, hitch a lift and then catch up with the rest of the party at the border. After some time, the aforementioned bus appeared in the distance and after much horn honking and light flashing, the three of us were disgorged and squeezed into the incredibly overcrowded vehicle full of people, children, chickens, goats and other paraphernalia. Back at Dudhwa, Balaram was already waiting with the passport and then we had a race in the jeep to catch up with our bus, just as it was reaching the Indo-Nepalese border.

Here I met Pradeep for the first time, impeccably turned out in crisp khaki trousers and leather jacket, Akubra and Raybans. Very impressive!

*He was delighted to see Ram and Dhan, and as the formalities and paperwork were taking some time, we were at leisure to wander and take photographs. For me this was a long-awaited opportunity. The surrounding scenes were wonderful: ladies cooking, mothers feeding babies, families crossing the border, bullocks, bicycles, holy men and chattering groups of young people. It was a photographer's paradise – all free of inhibitions and willing to talk and be photographed.*

*The formalities completed, we all piled back on to the bus and started the last leg of our journey into Nepal proper. There was a distinct change in atmosphere. We took the King Mahendra highway, the main east–west road across Nepal, which is recognizable as such in parts but in others is little more than a dusty dirt-track. We crossed river beds with people bathing themselves, their children and cattle to the left and right of us. Small groups of wide-eyed children shouted 'Bye' to us as we passed, the older people holding their joined hands up to their foreheads in the traditional 'Namaste' greeting which means 'I salute the God within you.' Surely one of the most beautiful greetings in the world.*

*Soon we saw the amazing Chisapani bridge in front of us, a vast expanse of metal technology spanning the river. We were nearly in Bardia. At the first barrier on the other side were smartly dressed Nepali guards in khaki trousers and shirts with white belts and bush hats. It was not quite clear whether they were soldiers or game wardens.*

*We drove on through a small, picturesque village and then transferred to jeeps and arrived at the lodge for a quick drink and shower before moving on to our tented camp. Pradeep took charge, obviously on his home territory, and we were thrilled to hear that the trackers had recently sighted the object of our quest, the two giant bulls, Raja Gaj and Kancha. As the sun began to set we piled into the jeeps, clean and refreshed for the very last leg of the journey.*

*Driving with the wind blowing through my hair, I couldn't believe we were actually about to approach our own tented camp in the middle of the jungle. Eight days in one place with our own elephants, the part of the expedition I had been dreaming about.*

*I will never forget the first sight of our camp. The sky was pink, the air was still and stretched along the river bank were our little tents in subtle shades of pinks and browns. In front of each tent there was a colourful plastic bucket and washbasin on its own handmade bamboo stand, and at the far end of the line was a large camp fire with the Raja Gaj Bar facing it. We were surrounded by rosewood and acacia trees and the smoke from the fire drifted lazily into the still evening. Dumping my bags, I persuaded the Colonel to come with me to the elephant camp which was about a minute's walk from ours. First we passed the cook's tent with hurricane lights glimmering in the dusk, then a long thatched lean-to which was home to the twenty-five or so mahouts who tended us and the elephants, and finally their mounts' quarters. A smouldering fire was in the centre and around were the five beautiful female elephants. The smell, the gentle sound of their swishing trunks as they ate and the occasional rumble and grunt overwhelmed my senses and I gave JBS a big hug of gratitude. He identified them for me: in front of us Madu Mala Kali or Honey Blossom, the matriarch who was older and temperamental, to her right Luksmi Kali, named after the goddess of wealth, then Sundar Kali, beautiful and supposedly the bravest, on the left Champa Kali, flower, and finally the cheeky, frisky, young Chan Chan Kali, who was to become my favourite. By then it was almost dark and the ambient sound of the jungle led by the tree frogs was deafening. I felt so privileged and happy to be there.*

*Arm in arm, we wandered back to a wonderful meal. Hari, the barman, served the best Bloody Marys I have ever tasted. The conversation was animated and we all looked forward to the morrow. After the others had gone to bed, I sat for a while with Pradeep, Dhan, Sandy and Jack watching the moon reflected in the still waters of the river and listening to the thrilling sound of tigers making love somewhere in the distance, 'Ahroom, ahroom'. Shortly after midnight I stumbled off to my little tent. As soon as my head touched the pillow I fell asleep, lulled by the gentle sounds of the jungle and the not so gentle snoring of our leader in the end tent. I dreamt of tigers and Raja Gaj.*

Going down to the elephant lines, I had handed round photos of the 1993 expedition that Sue Hilliard had given me for the boys. They were delighted to get them. Nepalese love pictures. Honey Blossom seemed pleased to see me too and put out her trunk straight away for the customary apple. My old phanit, Man Dhoj, had gone to Chitwan and his place had been taken by a slim, lithe Tharu named Dhuki Ram. He was born near the reserve in 1971 and was a happy, smiling and skilful handler. When I had ridden with him in the past, he had seemed very steady. I was pleased to find that he talked constantly to the old girl and used the ankush rather less than some phanits.

Pradeep had also told us some exciting news: more wild elephant had arrived to join the giants.

Adrian was back from his visit to Chitwan. Although his fossil hunt with John Edwards had gone well and he had obtained some interesting material, they had not found KK's site. Nevertheless the scientist seemed well pleased.

Waking for a call of nature at 3.30 a.m., I sat in my canvas chair for a few minutes listening to the night sounds. The moon was tucked away in the clouds and all was very still; even Honey Blossom had gone quiet. Then from across the phanta to the south came a splintering crash. Something large was pushing down a tree. As if to protest, my dear old lady gave a piercing trumpet. 'I wonder what's out there?' I thought as I slid back into my warm bed.

'You can see the difference,' observed Faanya as we climbed aboard. 'These boys are keen and efficient.' Coming from a lady who had lived in the African bush this was a well-deserved compliment for our phanits and their crews. Their whole demeanour was quite different from that of both the Indian mahouts and their elephants, who seemed bored to death with carrying tourists around the game parks. At Bardia, the Tharu handlers were much younger and bubbled with enthusiasm. They behaved like hunters eager to find their quarry and they knew the jungle and its creatures intimately.

The combined eyes, ears and sense of smell of a phanit and his elephant would seldom miss anything but, just in case they did, a naturalist or tracker stood at the back of each howdah. Every bent blade of grass, rustle of leaf or whiff of scent would tell them something. We carried no weapons and I was very conscious that in an emergency we were totally dependent on our phanits' skill and our mounts' strength to save us. A few hundred yards from camp a small animal poked its head up from behind a log. It was a yellow-throated marten which looked up at Honey Blossom as if to say, 'Hello, big fellow. What do you want?' The elephant eyed it disdainfully and slightly uneasily. Knowing her dislike of dogs, I wondered if she thought this might be one, but we passed on through the forest. A few minutes later a tiny fieldmouse shot across our path. Honey Blossom took not the slightest notice. 'So much for that legend,' I murmured to Paula.

Pradeep nodded towards one of the narrow, tree-clad islands

dividing the channels of the Karnali and in the mist we saw a line of huge footprints. Coming to the flood bank, it looked as though a back-acter on an earth-moving machine had torn down the rich soil. Giant feet had pressed deeply into the fresh earth where the king elephant had climbed out. Pradeep shielded his eyes from the rising sun and watched a clump of acacia. Following his gaze through my binoculars, I could see one tree was shaking. Then a massive grey serpent rose from the long grass. The flickering tongue at the end was in fact a prehensile finger feeling its way upwards to the tastiest morsel. Raja Gaj's trunk was picking his breakfast although, having been feeding for most of the night, I doubt if he ever counted one meal as separate from the next. 'Where's Kancha?' I wondered, remembering the advice of an old phanit: 'You may love elephants but always be ready for the unexpected. You must watch your back and have an escape route planned.' But on this occasion we had no worry. Kancha was browsing fifty yards from the big fellow and, as we watched, he coiled his trunk round a tree, slowly pushing and pulling. Then, with all the time in the world, the tusker placed his forehead on it and with no apparent effort pushed it over. Keeping one large brown eye on us, he began to strip the acacia of its bark, passing the succulent fibrous flesh back into his massive jaws. As if to follow this example, Honey Blossom seized a clump of grass from the forest floor, twisted it out of the ground and dusted off the loose soil against her foot before stuffing it into her mouth.

'Can we get some dung samples?' questioned Adrian.

'If they'll move on,' I answered.

Raja Gaj's tusks seemed to have grown longer and curled upwards. In 1993 Chris Thouless had estimated their weight at between sixty and seventy pounds and their owner to be in his fifties. The King looked more mammoth-like than ever and, as he raised his trunk to feed, the dome on his head became even more pronounced. Leaping into action, Rula got some excellent photos of this which were extremely important for our research. 'I guess he's quite wonderful,' said Paula who, being a petite lady, had been selected to ride in my well-filled howdah.

Using the Polaroid, we took some snaps to check shoulder heights and measured tracks. Raja Gaj's footprint was still twenty-two and a half inches and later we found the shoulder estimation, also done by Polaroid, came out at eleven foot three inches. 'We'll come back later,' I said as we moved off quietly through the grass.

An ochre-grey jungle cat scuttled from under our feet, the distinctive striped thighs and ringed tail standing out as it ran across the pebbles of a dry watercourse. 'Not very common,' muttered Pradeep. About three feet in overall length, it had a shorter tail than a leopard and as it stopped to cast a glance at us its pale green eyes gave it a cold, cruel expression. Known throughout northern Africa and much of Asia, it hunts more by day than most cats. Nevertheless it was quite a rarity. Our mammal team, keeping lists like train-spotters, noted it with glee.

Swinging round in a wide circle, we gave the bulls time to change position before returning. Approaching into wind through a thickly wooded part of the island, I wasn't especially concerned since they had been browsing in the opposite direction. But then my eye caught something white and for once neither Dhuki nor Pradeep saw it. Barely twenty yards away, almost covered by the leafy umbrella of a huge tree, were the tips of a pair of enormous tusks. They swayed gently from side to side. Before I could speak, Honey Blossom stopped. We froze and I could feel my heart pounding; never had we been so close to Raja Gaj. Behind us Chan Chan and Champa had closed up and halted. Luksmi and Sundar were on the flank, moving steadily ahead. Dhuki's unseen toe signals sent our old lady into reverse. As one and with extraordinary grace, the three cows retraced their footsteps until we had room to turn and go around the giants. Only then did we utter a word. It had been far too close. 'We damned nearly walked right into him,' said Jack, a bead of sweat trickling down his forehead.

After a wider swing we reached the dung heap and Adrian jumped down, polythene bag in hand, to scoop up his samples with a plastic knife and fork from the picnic kit. Dhan climbed a tree to watch for Kancha whilst the rest of us stood guard and took footprint measurements. In ten minutes the work was done. I went up to Dhan's tree with Honey Blossom to pick him up but he preferred to climb on to Sundar Kali.

'Don't you like my old lady?' I joked.

Dhan grinned, 'I don't think she likes me. She has attacked me three times.'

It was a timely reminder not to take any chances with this matriarch.

'There are some new elephants across the river,' beamed Ram, who had been talking to a game scout.

'How many?'

'He says two or three, but he's not certain. He thinks they're all bulls.'

The afternoon programme was postponed and, clutching binoculars and cameras, we clambered into our howdahs. It only took a few minutes to wade the shallows and form a line across the island. We were rewarded almost at once by a great crashing of heavy bodies in the undergrowth. 'Going right,' called Dhan, who had seen two young tuskers break cover. Clearly nervous, these elephants were frightened. The bush was denser than any we had experienced and it was impossible to move quietly. After two hundred yards the larger male doubled back and, by coming out into the river bed, gave us the slip. From a quick glance, he seemed to be in his twenties and the dome was not especially developed. We pressed on after his chum and almost at the tip of the island found him tangled in the creeper and undergrowth, his back to us as he struggled to free himself. 'He's very young,' said Pradeep. Indeed, the little chap was smaller than our ladies, probably only around fifteen.

Then we heard the most extraordinary sound. 'Yap, yap, yap!' It was just like a puppy dog.

'What on earth is that?' I asked.

'It is the elephant,' said Pradeep. 'They make that noise when frightened. He is calling for his friend.'

Backing across the open clearing, the five females had formed a crescent behind the juvenile when, with a crash and tearing of branches, he extracted himself. For a moment he stood shaking greenery off his head. To his relatively poor vision we were probably five indistinct blobs. Now was the time to show his courage. With a shrill trumpet, head held high, ears forward and his trunk waving wildly, he came straight at us. The ladies watched with interest. At about twenty-five yards the youngster skidded to a halt as he focused and realized he was charging a line of cows.

As he looked left and right, his ears fell and his trunk drooped. Without a sound he turned and crept back to the cover. Everyone burst out laughing and the poor little chap gave a few yaps before fleeing. We named him Bahadur Guj or 'brave one' and his older brother we called Div Guj or 'bright' because of his lighter colour.

Back at camp Adrian pickled his dung samples in vodka.

'Perfectly good alcohol,' grinned the scientist.

'What a waste,' groaned Rula.

Round the fire that night, we persuaded our Nepalese friends to relate some of their tales. Dhan told how as a small boy he had loved animals and started working at Tiger Tops in Chitwan where he had been apprenticed to an old phanit to help look after a huge, tame tusker. Sundar Prasad was ten foot six inches at the shoulder and had been injured by a charging rhino. As a result he hated rhinoceros and was very aggressive. Dhan's job was to cut grass for him and clean his quarters.

He was working close to the bull one day, when without warning it shot out its trunk, seized him around the waist and hurled him to the ground. 'Luckily he was chained,' explained Dhan, 'otherwise he might have killed me.' However, by the time the old keeper had appeared Dhan had picked himself up and, being a determined lad, simply went on cleaning the stable as if nothing had happened. Then, talking quietly to Sundar Prasad, he fed him some succulent grass. It took him six months to gain the tusker's confidence and get him to respond to orders. 'I won,' grinned Dhan. 'Eventually I could ride him and he would obey me. He would even kneel down. Once they do that you know they have submitted to your will and will do anything.' He went on to explain that it takes time and that elephants do listen to you and that you can tell they are listening because they will put their ears forward when you speak. 'There has to be chemistry between man and elephant. Some people will never have it,' explained our friend.

In 1989 Dhan had been loaned to the Cricket St Thomas Wildlife Park in Somerset to train elephants. His charges were virtually wild and it took him seven months to build up their trust. He did it by going into the cage and spending about half an hour each night talking to them, but 'you have to believe in it,' he said, the firelight playing on his swarthy features. 'And be very careful. I was always ready to run.'

As we saw with our lady elephants, they will only respond to those they know. They have many human emotions, especially jealousy. In a European zoo a young male elephant called Bimbo was given special attention by an older female. However, when a calf arrived the female switched her attention to it. Bimbo's reaction was to stick his tusks into the calf when no one was watching. This produced loud cries for help from the baby. In our herd, Luksmi hated the cheeky Chan Chan, and Honey Blossom's unpredictability was also a cause for caution, although I never saw her behave with aggression. However, the more I got to know her the more I found myself watching her every move. Other expedition members had no wish to ride her. 'She's got a broken spring,' complained Pat, preferring the rolling motion of Champa. But there was something very wise and dependable about the matriarch. She was also a glutton. We had paused on a march and were sitting on the ground enjoying a spot of lunch. I had unwrapped my food and having eaten one meat roll, reached for the other. All that was on the paper beside me was a slice of spam. Six feet above, Honey Blossom munched gently, her eyes looking up to the sky as if to say, 'It wasn't me.'

'You're a ruddy thief,' I told her.

From the depth of her throat came that old rumble and I'd swear she smiled.

Dawn was breaking but the heat hung in the trees. Although early in the year, it was still 65°F at 6 a.m. In the half light we trooped out, heading north in search of more newly arrived wild elephants. We'd only gone fifty yards when 'Chuff, chuff, chuff,' and a large rhino came trotting out of the grass thirty feet away and, passing through our line, dropped a load of dung before wading straight into the river. He seemed quite unperturbed by our presence or the close proximity of the camp. One of the boys from the camp spotted the steaming manure and ran out to scoop it up in a large leaf. Rhino dung is a highly prized laxative and when mixed with tobacco and smoked it is said to cure coughs.

In the days that followed, there were more meetings with Raja Gaj and Kancha and now the new wild bulls had joined them.

Adrian noted that neither of the old tuskers had body hair nor eyelashes while Bahadur and Div Guj, like our cows, had short hair on the top of their heads as well as thick strong hair at the tip of their tails. 'Why should this be?' I wrote in my log. It seemed the more we found out about the monsters, the greater the mystery.

Every hour of our day was filled with report writing, repairs to kit and washing the dust out of our clothes and hair. The weather was fine and warm, our only problem being dust devils, powerful vortexes of air that appeared out of nowhere and would easily uproot a tent. Poor Graham lost his to one that came spinning and swirling through the camp. We also helped with the elephants, preparing their food and scrubbing the ladies in the river at bath-time, a truly enjoyable chore. Rula almost lived in the elephant lines; she was totally absorbed by her affection for these great beasts and in the evenings she would write down her experiences:

*Since Jack needed pictures for* Hello *apart from safari snaps, and since I refused to pose in different outfits draped over interesting looking trees etc, we agreed that the photographs should be with the elephants. For me this was another dream come true. I could hardly be torn away from the elephant camp, wanting to find out as much as possible about the relationships and lifestyles of the phanits and their charges.*

*Jack wanted a photo of me climbing up using the trunk and ears method. The phanits made it look so easy. The idea was that Luksmi Kali should be positioned close to the edge of the river bank with the Himalayan foothills in the background. Her phanit gave the order for her to put her ears forward and I was told to place one foot on the upturned trunk and hold on to her ears with my hands. She slowly raised her trunk, elevator style, until I reached the top of her head then I would smartly turn around and sit astride her neck. That was the plan.*

*The first time the light wasn't right, the second time I wasn't looking at the camera, by the time we got to the third attempt Dhan said to Jack, 'You'd better get it right this time otherwise Luksmi might get fed up and just fling Rula right over her back!' Luckily the next shot was more or less perfect.*

*Riding on a howdah is one thing, riding bareback slightly behind the neck as the Nepalese phanits do is a different feeling altogether. They*

*have a piece of sacking under their behinds and their feet in macramé*
*type stirrups just behind the elephant's ears, and it is the pressure of*
*their bare feet pressing and prodding, coupled with the verbal commands,*
*that tell the elephant to move backwards, forwards, left or right. There*
*are no reins. The phanit usually carries a bamboo stick in the right*
*hand and the wicked-looking, metal ankush or bullhook in the left.*
*Thankfully these are very seldom used, but in cases of extreme dis-*
*obedience, a sharp thwack on the skull with the aforementioned instru-*
*ment quickly shows the elephant who is master. It became standard*
*procedure when I was with Pritni, who was Chan Chan Kali's phanit,*
*that if ever I saw him lift the ankush I would threaten to cuff him round*
*the ears.*

*My first attempt at riding bareback in just a swimsuit and T-shirt*
*was quite a frightening experience. The elephant's shoulders underneath*
*my backside felt like huge pistons and since there were no stirrups it*
*was very difficult to find a point of balance. It is a movement completely*
*different to that of a horse, since an elephant walks by moving its front*
*and hind right leg followed by the other front and hind left leg. Conse-*
*quently one gets a sort of rolling motion which feels very unsteady. Also*
*one is very high off the ground. On my first few attempts I clutched*
*desperately on to Chan Chan's ears but after a while I became more*
*confident and following Dhan's instructions managed to shift my seat*
*slightly further back and take the motion into the small of my back. I*
*had seen phanits stand, crouch and even lie flat on their bellies on top*
*of elephants with complete nonchalance. I was determined that with*
*practice and perseverance I would become more adept. I wanted to train*
*as an honorary phanit. I'm sure not many actresses have that on their*
*Curriculum Vitae!*

Tiger were all around. Mr J. B. Karki, the warden, reckoned there
were about thirty within a mile radius of our camp. At night we
heard them roaring but for the most part all one saw was the
flash of an orange backside or tail as 'Mr Stripes' bolted through
the grass. However, from the Babai came sad news that a local
woman had been taken. Led by Pat Troy, whom most now
referred to as 'The Major', Adrian, Paula and Wendy B. had gone
there to look for signs of elephant when they also found the
pug marks of the killer. Ram Din was able to point out that the
prints indicated an injured foot. Wendy wrote out a report
for me:

We had barely gone a hundred yards, when we came upon tiger tracks. Our guide, Ram Din, made an examination and pronounced them to be from the man-eating tiger. Being more used to an amble in the Surrey woods, I thought he was winding us up. However, when we inspected them, there were clear recent pug marks with one toe showing signs of injury which would mean that the beast could not catch game. Humans were much easier. Not only that, but they headed in the direction we were intending to go. Adrian Lister, who knows more about these things than we do, suggested we turn back, but we were all intent on continuing and did so. Funnily enough, I know we should have been worried but it was a sunny day, the river was flowing gently beside us and it did not seem possible that we were in any danger.

We criss-crossed the river, wading waist-deep into the water, and saw evidence of rhino both from their pug marks and also their dung heaps. A curious thing about rhino is that they always defecate in the same place, possibly as a signal to other rhino not to enter their territory. The dung heap we saw was four or five feet high. Eventually we found four huge fourteen-foot gharial basking on the far bank. They are very shy and soon slid into the water out of sight, their long pointed snouts causing a wide bow wave.

Now it was time to return before it got dark and we hastened back through pretty woodland beside the river. The trees and palms were all a lush green, many hanging with moss. At one stage I had to fall back due to a call of nature. Crouched behind a bush in the seclusion of the jungle, a gentle breeze moving the grass and palm fronds, my imagination really took over and I could just picture the man-eating tiger sizing me up for a good meal. I hastily rejoined the others to continue the punishing pace set by the Major, grateful for their company.

Whilst on the afternoon sweep we came to a patch of deep fern where Dhuki located the bones of a spotted deer, killed by some predator. Gleaming clean and white they were in perfect condition. Adrian wanted the jawbone and with great precision Honey Blossom picked it up and handed it over her head to him. 'Makes zoological work so much easier to have a trained elephant to collect for one,' smiled the good scientist.

I noted that Honey Blossom showed no reaction to handling the bones. This confirmed the opinions of Cynthia Moss, whose research on the African elephant is well known. She points out that elephants do have a strong interest in the bones of their own species but none at all in those of other creatures. When confronted with elephant remains they will often carry them away to be dropped elsewhere. Apparently the skull and tusks are of special interest and she suggests they may be trying to identify an old colleague or relation. It set me wondering about elephant emotions as we plodded on with Adrian and Wendy B.

Suddenly a cloud of large black insects erupted in front of us. There was chaos as we swatted the attackers and thrashed our arms to drive them off. Honey Blossom had trodden on a hornet's nest. Adrian and Pradeep cursed as they got stung, but although Wendy had several in her hair she moved with great caution, trying to ease them out with her sunglasses. Then I remembered, she was allergic to bee stings.

'Whoops, I've been stung,' she said calmly.

'Have you got your antidote to hand?' I asked.

'Afraid not,' she replied. 'The serum is with the Doc and Paula has the syringe in her nurse's medical kit.'

Both were some distance away.

My assistant in the Darien Gap Expedition of 1972 had become very seriously ill after an allergic reaction to a hornet attack and I knew this was no laughing matter.

'A hornet is more wasp than bee,' remarked Adrian.

'One has an alkaline and the other has an acid sting,' added Wendy. 'Don't ask me which.'

We began to look for Michael Wilson, but luckily after thirty minutes Wendy seemed to be all right. 'A Bloody Mary will put me straight,' she grinned.

Adrian was especially interested in the two new bulls. The trackers said there were probably more, but the problem with studying them was that they were usually in the company of Raja Gaj and Kancha. Now there were four bulls together it was not possible to rely on outnumbering and confusing them as a means of defence. Whenever we approached, Kancha, the royal escort, would see us off.

However, on a warm afternoon we found Bahadur and Div Guj feeding alone in a bamboo grove at the edge of a wide phanta. 'Yap, yap,' chirped Bahadur, giving his alarm call as they dived into the tall grass. We only had four riding elephants that day, so I asked Robert and Faanya with Sundar Kali to stay put whilst the rest of us outflanked the young tuskers and lined up in cover on the far side of a dry river bed. From here we should be able to get a clear view of them crossing the open space and obtain perfect footprints from the mud on the banks. Having given us time to get into position, Robert moved Sundar forward to drive the bulls towards us. Advancing into the tall grass, she was shaken to find that Div Guj had moved round and was now watching her from one side. There was no sign of his pal. Suddenly, with a crash Div came plunging through the grass straight at them; being smaller he was concealed until he was almost upon them, but Prem, Sundar's phanit, did not wait. A flick of his toe sent the fast little lady turning out of harm's way and up to the tree-line. Sundar could really move and the Roses hung on for dear life as they were hurled about in the howdah. They soon left their attacker behind and, as luck would have it, he withdrew to the watercourse where we waited, giving us perfect photographs and clear footprints.

It was time to pay our annual visit to Gola, the village most often raided by elephant and rhino from the reserve. So we set out across the first tributary in fine style with the water swirling around the ladies' stout legs. Village children lined the far bank awaiting us. However, the main channel, the size of the Thames, was deep and running fast. Pat, with his Royal Marine background and particularly with his SBS experience, volunteered to test the crossing on Chan Chan. Doc Wilson went too and, as we watched, the recce party waded into the torrent. They were half-way across before the gallant little elephant turned to face upstream. The tossing, rushing water was almost up to her eyes and her feet could hardly keep in contact with the river bed. Pradeep looked worried, 'It's no good,' he said. 'The current is too strong.'

'Come back,' I yelled, but then realized that was easier said than done. Pat looked apprehensive and Michael's feet were already awash. From amongst us, Sundar Kali trumpeted encouragement and step by step Chan Chan edged her way back. When she reached the shore, flanks heaving and water pouring off her glistening body, we breathed a sigh of relief. Then, seeing the children starting to run northward, I looked towards the mountains. Coming out from behind an island were the young bulls, closely followed by Raja Gaj and Kancha. They were heading for Gola. Cameras exploded into action.

The crop raiders waded straight into the river. The younger ones swam ahead using their trunks as snorkels, the two big fellows forged across, Raja Gaj hardly getting more than his legs wet and creating great bow waves against the current. As they emerged on the far side we got a good indication of their relative size by the water line on their heaving bodies. The smaller tuskers had been completely submerged, but the water had reached only halfway up Raja Gaj, and Kancha's shoulders were still dry.

'It's like something from a Cecil B. de Mille film,' said Sandy.

'Oh God! The children!' gasped Wendy Stephens, who, eyeing some egrets on the far bank, had seen the vast gaggle of kids, many of them tiny tots, rushing headlong towards the approaching elephants.

'We must do something,' cried someone, but there was nothing that we could do.

'Look out! Hatti!' yelled Rula, but the children plunged on regardless. Some had picked up sticks and above the noise of the river we could hear them shouting.

'They're trying to drive the bulls back,' said Sandy, who had recorded the whole scene with her long lens. Watching impotently we held our breath, expecting at any moment to witness the most terrible slaughter.

Now the tuskers were up the bank and sheltering in the shade of a patch of jungle. Only Kancha, by far the fiercest, remained at the edge of the trees, although we could see Raja Gaj's huge arched back towering in the greenery behind him.

The youngsters were only yards away when the King's escort made his first charge, lumbering out of the scrub with trunk waving and ears flapping. Agile as a pack of hunting dogs surrounding a wildebeest on the plains of Africa, the kids darted in to hurl sticks and stones, nimbly dodging the frustrated tusker's thrusts and lashes.

Dashing in and out was just a game. The girls had joined in too and seemed to be out-braving the boys; even toddlers were there waving twigs and adding to the cacophony of sound with high-pitched screams. Miraculously no one was hurt and when the elephant retreated deeper into the trees, the children went home, sure they had won the day. But that night when they were fast asleep, the moon lit up the maize fields as Raja Gaj led his merry band out to feast until a dozing guard awoke to hammer out the alarm on his great brass gong. Within a minute the crash of firecrackers and the shouts of the villagers could be heard in our camp, a mile away, as the people fought to save their hard-won crops.

'What on earth can they do to protect themselves?' asked Paula as we drained the coffee jug.

Already on this expedition we had found a pumpkin baited with insecticide left on the trail in the hope of catching an unwary elephant. Not that this was likely to have much effect: Ivan Sanderson tells of the 'perfectly uncanny skill' that elephants have in 'detecting anything that has been tampered with, as many carnival men have learned when they have tried to poison elephants that have been condemned to death. In one case a creature ate every bag of peanuts out of a trolley from which she was accustomed to steal such delicacies daily, except the few that contained the tasteless and odourless poison planted there to kill her. These she hurled aside with rage and contempt.'*

Electric fences would be broken down. I've seen African elephants throw logs into the wire and in Kenya's Aberdare National Park two young bulls, having filled a deep ditch with earth, hurled a squealing baby elephant into the electric fence to break it. Their living battering-ram having done its work, they sauntered over into a nearby vegetable garden for a meal. Fire and fireworks are effective for a time until the beasts learn they are relatively harmless. Charlie, a massive Indian elephant used by the late Sir Billy Butlin at his holiday camps, would perform a trick of stamping out a small fire and would kick away a firework.

* Ivan T. Sanderson, *The Dynasty of Abu* (Cassell, 1960)

'They are too intelligent to be fooled for long,' remarked Adrian, looking up from his dung samples. 'Almost anything you place in their way will be overcome in time.'

'The only way to stop a really determined elephant is with a heavy bullet,' said Pradeep. 'And we all pray that some terrified villager won't resort to that.' Luckily, most farmers only had ancient muskets, but poachers armed with modern weapons were just across the border and one of Tula Hatti's brothers had been shot several years before.

Fortunately, elephant have always been well protected in Nepal. To the Hindus, who make up a large proportion of the population, they are sacred and regarded as the incarnation of the deity Ganesh, god of good fortune. As such, it is unthinkable that they should be harmed or molested. Moreover, in days gone by the rulers of Nepal had learned to appreciate the value of the great creatures as transport and load carriers, for both peaceful and warlike purposes. Wild elephants were not too difficult to catch and the Tharu were especially skilled at training them to work. Fodder was plentiful and in the Terai they thrived; elephants had even been used on expeditions high into the mountains and had assisted an ambitious building project. It was therefore forbidden to hunt or harm elephants out of pure economic necessity.

For the present, this Himalayan Kingdom's wildlife policy continues to protect the elephant, but the local farmers were growing tired of sharing their crops. For how long would the villagers of Gola be prepared to suffer without striking back? We feared the poisoned pumpkin was just the start. What if more elephants were to join Raja Gaj's herd?

In our small way we helped by equipping the anti-poaching unit in Bardia with items they needed to make them more effective, and Robert Rose kindly donated the cash to buy plaster of Paris for use in recording pug marks. The Warden accepted it all gratefully and we promised more help in the future.

In an effort to help the people who live around the reserve, we had brought pencils, crayons and books for the school and simple medical items for the clinic. We felt, as has been found in Africa, that if one can let the locals have some profit from their proximity to wildlife it might deter them from poaching or allowing poachers access through their territory.

The last night in camp is always a little sad. Teams, built up by being squashed together in a howdah for a total of 150 miles in seven days or sharing a tense moment in the forest, are about to be broken up. The next day we would start the long haul back to the stress and strain of civilization, leaving behind our beloved riding elephants and those who looked after them. To ease the pain we danced, the elephant boys sang and Wendy B., in her role as entertainments officer, produced a splendid game: a jungle frog racing derby. Cardboard frogs raced along strings jerked tight by the contestants. The rules were very simple. There were four cardboard cut-out frogs with a string running through them. The object of the game is to hop them along the string and over the line. The rules were explained to the elephant boys and cooks, the most important being that the whole frog must cross the finishing line. On our hands and knees in the dust we ran a series of heats, semi-finals and finals. The Nepalese howled with delight. In the end it was the elephant boys versus the doctor in a needle race. The Doc won the day and the prize of a green lollipop. When we left the camp the game was donated to our helpers. Doubtless, it is still being played in the Tharu villages.

Throughout the day a vast pit had been excavated and now this was filled with glowing embers over which a huge pig was turned gently on a spit. Globules of fat fell spattering into flame as they struck the fire. The smell of roast pork, cased in the most fantastic crackling, was irresistible. Dinner was, as always, outstanding. Rum, J&B and beer flowed. From a nearby phanta came the mournful 'Ahoon, ahoon!' of the big cat, seeking his mate.

Having seen it all several times, I doubt if my impressions are always the most telling and I felt Wendy B. summed up the final days pretty well in her diary:

Dismantle the camp and drive to Tiger Mountain's Karnali Lodge for the night. What a treat to have a hot shower and change. In the evening a few of us walk to the nearby village. I take the tape recorder and get the children to sing and talk into it. They love it and we have such fun together. They take me to their den where they have their own recorder but no batteries. The village is so pretty it could have been made for a film set: thatched roofs, clay walls with painted patterns, wooden poles draped with drying straw and bunches of sweet-corn, chickens, goats with kids, pigs with piglets, darling smiling dark-eyed children in ragged clothes and bare feet, colourful adults, the ladies elegant in their saris. Rula and Jack sit down and have rice wine. Hang all the hygiene, this is the last day. We all get a red blob on our forehead. As we head home we pass a man with a child on his back. He asks for help. Our doctor diagnoses a broken leg and the child is taken back to be treated with a splint. As we walk back, we notice that there are platforms on trees for sentries to watch for wild animals getting at their crops. Farmers in England worry about deer and rabbits. Imagine the destruction a rhino or elephant can do. At the lodge I meet a couple from England who have a lot of mutual friends. I find I resent the intrusion of my other life into this idyllic setting. However, all too soon we are flying back, over the mountains and into Kathmandu and the Yak & Yeti Hotel.

*Chapter Nine*

# FOSSIL HUNT

'STEGODON, they've found a stegodon,' beamed Adrian Lister, looking like a cat with a double helping of cream.

Rula, now in an elegant long dress, raised a green eye above her ice-cold vodka. 'What on earth's that?'

'It's a type of mastodon, a primitive and distant ancestor of elephants,' went on Adrian. 'What's more, I've just met the Director of the Natural History Museum and he has shown me the skull of *Elephas planifrons* which was dug up by a German palaeontologist in East Nepal a few years ago. This is a fossil species more closely related to the Asian elephant.'

'How old is that?' enquired Pat Troy, who had just come into the bar looking incredibly smart in a safari suit.

'About two million years,' said Adrian, who went on to explain that his day in Kathmandu had been most productive. 'I saw a collection of fossils of exactly the type that I had been hoping for, proving that exciting material is indeed to be found in this region. I also obtained scientific papers detailing these finds, including the names of previous excavators, and some indication of the localities where they have been successful. Finally, I had a most useful and encouraging meeting with the Curator and Director of the Museum. They are interested in the possibility of me excavating further fossils – for them of course.'

'Do you think there's a link with Raja Gaj?' I asked.

Adrian looked thoughtful, 'It's too early to say, but there may be some genetic connection.'

Mash had joined us and was clutching a large brown envelope. 'I thought this might interest you,' he said, taking out a pile of photographs and maps. 'Have you ever heard of the Rani Mahal?'

The name rang a bell. 'Isn't it some legendary palace or temple thought to be up in the mountains?' I said.

'Well, sort of,' replied Mash. 'In fact it is a palace built by one of the Rana ministers who was exiled from Kathmandu for plotting a coup. I don't know a lot about it, but doing a recce along the Kali Gandaki a few weeks ago, we came round a bend and saw this.' He flipped a large colour print on the table.

There in front of us was a scene straight out of an Indiana Jones film, an amazing Gothic-style palace perched on a cliff overhanging a clear blue river. In spite of being partly overgrown and somewhat derelict, it was basically intact.

'Some local people told us that giant elephants were used to build it,' said Mash.

'What an extraordinary place. Has anyone been there?' queried Pat.

Mash explained that until recently it had taken three days to carry rafts to the upper reaches of the Kali Gandaki and so few outsiders visited the river, but now a road had been built from Pokhara to Baglung, which meant one could drive a truck to the water's edge, making it possible to sail downstream to the Rani Mahal.

'Let's go down to Thamel market and see if the bookshops have got anything about the place,' I said.

The second shop we tried produced a faded volume of Nepalese history in English. I happily paid out seventy rupees and we started reading it as we drove back to the Yak & Yeti Hotel.

Dhir Shumser, a Commander-in-Chief of the Nepalese Army who died in 1840, had fathered seventeen sons. The second was the highly ambitious Khadga Shumser who set about restoring the family's political fortunes by bumping off the opposition – mainly uncles and cousins. Although only twenty-four, he was already a General and Commander-in-Chief and becoming steadily more powerful. By now his elder brother Bir was Prime Minister and, fearing he would soon receive the same treatment from Khadga, banished him to Palpa, giving him the position of West Regional Commander as a consolation.

Removed from the scene of power, Khadga sought solace in his second Queen, Tej Kumari. By all accounts she was attentive and loving. So much so that the ruthless politician became known as Khadga Shumser the Lover. Every day he would take his wife with him on his horse, riding around Tansen where his head-quarters were located. Even today old people of the region recite the love story. Apparently the General would control his horse with the reins in one hand and hold his lady's waist with the other. Our booklet said, 'She, too, used to embrace her king frequently at her back.' Obviously the horse was pretty docile! It is only two and a half hours' walk along a footpath from Tansen to the Kali Gandaki and the quiet gorge became the lovers' favour-ite spot. Folklore relates that the couple would sometimes become so engrossed in one another that they would remain lost in a firm embrace until after sunset. At such times their guards feared to disturb them and this meant a difficult trek home in the dark, so the soldiers took to carrying lanterns and torches on such outings.

Desperately in love, Khadga would do anything for Tej Kumari and even offered to invade Kathmandu. However, the Queen was deeply religious and peace-loving and would not hear of it. Instead she asked him to build her a palace at their much loved site beside the river, making it a place of pilgrimage when she was dead. Shumser was greatly disturbed by the suggestion that she might die. However, he could not have foreseen how soon this would be. A few days later his wife went up to Ridi, a town beside the Kali Gandaki, to take a bath, probably at a hot spring. Tragically, there she died.

Overcome with grief, his only fear was that he might pass away without fulfilling his Queen's last wish. Thus Khadga sent to Calcutta for British engineers to design and build him a palace or mahal as Tej Kumari had requested. No expense was to be spared.

The foundation stone was laid in 1893 at the junction of the Barangdi and Kali Gandaki rivers. The builders imported almost all the structural fittings from abroad, even nuts and bolts, and to get these heavy loads up from Tansen it was necessary to use pack animals. Rumour has it that the General obtained some giant elephants and the first three years of the project were spent in cutting an elephant passing track over the mountains. Up this precipitous road came raw material and supplies. Finally, Persian carpets, furniture and fittings from London, including candelabra, arrived. The twenty-five-room Rani Mahal was completed in November 1897 and was provided with a system for fresh running water and even an electrical generator.

In the perfumed garden, poor Khadga, still pining for Tej Kumari, would seek his beloved. It is said that he would take a bath at midnight and talk to her by the river. He claimed she responded, but soon political jealousy and suspicion from his younger brother, Chandra, who was to become Prime Minister, forced him into further exile in India where he died in 1922. It seemed that from then on his mahal gradually deteriorated and was swallowed up by the jungle.

'We should see this place built by giant jumbos. There may even be fossil remains of earlier animals in the gorge,' suggested Adrian when I told him the story.

Back in Britain, Rula and her husband Dennis Waterman hosted our reunion at their home. There was sad news from Nepal. Colonel Hikmat Bisht had faxed Peter Byrne to announce the death of Tula Hatti. The poor beast had walked into a booby-trap bomb set just over the Indian border by poachers looking for deer. A foot had been terribly damaged and, when discovered by farmers, he was lying in a pool of water, bleeding profusely. From within Nepal the good Colonel and the Sukla Phanta Warden did all they could to get help to the stricken animal, but cross-border bureaucracy and the initial delay of the incident being reported to the authorities beat them. So died one of the greatest elephants that ever lived.

On a more positive note, we were encouraged by Adrian Lister's findings. 'I've done some research on another fossil that has been found in Nepal,' he said. '*Elephas hysudricus* is the real ancestor of the Asian elephant and when I went to look at an artist's view of the skull of this creature – that is to say one with the flesh put back on it – I saw this picture.' The slide that came up on the screen showed a heavily domed skull that looked the image of Raja Gaj with his trunk raised, feeding on a tree in Bardia. We gasped. Rula then produced a transparency, taken on our last visit, that was almost identical to the drawing. It was quite uncanny.

'To get more conclusive results I need better samples for DNA testing,' stated the scientist, 'and if we could find some fossils of early elephants it might help us to establish the origins of our large friends in Bardia.'

'Here we go again,' said Julian. 'I'd better start planning.'

The 1995 expedition would last three weeks. Mash had got some information on the Kali Gandaki and it seemed that local villagers often found fossils in its deep canyons. We would study this valley and also examine the Rani Mahal, then we would move to a camp near Ghidhniya village in the Siwalik Hills, east of Nepalganj. Here an American expedition had made some discoveries around twenty years before. Finally, we would return to Bardia to collect dung from which Adrian still hoped to get DNA. In March, Rula had written to say, 'Withdrawal symptoms already present as slowly the silica dust of Bardia has washed out of my safari gear. It was without doubt for me a truly magical, worthwhile experience and a mammoth personal journey. I hope you will consider me for future expeditions.'

So she agreed to join us again and shoot a video film with the latest compact camcorder that Panasonic kindly offered to lend us. Her sister Anna Lubienska, a gently spoken, London-based charity worker, also a redhead, would come too and volunteered to handle the sound recording for the BBC Natural History programme. Their friend Gary Hodges, the accomplished wildlife artist, was dedicated to conservation, so we recruited him.

Pat Troy would fly the Jersey flag with me again and Adrian would direct the zoological and palaeontological work. Dr Ken Reed, a micro-palaeontologist from Australia, who had worked all over the world with oil companies, would use his expert knowledge in the search for fossils.

David Jenkins, a well-travelled former Royal Marine who had turned to medicine, volunteered to be the doctor. Brook Hanson, the enthusiastic younger son of Lord Hanson, who had spent a year helping me to launch Operation Raleigh, was back in Britain and he volunteered to be the recce officer.

An old friend, Julian Brown, a retired barrister, had been our master of horse in Mongolia earlier that year. Now he was keen to try his hand at elephants. Julian also knew a great deal about historic buildings, which would be of benefit when examining the Rani Mahal.

Carol Turner, my patient assistant, would cope with administration, and Wendy B. could not resist the opportunity to extend her plant study and try out a new game of jumping elephants.

Then we had a call from the *Sunday Mirror* asking if they could join us for the final week of the expedition, so I met their people at the Wig and Pen Club. David Rowe, a young feature writer, had the gleam of adventure in his eye and Geoff Garratt was a highly experienced photographer with a good sense of humour. Neither of them was put off by the picture of Raja Gaj that glowered down at them from the Club's wall.

To encourage us, a fax arrived from Pradeep in Tiger Mountain's Kathmandu office. 'On 21 November, sixteen elephants were seen crossing the Karnali River in front of Gola village. Among them were males, females and six young calves about four to five feet in height. We are not sure if the five new ones we saw last year are among the sixteen, but I doubt it as the sixteen were seen coming into the reserve. If these are all new there could be twenty-three elephants there including Raja Gaj and Kancha.'

Carol flashed the news to the members of our team. 'Now you are really outnumbered,' commented Julian Matthews from beneath a pile of papers where he was organizing a new expedition to Mongolia. He had a point and I remembered what had befallen Alexandra Dixon when she approached a herd with calves.

'I don't want to report you being squashed flat,' smiled Sarah-Jane Lewis, our industrious PR lady, 'but at a time when elephants are threatened, it's great news to hear of an increase. Where do you think they are coming from?'

'Well, if they cross the Karnali they must be from the west, so they must have come up from Dudhwa or Sukla Phanta,' I said. 'Perhaps they are Tula Hatti's old herd.'

Indeed, the low frequency calls on the elephant telegraph could be saying, 'Come and join us, we are guarded by soldiers and there is plenty to eat.' But how many elephants could the Bardia reserve accommodate?

\*      \*      \*

Having matters to attend to in Delhi, I went out ahead of the expedition and when I arrived in Kathmandu, Dal, Tiger Mountain's 'Mr Fixit', met me with the news that the Royal Nepal flight from London had been delayed. It came as no surprise. 'They should be here at 2300 tomorrow,' smiled Dal, as he loaded my gear into the car. Well, it gave me more time to get organized, and I spent the day buying locally made tin trunks for the carriage of our more fragile equipment, and in the Shangri-La Hotel marking up my maps and conferring with Mash, Pradeep and the Tiger Mountain staff. Tej Rana, an experienced river guide who had been with us on the Karnali, would lead us down the Kali Gandaki. He had replaced Megh who, having married Sally, had set up his own white-water rafting company, Ultimate Descents. I heard all about it when Megh and Sally dined with me that evening, bringing their one-month-old daughter, Tara, with them. Whilst we were eating, a waiter obligingly wheeled Tara round the restaurant. What service!

The team arrived at 11.20 p.m. unbowed by the delays and the long flight. They brought with them our freight, including a couple of wheelchairs urgently needed by Megh for a local charity. Most had slept during the journey, which was just as well as there wasn't much time to enjoy the hotel beds that night.

An early morning stop in the Thamel bazaar allowed us to make a few purchases and order some local tunic tops that would have Gary's special expedition designs embroidered on the front by the time we returned to Kathmandu. Then it was on to the Natural History Museum.

'Well, there it is,' said Adrian proudly as we gazed through the glass case at the yellowing skull of the fossil elephant. Ken's eyes lit up as he passed showcases of ammonites, whereas Anna and Gary were looking sorrowfully at some moth-eaten stuffed birds on display. Brook and Julian Brown examined the fangs of a leopard mounted in an aggressive pose, whilst Doc David was outside photographing a pair of rhesus monkeys from nearby Swayambhunath Stupa playing around our bus.

The curator waved us off and called, 'Good luck!' as we drove on to the road to Pokhara. It had recently been widened and is now one of the best in Nepal. It has a good surface, reasonable camber and, thanks to the speed it allows, is lethal. Head-on collisions are common.

The lunch stop at the Blue Heaven Café, not far from 'Snell's Nose', gave us a chance to stretch and to soothe our shattered nerves, but we had more time to kill later when we reached a landslide. 'It happens all the time,' groaned Tej, as we joined the queue of slow-moving trucks waiting for a road gang to clear a way through. At the scene of the slip, hundreds of men and women, covered from head to foot in dust, dug and shovelled to remove debris. Their task seemed monumental.

To increase output, each shovel was operated by two people. As one held the handle the other pulled the shovel through the rubble with the aid of a length of rope. The road was being completely rebuilt and, to make a retaining wall, large rocks were being mined across the river. Oil-drum rafts held captive on wire cables plied back and forth to bring the stone across. There was even a tethered raft carrying a turbine being driven by the current to provide electrical power.

Whilst we waited there was a chance to take in our surroundings. Nothing is wasted in this Third World country: the paper used for cones by boys selling peanuts at the roadside was covered with sums – it had been taken from their arithmetic homework books. Wood is the only natural source of fuel and building material and deforestation is a huge problem, causing alarming erosion of the thin soil. There is now an attempt to control wood-cutting: anyone wishing to build a house must first seek permission from the local village headman and is then limited to two trees which may be cut to build the framework. Moreover, some replanting has been undertaken. Bottlebrush trees with bright red flowers and Indian rosewood are being planted beside the road and rivers, the saplings protected by wickerwork cages.

The roadworkers waved frantically at drivers moving round the detour at more than walking pace. Two hundred feet down the bank was a truck that had gone over when the road collapsed. It served as a potent reminder.

To make up time our young bus driver kept his foot down. As the vehicle was left-hand drive and the Nepalese drive on the left, overtaking was hazardous. However, the lookout, a handsome lad standing in the door, whistled and yelled whenever it was safe and we hurtled forward to overtake. No wonder the Nepalese called him 'the human traffic light'. Beneath my window a seven hundred and fifty foot drop fell away into the Trisuli River. 'Is this part of the adventure?' exclaimed Rula after a particularly near miss. Stopping only for speed checks at police posts, we ploughed on in order to reach Pokhara before dark. At one point we took our life in our hands, as do hundreds every day, crossing a particularly challenging steep, rickety construction known as the suicide suspension bridge. ONLY ONE VEHICLE AT A TIME, says the notice as you approach this precarious construction, and there are strict rules concerning troops walking across – if they marched in step the bridge would collapse.

The bone-shaking journey took nine hours and one snoozed at one's peril because it took every tensed muscle to remain seated. As the sun was setting everyone slumped with fatigue, trying to wedge themselves into a corner in the hope of snatching a brief doze. We suddenly crashed in and out of one especially severe pothole and were hailed on from above. The source of the cascade turned out to be our supply of bottled mineral water which became dislodged from the luggage rack above our heads, and at the same time we were pelted with metal and bits of plastic from the overhead light fitting, the screws of which were loosened by the constant vibration. Brook, being rudely awoken by this involuntary shower, asked earnestly, 'Which way is the river flowing now?'

The first foreigners to visit Nepal heard rumours of an untouched Shangri-La only seven days' march to the west of Kathmandu. When some of them reached Pokhara they found a place of amazing beauty where abundant tropical flowers grew beside a clear blue lake above which the snow-capped Himalayas lined the horizon. Even though it was dusk when we reached the town, the beauty was awe-inspiring.

The Pokhara Valley is at 2,900 feet and to the north the peaks of the Annapurna range rise to almost 23,000 feet. Between the town and the mountains there is barely even a hill. Nowhere in the world is there such a rise in height in such a short distance.

Until an airport was built, the valley remained isolated and remote but truly a place of pilgrimage. Although one can now reach it by plane much of the old magic remains. Arriving at dusk we just had time to cross over the lake on a hand-hauled ferry which delivered us to the Fish Tail Lodge in time for supper. In the bar, G&T in hand, was a freshly laundered Wendy B., who had been trekking in the area for a few days. 'Good trip?' she enquired as we staggered in.

Built on a promontory jutting out into the lake and living off its reputation of having once hosted the Prince of Wales, this must be the finest place to stay in town. We were hungry and the food was tasty.

'Do you wish to be woken to see the sunrise?' asked the receptionist. Needing sleep, I hesitated, but next morning was very glad that I had said 'yes'.

When my call came I pulled on a sarong and sallied forth into the picturesque gardens. Carol was up too and, cameras in hand, we waited in the pure, cool air for the sun to touch the distant peaks. As it did the surroundings appeared as if the lights in a theatre were being raised. In the garden dahlias, roses, nasturtiums, red and white poinsettia trees, giant alyssum and marigold provided a profusion of colour. Across the lake, jutting out of the land mass of mountains, rose a near replica of the Matterhorn. Machha Puchhare or the Fish Tail stood alone, slightly pink in the first rays of sunlight. The lower mountain peaks paraded to the left and right, each in turn becoming illuminated and reflected in the still waters of the Phewa Tal Lake. As I extended my lens to wide angle, bougainvillaea and stately trees edged the picture. It was a scene that any artist would have found challenging. No wonder this was called 'the most beautiful spot on earth'.

Before we set off next morning, Jimmy Roberts, the retired Gurkha Colonel, who is a legend in mountaineering circles, dropped by for a chat. I had first met him twenty years before when he was still climbing. In 1957 Jimmy managed to persuade the Nepalese to grant him permission to attempt Machha Puchhare. He found the local Gurungs regarded the mountain as sacred and were not at all keen on it being climbed. As it was, Jimmy's expedition was forced back a mere two hundred feet from the summit by a virtually impossible pitch. Some while later the government asked him to nominate a peak in the Annapurna sanctuary that should remain forever sacrosanct. He put forward Machha Puchhare.

Few outsiders knew Nepal and respected its culture more than Jimmy Roberts. Although he was now much older and hindered by rheumatism, no one who gathered around him that morning in sight of the holy mountain could fail to be moved by his words as he described the country he had grown to love.

In view of our short time in Kathmandu the chance for some shopping in the busy streets of the old town was appreciated. Cars, bicycles and dewy-eyed buffalo jostled for their right of way with porters, sherpas and heavily laden women. The land is more lush and the air cleaner than in Kathmandu. The atmosphere was certainly more relaxed and, wandering among stalls and shops, I could see why so many were attracted to Pokhara.

'I've just surprised the crowd by handling a snake,' said Wendy B. rather proudly. 'Of course it's only a python, but I bet they don't realize it's harmless.'

Snake-charmers are not very common in Nepal, so we joined a throng gathered around a circus of serpents. Four cobras, with hoods extended, swayed and undulated from wicker baskets as their owners played a tuneless dirge on their flutes, beating time with their feet. A couple of six-foot pythons slithered across the ground, forked tongues flickering, causing the audience to jump back in alarm. We tossed some rupees into the collection bag and moved on to see a Tibetan temple, Tashi Pakhel.

Since the Chinese invasion of their homeland, some thirty thousand Tibetan refugees have poured into Nepal. Many have settled in the Pokhara area and at the top of a low cliff on the outskirts of the town we found a mini-Tibet with whitewashed houses, prayer flags and other trappings of their culture. The monks and their attendants seemed genuinely pleased to see us.

Rula had been to Tibet the previous October and it had made a huge impression on her. In her journal she wrote of her visit to Pokhara:

*It was such a wonderful feeling to discover a little pocket of people I'd spent three weeks amongst earlier last year. Small seated groups of men and women, twirling their prayer wheels and chanting, 'Oh mani padme hung': peace to all sentient beings. That same serenity and peace*

*in their eyes even though in exile. They invited me to sit and chant with*
*them and I sat cross-legged in the warm sunshine. I pulled out my beads*
*and intoned the time-honoured chant with them. One particularly old*
*man produced some ancient Tibetan coins with great pride and laid*
*them on the ground in front of me. I offered him a few dollars but he*
*quite sternly let me know they were not for sale. Slowly and painfully*
*struggling to his feet, he then motioned me to follow him, and still*
*fingering his beads he put his arm through mine and slowly guided me*
*to the temple. It was empty save for two young monks tending the butter*
*lamps. The great Golden Buddha 'Sakyammui' gazed down at us from*
*his enormous height and we both knelt and made the traditional pro-*
*strations. He then pointed to my hand which still held the money and*
*gestured to the donation box. I rose and put in what little money I had.*
*He smiled, gave me one of his old coins and touched his forehead to my*
*hand. Very moved, I walked slowly back out into the sun with him,*
*turning the large prayer wheels at the top of the stairs. I showed him*
*the little Buddha hanging round my neck, he smiled and we both touched*
*our foreheads in the traditional greeting, 'Namaste.' Leaving the peaceful*
*little courtyard having purchased some pretty bangles, I turned for one*
*last look. He was still standing bowing and nodding towards me with*
*a bemused look on his face.*

Whilst Rula was in the temple I made the mistake of admiring
a silver cruet set offered by a souvenir seller at the gates and was
at once pursued by this highly persuasive lady who refused to
believe I wouldn't buy it. As our bus was about to leave she
accepted six dollars, little enough for us, but by her expression it
was a fair price. The new road to the Kali Gandaki ran through
endless terraced fields and neat hilltop villages of terracotta
houses with thatched roofs. A picnic at the roadside, drinks from
a little tea-house, and impish smiling children to carry off some
of our endless supply of hard-boiled eggs were other treats. Anne
gave the kids a postcard of Big Ben. They turned it round and
round looking totally perplexed, but in exchange she asked if
they had a loo she might use. A key was duly produced and she
was directed to a corrugated iron structure – and rather regretted
the experience.

The Kali Gandaki, named after the goddess Kali, is an especially
holy river and cremation on its banks is considered most aus-

picious. It rises in Mustang, a chunk of Nepal that juts into Tibet. Flowing through steep-sided canyons between two of the world's largest mountain massifs, it is believed to be one of the deepest gorges in the world, for at its mid-point it is 18,500 feet below the flanking summits. For centuries it has been a route for traders and pilgrims between India and Tibet. I wondered if the Nepalese invaders with their elephants had gone this way.

Slicing through the Himalayas, the river might provide fossil evidence of early elephants and Adrian had heard of a number of possible sites. The only way to travel through the gorge is by boat, so we planned to launch our fleet near Baglung village.

Tej's boys had the camp set up when we rolled in and the four Avons were already inflated. Supper, an incredibly delectable meal of mutton and vegetables with a subtle flavour, was enhanced by liberal dollops of chilli garlic sauce, my favourite dressing. Now Adrian was to go ahead to the known fossil beds east of Bardia while Ken Reed would direct our search along the Kali Gandaki; we would then rejoin Adrian in Bardia. That night the temperature plummeted and the camp went quiet as exhausted travellers climbed into their sleeping bags.

It was 10.55 a.m. on Tuesday, 21 January 1995 when we cast off. The river level was very low and bouncing through some minor rapids we felt the boulders on our hull. A grade three plus with a nasty hole kept us on our toes. In her boat, Anna was bailing furiously until someone pointed out that the boat had a self-bailing floor so there would always be a few inches of water in it. Waterfalls tumbling from the cliff provided a marvellous backdrop.

Having pioneered white-water rafting, I am always fascinated to hear how newcomers find it. Carol, my assistant, who was experiencing it for the first time, wrote in her log:

Rafting turned out to be a sometimes exhilarating, sometimes very peaceful, quite chilly and timeless business. We had to stop before each rapid, clamber out and struggle over the boulders along the shoreline to the rapid to assess its strength and the technique required to get through. It was fascinating to watch the expertise of the boatmen wielding their enormously long and heavy wooden oars and directing the paddling as the rafts spun round, flopped over huge boulders, heaved and cavorted over the rapids. The paddle boat was the greatest fun when it came to rapid-running, as it bucked and kicked about in a mad fashion, plunging down at the front and shooting up at the back as we frantically paddled, half the time with our paddles out of the water as we were flung up in the air, hanging on by our toes tucked under ropes in the bottom of the craft used to strap down our stores. Sometimes the passage of water between rocks or the sides of the gorges was so narrow, we had to duck to avoid being hit as the raft was flung against the rock face.

Ken, Julian and I looked after the survey work aided by a small optical range finder I had been sent by the American manufacturers, Ranging Inc. The speed and accuracy of Ken's compass readings made all the difference. His global experience with oil companies was clearly of value. On the sides of the gorge he moved like a mountain goat, leaping easily from rock to rock and giving us a running commentary on the geology. He certainly made a rather dry subject interesting.

We camped just past the Modi Khola junction and walking back up the valley saw a funeral in progress on the far bank. As we watched, the body was buried under a pile of rocks at the water's edge whilst nearby the deceased's two sons had their heads shaved for mourning. During the ceremony a conch shell was blown repeatedly, its mournful sound echoing between the cliffs of the gorge.

'He would have been a low caste person,' said Sundar, 'otherwise he would have been cremated. Only the wealthy can now afford the wood to burn their dead.'

Nearby a flock of vultures perched on the boulders, hunched scrawny birds with long bald necks. The loathsome creatures sharpened their beaks on the stones and stepped daintily from rock to rock as they waited for the mourners to disperse.

An impressive suspension bridge spanned the river just above our camp. Many decking planks were missing and the ironwork was pitted with rust. Rula found a small shop on the far side and was overjoyed to replenish her stock of cigarettes. Meanwhile I used the bridge to calibrate the range finder and Sundar asked some farmers about fossils.

'Any luck?' I enquired.

'They do not know of anything here, but say there may be some near Ridi,' replied Sundar and then went on to tell how the original footbridge had collapsed fourteen years before, plunging thirty-five people to their death.

Back in camp, Wendy felt we needed cheering up. She seemed to have a limitless supply of amazing kit and appeared in a king-fisher green towelling dressing gown, armed with a full-size dart-board which was then erected on an oar stuck in the sand and the boat boys set to in a needle-sharp match.

The rapids proved sporting but nothing really serious like the Karnali. Stopping for a couple of nights near Purti Ghat, we visited a small cave nearby said to contain fossils, but although Ken found stalactites and Wendy discovered some interesting plants that stung and irritated, there were no fossils.

News that we had a doctor with us soon spread and at every stop David Jenkins, Rula and Anna set up a temporary clinic. There was not a lot he could do and there is always the fear that if you give out modern drugs for the short time you are there, the people will stop using their traditional medicines and, not being able to get a regular supply of western drugs, will, in the long term, be worse off.

Our camp attracted a lot of villagers who used every spare moment to come and watch us aliens go about our daily tasks. Wendy remembers her experience:

On our second morning, I was the first out of the tent. I unzipped the flap and climbed out into the cold fresh air clutch-ing a flannel, toothbrush and paste in my hands. To my surprise I was confronted by six dear, sweet, smiling children aged between five and eight. They put their hands together in the traditional greeting; 'Namaste,' they chorused in their high-pitched little voices. Then with great purpose I headed towards the river to do my ablutions. To get to the water required a certain amount of rock-hopping and I had not chosen a very good route. However, I eventually arrived at the edge. I was

just about to put my flannel into the water when I noticed
something white below the surface. To my horror I realized
that it was the bones of a human hand from a burial upstream.
I decided to try a different location.

Whilst our medical team did their best to help the people, I
asked about fossils. The locals drew pictures of ammonites, the
strange spiral-shelled molluscs turned to stone which were evidence of the area's sub-marine origins, but they also spoke of
something else called a shaligram. Not even Ken knew what this
meant. I asked Carol, Rula and the others if they would go up to
the town and see if they could get more information.

On their return they reported that Purti Ghat was a charming
old trading centre, looking exactly like a Biblical illustration
perched on pinnacles of rock, the two parts of the town connected
by a swaying suspension bridge. An irrigation system feeding
water from a mountain stream to the little terraced areas of cultivation on the outskirts was extremely efficient and wheat and
rice grew lushly. The stream rushes right through the middle of
the place underneath huge flat paving slabs and the town, which
grew up around a trading post built by people of the commercial
Newar tribe from the Kathmandu Valley about one hundred years
ago, had an air of sophistication and order about it, although
hygiene was as lacking here as everywhere in the countryside.
'They tend to just squat wherever they are,' said Carol.

Climbing down the track into the town, the first shop they came
across was a travellers' refreshment and resting place, serving little
glasses of sweet, fragrant, peppery tea. They also offered sugary
ring doughnuts and brilliantly coloured strings of sweet rice. Happily, they found some very refreshing bottles of beer in a shop
on the village square over the other side of the little town, quite
expensive, but not surprisingly, as it has to be carried all the way
up from the road, some nine hours' walk away. Some thought
they would test the postal system, so bought paper and an envelope each, and with rather more amusement than faith, posted
them for delivery to England. To their amazement their letters
arrived within about a fortnight.

The houses, all joined into a long terrace lining the steep streets,
are built on three or sometimes even four levels. The large school,

which normally caters for 800 pupils with seventeen teachers, was preparing for the annual Government Board exams; over the nine-day examination period the school's ranks would be swelled by an influx of students from smaller hill schools in the region. The bank rather impressively sported an armed guard at the entrance. He stood with folded arms looking menacing, though there has never been so much as a hint of a hold-up. Pat Troy decided to change a five-dollar bill into rupees, which sent the system into a flat spin. His note was eyed and closely inspected with deep suspicion by the banking clerk and passed round to everyone gathered, but finally the guard, brandishing his shotgun in front of the huge crowd which had gathered, approved its authenticity and, after much signing of documents, a transaction was brought about.

In the village square they found the locals whiling away their time around a table with pockets at the side, playing a game which is similar to billiards, using not cues and balls but pittances – rather like shove ha'penny – the colour of the pittances determining their score value. They stopped to admire the long coils of highly coloured glass bangles being sold by a lady who insisted that Carol should decorate her arms by wearing some. She pointed out that she would never get them over her wide-boned hands, but was assured that the lady was an expert fitter. As a result she returned clanking, having undergone some severe torture to get them on. There were also two goldsmiths in town, beating away, making earrings and nose-rings in almost feather-weight orangey-coloured gold. Nepali women carry all their family wealth in jewellery which adorns their heads, hands and arms. It was a fascinating visit to a remote settlement far from the beaten track, but there was no news of fossils or shaligrams.

After Purti Ghat, the Gandaki was less turbulent for quite a way, although the lack of sun in the gorge made it colder. The camp fire was greatly appreciated as we stood around the blaze of driftwood, warming ourselves and trying to dry clothes. Nevertheless it was an area of great beauty.

Soon it began to warm up again and Carol wrote in her diary:

Such luxury, therefore, to find a pretty fall of water which was really quite warm. Lovely wild flowers including little white ground orchids growing amongst the lush ferns. Deforestation is very evident with no replanting – what will the hill people do when there is no more wood to burn?

Wonderful sounds across the water: a woodpecker, gentle faraway human calls and a deep horn being blown across the valleys. A peaceful day's rafting, drifting along great stretches of mirror-like aquamarine water which contrasts with the bright citrus green of the moss and ferns on the rocky banks. The Avons only need six inches of water to glide over the boulders of the river in spite of the enormous weight they are carrying. In this calmer stretch we come across a few dugouts which the people use to cross the river, but they cannot handle the rapids. Monkeys dart around in the undergrowth and we pass groups of gold panners. Sadly, this beautiful gorge is soon to be flooded to provide hydroelectricity – which also will mean no more rafting. We pass many burial places and a tiny, very holy Hindu temple on a hillside to which the people travel for days to visit and below which there are signs of cremations. Egyptian vultures plentiful.

A tiny fieldmouse had been hiding in the bottom of one of the boats, very squeaky and frightened. Wendy and Gary made a dive for it and managed to catch it – rather gingerly in case it was rabid – then, after it had had a little sleep in her hand, Wendy took it off with great ceremony to what was considered to be a suitable spot to release it.

The valley opened out when we reached Ridi and the colourful, solidly built houses rose up the sides of the steep dry hills. The current slackened as we drew near the broad beach where a great many people had gathered for a puja (or religious festival). On the water floated dozens of leaf bowls, beautifully sewn together and carrying offerings of food to the gods. It is here that a renowned temple, the Rikheswara Narayana, houses a statue of the god Vishnu. Local tradition has it that this was originally the size of an infant boy but in the course of years it has assumed the appearance of an adult god.

There was just time for Sanu, our excellent cook, to replenish our fresh food for us and do a little shopping in the narrow streets. We also asked about shaligrams and were shown some black rocks that had been polished by the river. 'Not fossils,' muttered Ken, turning one over in his hand and making a close inspection with his magnifying glass.

Back on the beach David found a human shin bone. 'This is a place of cremation,' confided Sundar as we waved farewell to the smartly dressed worshippers on the water's edge and pulled out into the flow. Soon Ridi had disappeared behind a jungle-covered headland.

Lunching on a strand of silver sand, we relaxed in the hot sun, but seeing a fish jump I got out my rod. A mahseer followed my lure right into the shallows but declined to bite, so I handed the tackle to Dhan Gurung, a big muscular boatman. Alas, he also failed, so Tej took it over and with his first cast had a plump two-pounder on the hook. A cheer went up and thereafter we fished at every stop.

It was mid-afternoon when Wendy, who was keeping the navigation log, called out, 'The Rana Palace should be around the next bend if our reckoning is correct.' Almost as she spoke we had our first view of the splendid building, standing out on a bluff a hundred feet above the river. The roof was gone, revealing heavy timber rafters set in the Gothic-style edifice. Trees and creepers were entwined in the brickwork. A wide stone staircase led up from the water to terraces and a pillared façade gave it a truly regal appearance. Beyond it and across the river stretched the longest suspension footbridge in Nepal, said to be two hundred and twenty-two metres in length.

Sweeping across the current we landed on a sandy shore opposite the palace and, forming lines, unloaded our gear. Whilst the camp was being made ready, Brook shot off for a recce of the palace and on return said, 'It's quite amazing, just like something from a Hollywood drama.'

Anna, who had been further along our beach, had seen burial mounds. 'We are camping in a graveyard,' she said, cheerfully.

The best view of the Rani Mahal was in the morning when the sun shone directly on it. Working in several teams we surveyed the site and examined the fabric. Julian Brown put his experience of ancient buildings to good use while some of the more intrepid climbed to the upper storey of the crumbling ruin. Ken found a water system, complete with a cistern on a knoll behind the palace, whilst David and Pat discovered the best viewpoint from a hill opposite.

The palace was constructed with bricks made of the local rosy red clay, which was perfect building material for the very romantic Italian Baroque style of design. Before the foundations were laid, a small river running down from the hills into the Kali Gandaki at the foot of the rock which held the palace had to be diverted, for fear of it eating away at the foot of the rock. Sadly, with the lack of upkeep, this tributary is returning to its natural course.

Stables and barrack rooms made up the lowest level, with steps leading up to the temple courtyard. We later learned that there were about three platoons of soldiers billeted at the palace, with more at Tansen; all wore simple local clothing apart from their commander who sported European-style military uniform.

A three-shrined temple was roofed with three huge bell-shaped spires which had originally been coated with gold leaf, but this had been pillaged some years ago. Two of the shrines are dedicated to the god Shiva, the middle shrine containing a beautiful gold-painted statue of Shumser's Queen. Three priests, each responsible for one of the shrines, worship there daily, and are supported by the regional government, with gifts of rice from the local people. An old man appeared from nowhere and seemed to be some sort of caretaker. At the corner of the temple's roof, I noticed threatening bronze cobras jutting out from the gutters.

Climbing a flight of broad steps we came to a magnificent paved terrace with two lily ponds, one on either side of the main thoroughfare. Originally the terrace was lit at night by metal lampstands. An ornamental archway decorated with badges depicting flower shapes led to a little look-out point higher up on the rock face with a magnificent view of the whole sweep of river below. On the terrace beneath this lookout point, a shady retreat was used for relaxing and taking afternoon tea. Now the ponds have been drained, the flower beds destroyed by goats and the great cast iron vases gather rust amongst the twisted wreckage of the corrugated iron roof.

Steps lead up to the colonnaded main entrance to the palace with enormous pottery plant pots either side of the massive wooden main door. The doorway is adorned with a small inverted V-shaped piece of metal known as 'karuwa', a traditional mark to protect the house and its inhabitants. This would have been made by the local blacksmith on an auspicious day and another special day would have been chosen for the placing of the karuwa. The columns were built of brick with stucco plaster and both they and the pilasters were decorated with blue paint against the cream of the main structure. Hooks were inserted in the walls for suspending lanterns to light the terrace.

At the front of the building, the high-ceilinged rooms were used for reception and administrative purposes with a stairway leading to the upper floor. Ground-floor sitting rooms leading on to the back veranda and terrace had fireplaces for chilly winter evenings. Chandeliers had hung in the main rooms, lit by an electric generator.

Steps from the main building lead to the kitchens and dining area at the rear. Two huge ovens catered for the large numbers to be fed, with shelving for the huge pots and pans used. Apparently even the royal couple were to eat their meals in the communal dining area.

Covered water channels had been laid high around the hillsides for about three miles, the water collected would have run gradually downhill into a multi-chambered filtration tank set on the rock high above the building. The toilet area was located at the back, between the main house and the kitchens. The loos consisted of bore-holes surrounded by stones, which were washed clean by running water into a drainage system.

Pleasure gardens, an orchard and vegetable gardens, now overgrown, were situated to the left of the palace, but flowers, mango and banana trees, and a mimosa tree survive.

A bronze bell was suspended on steel beams on which Brook found the words 'Dorman Long Ltd Middlesboro'. By now the aged keeper had put up a sign which read PLEASE REMOVE SHOES.

Rula and Carol investigated the track leading from the Rani Mahal into the hills. Although much reduced in width through lack of maintenance, its construction indicated that this was the original trail along which the elephants had brought in the building material. At the top of a long incline was a strange rock shaped like a recumbent elephant. A prayer flag flew from a pole above it and the surface had been daubed with red dye. A few houses clung to the rockface and the people called this sacred spot 'Hatbagda' (Elephant Rock). We could imagine Shumser's giant jumbos lumbering along this royal road bearing his British girders.

When the sun disappeared over the top of the mountains, we were still taking measurements. The others walked on as I packed up my gear. For a few minutes I was alone in the palace with only the hiss of the river and a faint breeze in the trees. The place had an aura of sadness and decay. In the century since Khadga Shumser and Tej Kumari had tarried here, Nepal had seen the coming of roads, dams, electricity, cars, planes, telephones, radios and television, but the forest was disappearing rapidly and wildlife was being stamped out. I wondered what had happened to the enormous numbers of people that had worked here. How many had died at the job? Where did the large elephants come from? All this effort, for what? As I strolled past the shrine something caught my eye. A shiny black cobra was slithering away across the flagstones.

That night Julian read out his survey report. He concluded:

The building is in such an advanced state of decay that restoration, though not impossible, would be a slow and painstaking task, necessitating the examination in detail of every part during the course of restoration to ascertain whether each could be saved or would have to be scrapped and replaced. The installation of electrical, plumbing and drainage facilities would be a major consideration and would depend upon to what use the building was to be put. It is inadequate to run as a hotel without the addition of a substantial annex in which to house guests, as the main building could only be used for accommodating public rooms. In view of the cost of restoration the proprietors would have to consider what infrastructure is needed to support any proposed use. If nothing else is done it will gradually crumble into a pile of rubble over the years.

When the Kali Gandaki is dammed above Ridi it will produce valuable hydroelectricity and have a considerable effect on the valley. The idea of the rebuilt Rani Mahal being a thriving tourist lodge bringing wealth to the region is certainly interesting, but having heard Julian's findings I doubted if the funds needed to refurbish the Lost Palace of the Ranas would be forthcoming. Perhaps it is just as well if the peace and tranquillity of this remote place is to be preserved.

We had invited a former Gurkha soldier whom Carol had met near the Hatbagda to bring his children to dance and sing to us in the camp and as night fell we heard the sound of chanting as a crowd approached the bridge. With the image intensifier we saw that it was a large group of men and no children. Some carried lanterns and others were bearing a pole beneath which swung a long load. 'Good heavens,' exclaimed Pat, 'I think they've got a body.' They had indeed and soon a burial party was at work on our beach, removing rocks and pebbles to make a shallow grave. Dhan Gurung went over to assist and out of morbid curiosity some of us followed.

A pressure lamp illuminated a macabre scene. Stripped to the waist, the sweating gravediggers struggled with the rocks. They used only their bare hands and lying beside the growing hole was the almost naked body of a youngish man, probably in his late twenties. Powders and potions were being applied to his skin and a single candle burned beside his head. Apart from his pallid complexion and the strange contorted angle of his neck, he looked as if he might be asleep, but he was very dead.

'The bus left the road and crashed into a ravine,' said Tej. 'Forty-three killed. This man is from a village nearby so the people have brought him here for burial.'

'How far have they carried him?' asked Anna.

'Oh, the accident was many miles from here, beyond Tansen,' replied our skipper.

Leaving them to their work, we returned to camp for supper. Earlier in the day, Mahendra had decapitated a goat, boned the meat beautifully and he now served it with a mouth-watering sauce, but we didn't eat much. However, the children's arrival and a spot of song and dance cheered us up. Julian, with his flowing silver hair and military moustache, was a splendid sight and Rula soon got all the boat boys joining in. We rewarded the dancers with copious quantities of bread and jam and some delicious currant cake that Sanu had created. Across the river a faint light winked amongst the ruins. Was it the old keeper of the shrine or perhaps the ghost of Khadga Shumser seeking his Queen?

Floating downstream next day we passed several pujas in progress. Colourfully dressed people smiled and waved. Men with great horns, some six foot long, sounded off long notes of greeting.

The rapids were fairly easy but a grade four tested our skill and gave us a good wetting. By now we were blasé at anything less than that and when our skipper said, 'Grade three coming up, hold on,' neither Ken nor I looked up from our survey work. Suddenly there was a splintering crash. Immediately the raft spun sideways, dipping into a yawning hole. We were almost on our side and water was pouring over the bow and pushing Ken across the gunwale. I seized him by his life jacket and held on until the craft righted itself.

'Very sorry,' apologized Tej, 'my oar broke as we went into the rapid.'

Our last night on the river. The evening meal over, we gathered around the camp fire and discovered what had kept Rula and Anna so preoccupied during the days spent floating downriver. Their 'Ode to the River Boys on the Kali Gandaki' was sung to the tune of 'The Teddy Bears' Picnic' and went thus:

> *If you go down to the Kali Gandaki, you'll have to use your eyes,*
> *If you go down to the Kali Gandaki, you're in for a surprise,*
> *It's cold and it's rough and it can be quite tough,*
> *But we set up our camp when we've had just enough.*
> *That's what it's like on the beautiful Kali Gandaki*
>
> *We pack and unpack and we eat and we drink*
> *We write and we photo and listen and think,*
> *We observe and we measure,*
> *Or just take our pleasure*

*While pootling about, relaxing at leisure.*
*That's what it's like on the beautiful Kali Gandaki.*

*Sundar, Tej and Wong are ace,*
*They point out plant, bird and special place,*
*Sanu, Mongol and Jerry too,*
*Amaze us nightly with a gourmet 'do'.*
*Dhan protects us and Asi helps*
*We experience, discover, observe and collate.*
*It's a helluva trip you'll love or you'll hate.*
*But it's special, unique and it's my cup of tea,*
*That's rafting the beautiful Kali Gandaki.*

*Ken is our expert on fossils and rocks,*
*While Wendy's collecting her plants and her moss.*
*Young Brook is obsessed with his Gurkha knife*
*And Rula is videoing all aspects of life.*
*It's all going on while rafting along*
*On the beautiful Kali Gandaki.*

*Julian and Carol work like dogs,*
*Gary and Anna're keeping bird logs.*
*Leaving Pat and the Colonel,*
*A fish and a mouse,*
*And David our doctor about the camp house.*
*That's how we live on the beautiful Kali Gandaki.*

*Rana palace and Ridi Bazaar,*
*A varied sixty kilometres rafting so far.*
*Stoke the fire, drink the rum,*
*Another scrummy meal fills our tum,*
*The moon's up, the day's done,*
*Each face glowing from the warm sun.*
*Thanks to the Colonel, Tej and his team*
*These past days like a dream.*
*So God bless Nepal and the beautiful Kali Gandaki.*

We left the river at Ramdighat where the road from Pokhara crosses the Kali Gandaki. Our bus awaited and in this we climbed up to Tansen, the administrative capital of Palpa District. Winding our way up the narrow cobbled streets, past red brick buildings of this important hill station and trading post, we eventually came to the Durbar whose massive gateway, the Mul Dhoka, was proclaimed to be the largest in the Kingdom (erected by Khadga Shumser during his time as Governor of Palpa). A renovated temple, built in 1815 to commemorate a Nepali victory over the British, was pointed out to us, but our main interest was Shumser's old palace, now the local government building. Going in through the great gate, I found a smartly dressed scribe, Yog-Presad, who spoke some English and knew a little of the region's history:

'Khadga Shumser used between twelve thousand and thirteen thousand soldiers to build the elephant road to the Rani Mahal and it was a British design.' Apparently the plasterwork at the palace was very special and originally the whole place had been painted blue and cream. 'You must see the Hatti-Sar,' said Yog-Presad, pointing to a twelve-foot-high phallic pillar by the great wooden gate. 'That is where the Governor tied up his huge elephants, but he also had many mules and donkeys.'

'Where did he get his elephants?' I asked.

'They were brought from Chitwan,' asserted the scribe. 'There were four of them, some were medium-sized but two were very big elephants and in winter, when it is cold here, they went back to the Terai.'

I asked about the difficulties of constructing the road.

'There were many problems, a soldier fell from the cliff and died, and Shumser's daughter was also killed when she fell into a well.'

He also knew all about the strangely shaped rock that Rula had seen on the trail.

'You see, the gate had to be big enough to get the elephants through,' explained Yog-Presad. It must have been over twenty-five feet to the lintel. A carving of the elephant-headed Ganesh, son of Shiva and the warrior god Karpikaya, ornamented the stonework surround.

'You could just imagine the Governor riding out in an ornate howdah on his giant elephant,' said Brook, who was measuring up the gateway.

Outside, the Durbar was full of fascinating old buildings and even the postboxes were ornate.

Some distance from Tansen, on the steep winding road to the lower foothills, we came across a group of sad-eyed people peering into the gorge and, fearing some accident, Asuk, our driver, halted. Tej jumped out to enquire and returned saying, 'This is the place where the bus went over.' We could not resist looking down at the mangled wreckage a thousand feet below. Unrecognizable, it lay wheel-less and half submerged in a tumbling stream.

'Forty-three dead, sixteen injured,' said Sundar, who had been talking to a bystander. 'There are still bodies to be brought up.'

'Poor devils,' said Carol, 'but it's a wonder anyone survived at all.'

As darkness fell we turned off the east–west highway and drove north for Rapti Dunn and the fossil base. The narrow, newly cut track, inches deep in fine dust, made the going hazardous, and we tried not to look over the edge as it wound up the hills. At precisely 8 p.m., as the boat boys had predicted, the swaying and shaking stopped and we had arrived in a sandy valley where Adrian had been scouting for signs of fossils. All were very relieved to reach the camp where a lonely palaeontologist and a hot meal awaited.

'A leopard was here last night,' smiled Adrian, happy to have our company, but after the terror of the road, that did not worry us unduly.

Over supper he went on to tell us how, whilst in Kathmandu, he had seen one of the holy men elevating a fifty-pound rock with his penis.

'I am sure it's genuine,' he said.

'Only fifty pounds,' muttered Pat, 'obviously not Marine-trained.'

From her cavernous rucksack Wendy produced the dartboard. Although the darts often got lost in the sand, the fossil hunters were quickly addicted. Jackals were howling as I climbed into my bed. The temperature had dropped to 45°F. 'Must be the damp sand,' I thought.

\*     \*     \*

Before Rula, Anna, Carol and Gary left us to our fossilizing and pressed on to Bardia to prepare the way and ascertain the whereabouts of the various wild elephants, Adrian insisted on showing them an extraordinary discovery. Only fifty yards from the camp was a large boulder covered with erotic drawings of men and women doing what comes naturally. He was told that the drawings were made by a celibate holy man, and the great stone seemed to guard the entrance to a valley with a shallow river, around which were piled enormous and curious shaped rocks, said to be the remains of a wedding party at which all the people were turned to stone. The locals feared this place and kept away.

'We are in the Siwalik Hills,' explained Adrian, pointing out the features on a map he had made in the sand. 'In the bands of sedimentary rock that break through the surface, there are fossils.' He produced a few small examples, told us how to search, and off we went. Two days of toil in the dusty valley produced only one relic of a prehistoric animal. This was a leg bone of an early, rather small horse which Ken's sharp eyes picked up. But we did see an extraordinary object. Returning from a visit to a leopard's lair, we stopped at a farm and were asking about fossils when the man of the house went to a potted plant in his yard and dug out an object the size and shape of a bantam's egg.

It seemed to be composed of some form of hard grey deposit with bands of dark green silica-like material spiralling round it.

'He says it is a shaligram,' said Kul Thapa, Adrian's interpreter.

Ken and Adrian looked puzzled and examined it long and hard.

'He claims it comes from an animal and belonged to his grandfather,' went on Kul. 'It brings good fortune.'

As we turned to leave, the farmer spoke again and our interpreter's eyes lit up. 'He says many years ago his father found some very large old bones near here, but they got swept away by the river.'

'It could have been *Elephas hysudricus*,' mused Adrian as we tramped home.

Back at camp, Tej and Sanu, Adrian's skilful cook, were slicing up garlic and ginger. A great feast was being prepared and after the daily conference we tucked into one of the best meals I have ever eaten in the field. The assortment of curried dishes, salads, vegetables, dhal, perfect rice, prawn crackers and fresh fruit salad, washed down with kukri rum and orange, was fit for a king.

Meanwhile a farmer had brought in a baby who had been trodden on by a goat. The child's femur was broken and by the light of a Tilley lamp, David splinted it. To cheer up the little fellow we pressed small gifts and rupees on his dad. Father and son departed with the equivalent of several weeks' wages. Luckily we were leaving early next day, for I could see we would have been swamped with casualties.

We slept like logs although Julian found a pack of wild dogs sniffing around when he answered a call of nature at 4.30 a.m.

Once more we entrusted ourselves to the skilful Asuk, who took us back down the tortuous track with care, using his horn liberally at every bend. Once on the highway, I dozed off. I woke as we crossed over the Babai Bridge. 'Oh look, there's an elephant,' said someone, and I glanced out of the window. Two hundred yards away, browsing beside the river was a tusker. 'Must be a government beast,' I murmured and we were well down the road before I came out of my trance-like state. The government did not have any tuskers in this area. 'Blast, we've just driven right past a wild bull and I was too stupid to realize it,' I cursed. One thing was sure, it was not Raja Gaj or Kancha so there must be a big male amongst the newcomers.

At the Karnali Lodge, our advance party waited. Pradeep, Dhan Bahadur and Ram Din were there too, plus our old pal Karan Rana who managed the lodge. It felt like coming home. A slim, attractive young woman, her blonde hair blowing in the breeze, walked across the lawn, smiling. 'Hello, John, I've come to give a hand.' It was Anna-Tara, Jim Edwards' daughter, whom I had known since she was a baby at Tiger Tops. Now training to be a naturalist, she was keen to meet the beasts of Bardia. It was extraordinary how few people in Nepal had seen the giants.

'What news of the big fellows?' I asked Pradeep.

For once he did not look so confident. There was a pause then he said quietly, 'We have not seen them for some days. The trackers think they are outside the reserve – somewhere.'

*Chapter Ten*

# ELEPHANTS GALORE

DOWN by the river the camp was set up as before. Honey Blossom looked well and as beautiful as ever. Dhuki had decorated her with chalk and oil for our meeting. I thought she had put on a little weight and said so. The phanit smiled lovingly and the old lady snorted. Luksmi, who was one of the older elephants, had been sold off and replaced by Raj Kali, a young, slightly nervous twenty-one-year-old. I had seen this coming. Luksmi's intense dislike of Chan Chan had been difficult, especially when the elephants were quartered and a phanit might well attend to one and then move on to another. Whilst Honey Blossom could be unpredictable, she had not caused trouble in this herd, although on one occasion when I rode Champa Kali instead because the matriarch had been given a rest for a foot injury, I noticed a distinctly cool reception on my return next day.

Around the fire we discussed the new plan. Speaking rapidly, Pradeep outlined the situation.

'Last month I sighted twenty-two elephants, including four or five small calves ranging from one to three months old. The trackers say they have seen nine small calves together in one group.'

'A nursery?' questioned Rula.

'Perhaps,' replied Pradeep, continuing his report. 'The elephants are seen most days, sometimes in small groups, sometimes in one large herd. There is a particularly aggressive bull who has chased our elephants on several occasions, making it difficult for us to get close.' He paused to listen to the whistling alarm call of a spotted deer which had sounded nearby.

'Tiger,' murmured Dhan, standing up and peering into the darkness.

'What about the giants?' asked Pat.

Pradeep replied, 'Raja Gaj and Kancha were sighted very near the tented camp on 28 December. They don't seem to be involved with the new herd. We are recording all sightings in a book. Last month was very good, and on 4 January three elephants came right up to the lodge at eight-thirty one evening and destroyed the banana trees. Everyone saw them. Before that a couple had raided the riding elephants' fodder stall. They always come after dark.'

'But no sign of Raja Gaj or Kancha recently?' asked Wendy.

'The trackers think they are living away from the herd and I'm sure we will find them,' replied Pradeep.

Summing it up, I said, 'Whilst we try to locate them, we should concentrate our studies on the new arrivals, but, being out-numbered, we must stalk them with care, especially where there are babies.'

Hari brought me a J&B. Like a London club barman, he always remembered people's favourite tipple. The rising moon was reflected in the river, and overhead the stars twinkled as the sparks of the fire raced up to meet them. 'God, this is a magical place,' I thought.

Ram was telling Carol about sloth bears. 'They really are mis-named,' he said, 'as they do not hang from the branches of trees. They are very aggressive, dangerous animals, standing around five and a half feet on their hind legs, three feet at the shoulder. They will hunt a man down and then claw out his face. My uncle was killed by one – he had no face left when the bear had finished with him.'

'How can you get away then?' asked my assistant.

'Well, it is better to climb a small tree because although the bear is a good climber, he cannot grip on a narrow trunk.'

He went on to explain that there were thirty to thirty-five in the reserve and, being omnivorous, they eat termites, roots, berries and plants.

'Not humans, I hope,' said Carol.

'No', he replied, 'not as far as I know, but they are much more feared by man than tiger or elephant.'

After the 1993 expedition, Henning Caesar, the German chemist, had written to me:

> Howdahs are not built for comfort. A person who bruises easily and cannot bear pain in stoic silence should not travel in a howdah, especially not in a fully laden one with three other people. It is a tight fit to say the least, and each step of the elephant pushes you against your fellow riders or, since that is socially unacceptable, against the wooden railings of the howdah. In addition, your colleagues carry cameras, binoculars, videos and water bottles, all hard and designed to dig into your ribs and kidneys. Tie towels round the railings to protect your elbows or bring your sleeping mat along, but the only comfortable way is to sit up there alone, behind the phanit, looking forward. The phanit does his best to bend branches out of the way of faces, but lower down your legs are sticking out sideways and the thorn bushes that the elephant shoulders out of the way tend to give naked legs a nasty beating. Recommended are long trousers, a long-sleeved shirt, hat, safety glasses and gardening gloves. Filming is something else: the sun is in your eye, the camera wants to focus on the tree in front, not on the bull behind, the elephant on which you sit is moving all the time, other elephants with passengers intrude into the picture, and you probably lack the language skills to tell the phanit where to go.

Having ridden almost a thousand miles on elephants over twenty years, I tended to agree and had given much consideration to the problem. One needs to be held firmly in place to stop the body being rocked violently from side to side, but the most needed support is for the back. Thus I designed a legless wicker armchair that would fit in the howdah and in which you could be held by a lap strap, so hands would be free to operate cameras, tape recorders, binoculars and to take notes as your mount lurched along. Pradeep produced a prototype, but it was too big for the howdah and when we tried it, Adrian seated behind me was squashed to death. He quite understood the need for his leader to ride in comfort, he said, but he would prefer not to be with me. So it was back to the drawing-board and instead I used my inflatable chair which certainly provided back support and gave a measure of stability.

The dawn sortie to the south revealed that the grass was higher than usual and we saw plenty of tiger spoor, but wild elephant tracks were all four to five days old and there were no large ones. At a creek we found three rhino: a male, a female and a calf. Like a herd of primeval beasts grumbling at being disturbed, they trotted off into the grass, heads held up. A porcupine hurried across the trail and scarlet minivets flitted about the trees, but it was not until mid-afternoon that we had more interesting sightings.

A tigress with cubs was known to be in the area just north of our camp and here, at about four o'clock, we came across the remains of a recent kill. Whilst we were examining it, Dhan's ultra-sharp hearing picked up sounds of movement close by and we moved forward cautiously in an extended line. Suddenly Ram gave the sighting cry, 'Yoo, yoo!' and, quickening her pace, Honey Blossom crossed a small stream on to a slight rise. This gave us a view across an open patch of grass and scrub. From his elevated position at the back of the howdah, Pradeep saw them first. A nervous young bull elephant poked his head out from a line of low trees; behind him two cows were using their trunks to steer their calves. Reminding me instantly of Walt Disney's *Dumbo*, the babies scuttled through the grass, their little trunks waving and their ears looking oversized. Our ladies watched thoughtfully as the herd crossed our front. Cameras and videos went into action. Adrian was scribbling a note. It was a lovely sight. In the fifth year of our search we had finally seen cows and calves in Bardia.

Plodding on in their wake, we hoped for another chance to observe them and pick out identifying marks, but they disappeared into the darkness of the forest.

'There was a tiger. Right by your tent,' grinned Sakali. 'The boys saw the pug marks when they were collecting the night lights this morning.'

Sure enough, near the path to the loo, barely thirty feet from where I slept, were the unmistakable prints of a good size tigress.

'I think it's the one with the cubs. She must have been hungry to come so close to the camp.'

I thanked him for this comforting news and unpacked the electronic alarm that I had used with some success in Mongolia. The Critter-Gitter is a battery-operated device that gives off a series of ear-splitting shrieks and its two red eyes flash wildly when anything passes through the infra-red beam. Being a little larger than a cigarette packet and having a detection range of forty feet, it provides warning of uninvited visitors and hopefully scares the pants off them. As I am the loudest snorer, my tent is always at the end of the line, so in future I would set up the Critter-Gitter at bedtime.

Mr Karki, the Warden, arrived as we were finishing brunch. With him was a smartly dressed Nepalese Army Officer, Captain S. R. Kharel. The Wildlife Department's anti-poaching unit, which was unarmed, had encountered poachers with weapons on several occasions. With great courage they had thrown stones at the marauders, but when this was met with rifle fire they had been forced to retreat. The army teams had no such problems. Recently three soldiers under Sergeant Ekbhadur Gurung had been on patrol in the north of the reserve. Hearing gunshots, they went to investigate and, coming across fresh footprints, they followed the tracks through the dense bush. Moving like the animals they protected, the patrol went slowly and silently forward. Hunting a man, who may be carrying a loaded AK-47 automatic rifle and knows the jungle like his own backyard, is much more frightening than closing with a dangerous beast.

They stopped frequently to examine the prints and listen. The forest was strangely quiet. The faint smell of cooked meat was the first indication that they were near their target. Then they spied a camouflaged hut. Built of branches and grass, it blended perfectly into the surroundings. The sergeant signed to his men to surround it before calling out, 'Come out with your hands up or we fire.' The effect was electric. A figure in tattered clothes burst from the hideaway. In his right hand was a rifle. The crackle and crash of the firing echoed up to the hills. The poacher lay where he had fallen. He was stone dead.

Sergeant Gurung was awarded citations by the government and the International Trust for Nature Conservation. The man had come from the mountains to the north. He was not a Tharu.

For years we had campaigned for the Wildlife Department's anti-poaching unit and the army teams to work together. Now,

Captain Kharel assured me this was happening. However, there were still poachers in the area.

A couple of gangs were said to be active in Bardia. They hunted deer for meat and so far had not gone for the bigger game. The patrol also looked out for people who came in to cut firewood. Apparently some had chainsaws which they tended to use in the rainy season when the sound did not carry so well. Other incursions were made by villagers collecting a plant they called 'Negro' which was sold in India for the manufacture of soap. Government programmes, aimed at educating the people to use alternative fuel, such as gas and kerosene, had helped to reduce the wood-cutting. However, the anti-poaching units, both civil and military, needed more resources.

We also heard that the man-eater whose tracks we had found the previous year had killed five men and a woman before he was captured and deported to Kathmandu Zoo. Later a woman was killed by a rhino. 'The people need protecting too,' commented Brook, whose special responsibility was for community aid.

Whether it was for our protection or the elephants, I was not sure, but Pradeep and several of his team had gone off to conduct a puja beside the river. This is a religious ceremony designed to ward off evil spirits and keep law and order in the various spheres of influence that the particular gods or goddesses represent. Pujas are performed on auspicious days, but extra ones may be arranged for a special purpose. In this case the aim was probably to see us safely through the impending hunt for Raja Gaj.

On top of the bank seven small altars of stones had been erected around one more prominent rock sticking up in the middle. This one represents Shiva, the god of all creation and destruction. Offerings of fruit, rice and eggs were brought forward. Vermilion and golden powder and flower petals were then sprinkled with the egg on the altars.

Then a chicken and a 'khasi' or castrated goat were brought in. The chicken's throat was cut and its blood allowed to pump over the altars. The goat was then held in the centre of the sacrificial area and water sprinkled over its neck. The cold water made the animal shiver which was considered important and a signal that the creature was ready to die for the god.

At that point, Pritni raised his kukri and with a single powerful swipe decapitated the goat. Our Nepalese team nodded in approval and pressed forward to see how the blood patterns were forming on the ground. The signs, considered with the goat's behaviour, would give an indication of the success of the worshippers' prayers.

When all were satisfied, the animals were plucked and skinned for supper whilst those participating were marked on the forehead with a small red blob resulting from the ingredients of the sacrifice.

Late that evening David Rowe and Geoff Garratt of the *Sunday Mirror* arrived from Kathmandu after a long haul by air and road. David's case had gone missing en route, but they were in good spirits. I was wondering how to tell them that we had not found the giants yet, when Pradeep came up to my tent.

'The trackers say they have seen Raja Gaj and Kancha,' he grinned. 'They are south-west of here, near the village of Monotapa. It is some way from the reserve but in the buffer zone. I'll send our elephants ahead before dawn and we can go downriver by boat and join them near the village.'

For a change we ate a cooked breakfast and then clambered into two Avons, which bobbed gently downstream. The sun was hot and I began to doze. Then Dhan called, 'Sunsh – Gangetic dolphin!' Seizing my camera, I adjusted the polarizing filter to soften the glare of the water and watched. It would be a great treat to see one and better still to get a photograph of this rare mammal.

The dolphin population is declining in all Nepalese rivers except the Karnali. In 1993, Brian D. Smith, a leading American wildlife and fisheries biologist, reported seeing thirty in the river. The overall decrease is an indication of the health of the country's waterways and it should be noted that other river dwellers including gharial, mugger, otters and turtle are also threatened. There are many causes of this: pollution, habitat degradation, overfishing, barrages and artificial barriers all play their part according to T. M. Takapa of the Nepal Centre for Riverine Lives Research Development (NCRLRD).

Fifty yards ahead, the surface of the water heaved, then over to the right a flash of smooth grey-green body showed for a split second. We held our breath. To get one in the lens was virtually impossible. We never knew where they would rise next, so I opened the zoom a little and, squinting through, aimed it straight ahead, finger poised on the button. Twice more the dolphin surfaced, then I got one almost in mid-frame. 'Click.' I had been very lucky.

The establishment of a dolphin reserve on the Karnali, between Chisapani and the Indian border, has been proposed by the NCRLRD and it is hoped this will be adopted whilst there are still some Gangetic dolphins to save.

When we reached the ladies they were being saddled up, having enjoyed a cooling swim. In spite of their long march they seemed fresh, frisky and eager to be off. It was as if they rather looked forward to meeting two handsome bulls.

The Warden's mount had joined us, so we had six domestic elephants; using walkie-talkies on the flank, we extended the line across an area of scrub and acacia. Pradeep waved his akubra hat, given to him by John Hunt the previous year, and we advanced in silence, like troops going into battle. It was mid-morning and the sun was high. David Rowe, squeezed into my howdah, eagerly surveyed the scene. Having come all this way to see the two giants, his only fear was that they might not appear. Geoff Garratt had a large lens firmly in his hand, praying for the shot that would fill the centre pages of the *Sunday Mirror*.

At first the bush seemed dead, then my radio crackled. 'Contact, we have a sighting!' It was Pat's voice but we could see nothing. Suddenly, out of nowhere and with a 'whroom', the giant bulk of the King rose slowly and deliberately from his bed. He had been lying down. 'It's prehistoric,' was all David said. Raja Gaj's massive bald head faced us from thirty yards. His wide forehead, topped by two bulging domes, was powdered with dust. His enormous tusks glinted through the leaves and I was sad to see the right one had broken; about a third of its length had gone, presumably in a fight. But with whom – who would dare to confront such an enormous beast?

Rula was filming and Wendy was taping as we circled him cautiously. 'Kancha,' hissed Pradeep, referring to the temperamental escort. The King's minder was standing in the shade of an acacia watching us. Resting his massive trunk across a branch, he dropped his lower lip, giving the impression of a smile. This position gave us a good view of the strange dome on top of his head that was like the artist's impression of *Elephas hysudricus*. We backed off and slowly circled round Kancha. The two giants seemed quite unconcerned. As we edged closer to the tuskers, Adrian noticed that Raja Gaj had lost the tip of his tail and I could see two puncture marks on his backside, the right distance apart to have been made by tusks.

'Look, Raja Gaj has five legs,' laughed Ram Din, who was riding shotgun on Wendy's elephant. In the interest of science, Geoff Garratt raised his camera, but there was too much shadow to get a clear picture of the biggest erection in Asia. Clearly the presence of six female elephants was having an effect.

'He hasn't even got eyelashes,' whispered Anna, whose elephant had come up beside ours. 'And d'you see, Kancha has a growth beside his left tusk?'

We continued recording detail until Kancha, his trunk scenting the ladies and humans, swaggered towards us. As his ears came forward, Pradeep decided the situation was becoming dangerous and shouted, 'Agutt, agutt!' (Go, go) The females turned and, fanning out in different directions, showed the aggressor their heels. After a hundred yards or so the bull stopped, sniffed some of our ladies' dung and returned to the shade of his acacia. It was simply too hot to be bothered with us, as long as we kept our distance.

Having pulled back, we dismounted and sent the ladies off to cool themselves down in the river. Dust devils whirled about the hot, open ground sending clouds of dry leaves twirling high into the air. The tuskers continued to feed in the cover.

Encouraged by the relative placidness of the bulls, Pradeep, Dhan and Indra Tamang walked forward to the edge of the scrub whilst we watched with interest. When they were fifty yards from the grazing giants, Kancha, who had been watching, lumbered towards them menacingly. 'My God . . .' said someone, but the naturalists stood their ground, and, out of bravado, Indra turned his back on the advancing bull that seemed to tower over him. I knew well that, in spite of their massive size and ponderous movement, an elephant can accelerate rapidly and a man in the open has little chance of avoiding a determined attack. In the jungle there are ways to escape, but for our trio there was no cover on a flat, featureless floodplain. I just prayed they knew what they were doing. When Kancha was twenty yards away, Indra faced him and, raising his arms, shooed him away, crying, 'Go back, go back,' in Nepali. It was quite extraordinary. Kancha stopped, sniffed the air and then backed off.

The tuskers had sauntered away, so, remounting, we moved over to where they had both been standing to gather dung samples and check some measurements. Pradeep had noted the branches at the level of Raja Gaj's shoulder and standing up on Honey Blossom, he dropped his tape from them to the ground. 'Twelve feet,' he exclaimed. It sounded a lot, but we had last measured the old boy two years before and it is known that elephants have two growing periods in their lives. He had certainly put on weight and might well have grown taller, but this was of less interest to us than his unusual skull, his lack of body hair and, in time, the DNA results.

Adrian had now shown that DNA could be present in dung, but the greatest care was needed to avoid polluting samples by human touch. Mindful of this, he now came equipped with proper sampling fluids and tubes.

As we headed back to the river, we met Raja Gaj once more. He was browsing quietly with his back to us. Wanting a better look at the injuries to his buttocks, we moved closer. His head was turned very slightly to one side and the piggy eye never left us. I was so intent on examining the old wound that I hadn't realized how near we were; it could not have been more than thirty feet. Raja Gaj flicked his stumpy hairless tail like a windscreen wiper across his vast backside and then, with a turn of speed incredible in so large a creature, he pirouetted round to face us, his great trunk stretched out until it almost touched Honey Blossom. Behind his raised and threatening tusks, his vast ears were spread wide. With legs apart to give him a firmer base, it was as if he was expecting to be attacked and was ready to retaliate. I heard David's gasp and even Anna-Tara had jumped in alarm. 'He won't charge,' whispered Pradeep. I was grateful for the reassurance, and later I was to thank my Nikon auto-focus for recording that incredible sight.

One thing was pretty certain, Raja Gaj had been in a battle. When bulls fight it is usually head to head. If one decides to break off the contest and turns away, he immediately risks a fatal thrust from his adversary's tusks into the soft area between his hind legs and upwards into the belly or his internal testicles. The wounds on the King's backside had healed, but I did not recall seeing them on the previous expedition. I doubted that he would have fought with Kancha, so it could mean that somewhere in the area was another giant tusker. Finding the two old bulls so far from their usual feeding grounds might mean that they had been chased away from the cows by rivals.

There were no reports of an especially large male in the reserve, but we had seen a wild bull by the Babai Bridge the previous week. There was another possibility. In the dark of the forest, a tuskless male or makhna might be mistaken for a large cow. They can reach an enormous size and as they do not grow tusks their strength builds up in other ways. A makhna has an exceptionally heavy trunk and with this can smash a rival's tusk as if it were a branch. The wound marks on Raja Gaj's behind might have been the result of a separate incident. I was still thinking this over when we reached the river.

We made our way back to the beach where we had left the boats, and ate our picnic, well entertained by the antics of our ladies cooling off in the water. There they stayed for half an hour, trumpeting and squealing, spraying water over each other with their trunks. Champa, Sundar and Chan Chan had come from India together and were obviously the greatest of pals. Honey Blossom bathed a little distance away and poor Raj Kali looked on shyly like a new girl on a first term outing. The government elephant eventually came over for a chat.

Gary stood, camera in hand, photographing every detail, doubtless composing a work of art entitled 'Three Girls Bathing'. It was an enchanting sight. David was already composing his article for the *Sunday Mirror* and Geoff was as pleased as punch.

'Now I've got the vital pictures, I can really relax and enjoy the rest of the expedition,' he said, lighting up a cigar.

Pradeep, Adrian and Brook, hoping Kancha would have left some fresh dung, returned to collect specimens. On arrival they had a long wait before he would oblige, and then they had to resort to throwing sticks in an effort to persuade him to move so that they could get at his droppings.

Making our way back to camp, morale was sky-high. Ram and Dhan kept us entertained with great stories of brushes with wildlife.

'A tiger can jump eighteen to twenty-five feet . . .'

'I came on a wild boar being attacked by a tiger and they both chased me . . .'

Dhan was in especially good form and took us through his days of training the elephants at Cricket St Thomas Wildlife Park and how he had ridden Millie around Somerset's leafy lanes, where she enjoyed willow, hazel and beech with the same relish as her relatives munched exotic plants in Bardia. But the conversation always came back to tiger.

'I had many lucky escapes at Chitwan,' said Dhan. 'Once when we came upon a tigress with cubs she chased us. The grass was too thick to get through and I lay down, hoping she wouldn't see me. But the animal ran right on to me, bumped into my backside and was right on top. Then she turned and went back to her cubs. I thought I was a goner.' He paused to sip his beer and, refreshed, went on. 'I was almost killed by a man-eater we called Number 118. As a resident naturalist I was sent to track a tiger that had killed a man cutting grass. I was riding Chan Chan Kali when we came across the tiger eating the body. With a roar he came at us. The elephant moved so fast I slid off the back and was left hanging on to her tail, bouncing along with the tiger right behind snapping and snarling. Somehow I pulled myself up.' Luckily for Dhan at this point the angry cat lost interest in him and returned to its kill.

'To get a better view I climbed off the elephant's back and up into a tree,' continued our friend. His colleagues sent the elephant off in a long sweep to look for the tiger whilst Dhan remained on his perch. Suddenly the grass swayed and parted. Dragging the carcass of the grasscutter, the tiger emerged and recommenced its meal at the foot of the tree. 'I watched in horror as the powerful jaws tore at the human flesh,' said Dhan. 'Then to my terror the beast looked straight up at me. I knew tigers could climb trees and my heart beat fast for my tree was not very tall.' Trying to shut out the blood-curdling sounds, Dhan prayed hard that the elephant team would soon return. When at last one elephant did come back the tiger showed no fear. Knowing a single elephant is little protection, he shouted, 'Go and get the others.' The naturalist then waited for what seemed like hours. Half the man had been consumed and Dhan wondered if he would become the dessert, when finally three elephants arrived and advancing in extended line drove the man-eater off with ear-splitting trumpeting. One of the mounts then picked up the bloody remains and placed them on her back before the sad procession returned to camp.

I poured myself a large scotch and returned to the fire in time to hear Pradeep telling of a tiger that had been crossing a trail right in front of an open jeep he was driving. The huge cat stopped and eyed him and his passenger, an American lady. 'I had to stop,' he explained. 'The tiger occupied the entire width of the track. Suddenly, to my surprise, the wretched visitor put up her camera and let off the flash. With a giant roar the tiger leapt straight on to the bonnet – and the windscreen was down!'

'What on earth did you do,' asked Carol.

'By some strange reflex I hit the horn,' said Pradeep, 'and the beast leapt off in fright. Its face was so close I could feel its breath.'

The bar did a roaring trade that evening and the trackers and elephant boys were given some well-earned rum.

Rain in the night improved tracking and, to give the elephants a rest after the previous day's exertions, we went out on foot and in a jeep. The vehicle group made a wider sweep and found fresh elephant dung for Adrian. Rula, David Jenkins and others were in the foot patrol and Rula recorded their experiences:

*Ram had promised for a long time to take me on a walking safari with particular emphasis on plants and flowers with medicinal properties and some tuition on tracking techniques. Ram, Dhan and Pradeep were all walking encyclopaedias, knowing the name of every plant, bird and animal not only in Nepali and English but nearly always in Latin too.*

*Ram, a tiny, compact, handsome man with huge smiling eyes and a mini plant thesaurus in his pocket, seemed to have a particular interest in the healing powers attributed to many of the plants in the jungle. He gathered us around him on the outskirts of our camp. There were Doc David, David Rowe, Gary, my sister Anna, Carol, conscientiously taking notes, and myself with the video camera. We would skirt the sal forest and along the edge of the huge, all-concealing elephant grass.*

*We knew there were elephants in the vicinity as just after lunch a young tusker had been seen crossing the river very close to the camp. Pradeep had also told us there were approximately thirty tigers within a one mile radius and we also knew that sloth bears were resident in this part of the jungle. None of our team had ever seen one, though there had been signs of their dens in the root bowls of trees and occasional scratch marks on the trees themselves. Ram had also told me that of all the beasts in the jungle he feared sloth bear the most. He had had several close shaves and he explained that though elephant, rhino and tiger will usually only attack if cornered or when protecting their young, sloth bears were highly aggressive and seemed to kill for pleasure.*

*So we ambled along in the balmy, peaceful Bardian sunshine keeping close to Ram, quickly becoming engrossed in the various botanical speci-mens he showed us. Plants for TB, curing earache, headaches, stems to be boiled for reducing fevers and leaves for stopping bleeding. A veritable jungle pharmacy. One story held particular charm for me. 'Sometimes,' Ram said, 'elephants get bad tummies and have much pain, then the elephant will take his phanit into the jungle to find this plant.' He pointed to a clump of rather ordinary-looking dark green leaves. 'The phanit will gather them and take them back to camp to treat the ele-phant.' I found this so touching, another example of how this trusting relationship between man and beast works both ways.*

*Suddenly Gary touched my shoulder. There, about fifty yards in front of us, a large grey shape, seemingly unaware of our presence, lumbered across our path. We heard a loud sharp crack. 'Elephant browsing,' said Ram. Slowly I took the lens off my video camera, secretly praying for the possibility of a good ground shot of a tusker. God, what a coup that would be, what a story to tell both round the campfire at that evening's debrief and back home.*

*I whispered to Ram, 'Can we try to track him?'*

*His smiling eyes lit up with enthusiasm and he whispered back, 'It is dangerous.'*

*I pleaded with him, 'Please, Ram, please.'*

*Some of the others didn't look too certain but finally we all agreed. To our right was the edge of the forest and to our left the eighteen foot elephant grass. Beyond was the river. Everything takes on a different perspective on foot. The huge trees with their tangled exposed roots poking out of the eroded soil reminded me of a film set for Narnia.*

We followed Ram quietly into the forest treading as carefully as possible. You would think that four and a half tons of jumbo would find it
difficult to hide, but it is extraordinary how quick and yet quiet they
can be, and all wild animals know how to use the environment to their
advantage. Suddenly Ram pointed to some freshly snapped twigs and
branches. Slightly to our left were several large piles of fairly recent
dung. It seemed our large friend was quite close. Adrenaline racing and
camera ready, we crept slowly onward. In front the trees had become
denser. Then we heard that unmistakable deep-throated rumble that
elephants use to communicate with each other and there, straight ahead,
about twenty feet away he pointed to a large patch of grey amongst the
dappled greens. It just looked like a boulder, immobile. He had his back
to us and so far seemed unaware of our presence. Anna, Gary and I
exchanged winks and I could feel the bubbling of nervous giggles beginning, not a good idea. This was not one of our domesticated ladies but
a wild tusker in his own domain with very little experience of man. I
could tell from Ram's face we had to be very, very careful.

Slowly Ram bent down and picked up a stick, motioned me to be
ready with the camera and then threw his missile off to our right where
the ground was slightly more exposed and better lit. There was a short
squeak, a vague movement of the boulder as I looked through the view-
finder and then nothing; no mad trumpeting sounds, no crashing through
the undergrowth, just empty silence. We stayed still for several minutes.
Ram was sniffing the air and looking around. He then said he thought
the elephant would double round behind us via the elephant grass and
did we want to follow? My immediate answer was in the affirmative;
real danger, real adventure and I was desperate for some footage. Ram's
words, however, made my spine tingle even though they were said with
a sense of humour. 'Remember my friends, all my life I have lived in
the jungle. I can run and I can climb trees. If anything happens you
are all responsible for yourselves.'

If elephants can successfully hide feet away from you in elephant grass,
what about tigers and even worse the dreaded sloth bear? Still our
intrepid band decided to bravely venture forth via the edge of the forest
into the dense, immensely tall and incredibly thick-bladed grass. In single
file, feeling very puny and vulnerable, eyes darting to the left and right
we crept through the sharp-bladed foliage.

Suddenly and with no warning, in a small trampled clearing no more
than ten feet in front of us, stood the big boy, staring at us intently with
trunk raised. We all cannoned into Ram. I was so transfixed I forgot to

*raise the camera. The bull began to take a serious interest, swaying his head and stamping the ground with his forefoot. Then he started to move towards us. I have always been told not to run from any animal and I know an elephant's eyesight is not brilliant, but the space between us was getting less and less and there were no trees to climb. Suddenly our diminutive little Ram started jumping up and down and waving his arms in the air shouting, 'Oi, oi, oi.' To my amazement the bull stopped dead in his tracks, ears forward and trunk up, emitting peculiar squeaking noises like a frightened puppy. Eyeballing us for a few more seconds, he then thought better of it, turned round and nonchalantly sauntered off, obviously bored with us silly little people disturbing his post-meridian stroll. I didn't get any footage, but it was a thrilling encounter and at least we lived to regale the group with it round the campfire that evening.*

It is an extraordinary fact that elephants do seem to like beautiful women!

At camp it was bath-time for the elephants again. In her diary Rula wrote:

*Today I am bathing Chan Chan! Back at the camp she slowly kneels down as I clamber up using her knee and ears. Once safely astride her massive neck with Pritni perching behind me, she gently gets up, sensing a novice is in the normal command position, and moves slowly through the trees to the edge of the river bank. Here there is quite a steep drop and I have to alter my balance as she slowly descends, conscientiously testing the ground with her trunk. The beach and the river are full of fairly large rounded pebbles difficult enough for humans to walk on and, though elephants have huge pads, they are nevertheless very sensitive. In spite of their massive, ungainly-looking bodies they hardly ever stumble.*

*We reach the edge of the water. Sundar and Champa are already immersed and blowing bubbles. Chan Chan, with an excited rumble at seeing her two friends, carefully plods into the water and stands swishing her trunk gently to and fro. Pritni gives the order, 'Baith,' meaning lie down. As if in slow motion, she slowly sinks to her haunches and I can feel the tips of my toes touching the water. She then bends her front legs. Still astride her neck, I gently shift my balance as she rolls very, very slowly on to her side. She settles down, legs stretched out with a contented sigh, head underwater, eyes closed and the tip of her trunk just periscoping up for the occasional breath. I am now crouching on her side. She gives a large, bubbly fart and relaxes even more, making herself comfort-*

*able on the pebbles and sneaks out her trunk to tickle Sundar Kali who is lying next to her.*

*I start to clamber all over her, scrubbing the thick leathery hide with my hands. I gently wash her eyes with those huge, sexy, spiky three-inch-long eyelashes. She looks at me with complete trust and contentment. Then I move on to her ears and her mouth and the top of her head where the bristles have trapped seeds and insects and other debris. Finally down her fat tummy, behind her knees and then her tail. This takes about twenty minutes. Pritni then gives the order, 'Sambaith,' which means up and turn over. Slowly, with a lot of grunting, she rises like a gleaming lump of ebony on to her knees, then falls slowly on to her other side and we start the whole process once again. This time as I am standing by her huge head washing her forehead she sneaks her trunk between my legs and blows bubbles while winking at me with a cheeky expression. It is such a wonderful feeling ministering to this four-ton baby and I feel very privileged. We play some more bath-time games and then with the setting sun glinting on her shiny skin, I get back on to her neck and we rise slowly up while the phanits, Champa and Sundar look on with amusement. As a final thank you she fills her trunk with several gallons of water and, to the delight of everyone watching, she slowly lifts it up and positions her trunk over my head and gives me a power shower. Shrieking with laughter we slowly walk out of the water and up the bank. By this time I am feeling confident enough not to hold on to her ears. Back at her living quarters she sinks down to her knees; once more I slide down and as I am feeding her the special ele sandwiches she gently puts her trunk round my neck and blows down the front of my T-shirt as if to say, 'Wasn't that fun! Let's do it again some time!' I did many times with her and the others and it never failed to be a thrill and a joy.*

A phanit's life may sound romantic but it is damned hard work as Rula was to find out:

*A mahout, a generic term for an elephant handler, has a hard but, I would think, very satisfying life. It is my ambition to train as an honorary one, a privilege rarely, if ever, bestowed on a Western woman. There are actually four grades of which the mahout, technically speaking, is the lowest. The rawat is the boss in charge of elephants and men's well-being in general terms, after him come the phanit, the official driver of the elephant, then comes the pachwa who goes out grazing with the elephants and chops down their fodder and bathes them. Last is the mahout who cleans the camp, the elephant tack and makes the all-important elephant sandwiches.*

*In actuality, all these roles with the exception of the rawat are inter-changeable and the ones at our camp all worked together with a great sense of camaraderie. Their day starts early, sometimes they even have to get up in the middle of the night, as did Madu Mala Kali's mahout for she had frequent attacks of the munchies in the early hours of the morning and would keep the whole camp awake with her persistent trumpeting and groaning.*

*When they arise before the sun they have to dust and brush down the elephants, muck out, which in an elephant camp is a huge job, stoke up the fire, dust down and prepare the tack and have the elephants saddled and ready for us – that is in a safari situation. We would arrive about 6.45 a.m. having had a cup of tea, warmly dressed and slung about with cameras, sound equipment, notebooks, etc. The eles were always ready standing at their posts, phanits usually mounted and wait-ing, sprucely turned out in their jungle green slacks and shirts, always barefoot.*

*Some of the other boys would already be making the special ele sand-wiches, delicious neat little parcels made from unhusked rice, molasses and salt painstakingly wrapped and tied in thin grasses.*

*Each elephant consumes approximately eighty of these a day to sup-plement its diet. In the wild these huge animals would forage for sixteen to eighteen hours of the day, but when out with us for an average of eight hours of the day these titbits are a necessary addition to their daily 600lbs of fresh fodder. This phenomenal amount has to be gathered fresh for each elephant every single day and it is a physically taxing and time-consuming operation. I was lucky enough to partake in one of these outings.*

*Dhan Bahadur, myself and three other phanits left the camp at about 4.30 in the afternoon on a day before our main party had reached Bardia so there was no mass safari. Atop the bare backs of Chan Chan Kali and Raj Kali we lumbered off deep into the sal forest. The sun filtered through the dense canopy throwing dappled highlights on the foliage and the occasional small group of chital browsing in the warm afternoon sun. Swaying gently and completely relaxed, I sat behind Dhan with my arms around his waist as he let Chan Chan slowly wind her way through the undergrowth, every so often breaking off some tasty morsel – like a sapling – to chew on or simply to play with. The two elephants rumbled to each other. It was peaceful and quiet and we stopped to watch a group of monkeys grooming each other in the boughs of the trees. It is such a very special feeling and so different from being in a Land Rover. Somehow being on an animal native to these surroundings one does not feel like an intruder nor a tourist. One feels part of nature, part of the scene and other animals take very little notice if one is silent. I found myself working out the film format in my head. I was making a teaser video of the trip with a dual purpose: one as a fun record for Discovery Expeditions and my fellow expeditioners, but more important, a rough sketch of 'A Day in the Life of a Mahout'. I think this relationship is so touching and extraordinary, a sort of wonderful compromise in a world where animals totally in the wild are in ever greater danger from poaching, loss of habitat and human encroachment. It is a centuries old tradition where respect, a careful balance of power and a mutual understanding and trust are paramount. I want to make a film of this and I will.*

*After about three-quarters of an hour we reached a glade deep in the forest, surrounded by immensely tall and luscious wild fig trees. The phanits dismounted and, using a type of curved knife, they shimmied up the trees, high into the canopy, forty feet up. With their kukris they hacked off great branches which came hurtling down towards us. Dhan and I piled them up on the ground in front of the elephants, who stood in the sunshine untethered, with their trunks entwined and their gentle eyes drooping in the heat. Chan Chan had her back legs crossed and looked very comical. After approximately an hour with two enormous piles in front of us, the phanits descended and nimbly climbed up on to the elephants' backs with the aid of an obliging upturned trunk and we started loading their dinner. Dhan murmured an almost inaudible, 'Utar', which roughly translated means pick up or give to me. Chan Chan picked a large branch, twined it round her trunk, lifted it up and passed it over her head to the phanit who then put it across her back. This manoeuvre continued until there were approximately five feet of tightly packed foliage and branches on the ele's back. This was then secured with several yards of rope and finally we all clambered up to the top which by now made us about sixteen feet off the ground. Slowly and with a much heightened, less secure but still comfortable seat, we waddled back to camp to unload. This was very simple. After we had dismounted, the ropes were untied and the elephant gently sat down, allowing the cargo to slide off her back to the single command of 'Baith', meaning down.*

*Each elephant understands between thirty and sixty verbal commands. They are extremely intelligent and share, and openly show, many human mood characteristics. They can be mischievous and cheeky, sad and depressed, volatile and bad tempered, lazy and frisky, sulky and cuddly and happy. They also cry with fear and pain and emotional hurt. Extraordinary creatures and I make no pretence of being totally besotted by them.*

*But back now to a mahout's day. When the elephants are working in a safari situation, the phanits and trackers come out with the group from about 6.45 until 11 a.m. The mahouts and pachwas back at the camp carry on with tidying and cooking the meal for our return. When we get back from the morning safari, the elephants are unsaddled and usually taken for a bath. Either before or after the bath, depending on the plans for the rest of the day, some of the mahouts go out on fodder-collecting trips. During their free time the mahouts' favourite pastime seems to be poker! The afternoon safari would usually start about 3 p.m. and finish about 6–6.30. The elephants would then get some of their elephant sandwiches and then they might be taken out to graze for an hour or so.*

*The elephants are also inspected daily for any health problems, bites or wounds particularly to their feet. Again I was lucky enough to observe and photograph three inspections and two resulting operations. On the first occasion the patient was Sundar Kali, who had a thorn embedded deep in her left forefoot. Her mahout gave the lie down command and she sank slowly to her knees and, with a great deal of grunting, fell over on to one side, all four legs out towards us. It was almost dark by now and the operation was lit by several hurricane lamps. Two mahouts sat near her head talking to her gently, her tightly coiled trunk remindful of a human clenching a fist or biting on a finger to help with the pain. The foot was bathed with water and then with only a Swiss Army penknife three other mahouts took it in turns to dig round the thorn trying to remove it. I got sent off for my tweezers. By now it was completely dark. On my return the hole in her foot was about half an inch wide and, though the thorn was visible, it was still deemed necessary to dig deeper so the thorn would not break or splinter. Sundar Kali was obviously in pain; every so often her whole body tensed and shivered and the mahouts kept a close eye on her trunk and other forefoot. One involuntary flick or kick could result in a broken limb or back.*

*There were huge tears rolling down her cheeks and I sat close to her great head and gently stroked her to keep her calm. Finally the offending object, about three inches long, was dug out and removed with my tweezers. Then a thin tube of bamboo was inserted into the wound via which some boiling disinfectant was poured in. Her huge bulk shivered once more as we all talked to her and her mahout gave the order for her to get up. Slowly she did just that, gingerly testing her foot and then graciously putting her trunk around one of the mahout's necks in a gesture of thanks, she rumbled softly and returned to her place and a few extra ele sandwiches. At the end of the day the elephants were chained by one leg to their places, their huge mound of dinner next to them. The mahouts have their well-earned dinner, followed by some more poker or maybe some games and dancing back at the 'human' camp.*

*So ends a mahout's day, a long hard one, but the response and communication between them and their charges seems deep and meaningful. Both seem to realize that they need each other and they certainly respect and love each other. They say a completely wild elephant can be tamed, safe and obedient within six months. The normal training period for a mahout is between two and three years.*

The Karnali was low enough for us to make a crossing to Gola, so we went over with a load of items for the school and village clinic. The headman was away but his deputy accepted the gifts and we spent a while with the people. They watched our ladies uneasily and we heard more tales of crop raiding.

It was St Valentine's day and I gave Honey Blossom a card decorated with a large pink elephant. Dhuki beamed with pride. I hoped he didn't think it was for him!

All day the weather had looked unsettled and at dusk lightning was flickering in the hills. At half-past midnight the storm broke. I awoke to my electronic tiger alarm going mad, having been set off by the flapping tent canvas. Coming from the Chisapani Gorge, the gusty wind and rain lashed the camp. Guy ropes heaved and strained and loose kit took off. By 1 a.m. I reckoned it was up to force seven and sleep was impossible. Items of clothing were flying everywhere as we struggled to keep the office tent and the lab intact. My spare glasses had gone; I later found them broken, in the elephant lines. One of the ladies had trodden on them. I hoped my insurance company would be sympathetic.

At dawn we surveyed the damage and said goodbye to Pat's

group, which was heading up Babai River to look for more elephants and check on the state of the gharial.

A castor oil seed, thought to be quite poisonous, had got into
my eye during one of our plunges through the bush and was
causing it to water madly. David Jenkins applied drops which
helped, but my sight was affected.

A meeting with two young bulls livened up the day. The bigger
one had beautiful, straight, sharp-pointed tusks and carried his
head high. 'He's in fine condition,' murmured Adrian, as a game
of cat and mouse developed. We saw him scent the ladies' dung
with great care, before turning back.

'I think he will pay the camp a visit,' said Pradeep.

I was admiring a four-foot Indian monitor lizard in a phanta
when the alarm went. 'Yo, yo, bagh, bagh!' The tiger, a big powerful male, bounded off eastward and, as the bulls had gone, we
followed it. Entering a patch of shady jungle, we heard a langur
cough – always a reliable indication. The monkey was right beside
us and when it leapt, it landed with full force on what turned
out to be a rotten branch which snapped instantly, tumbling the
langur on to the ground with an awful thump. 'Aaoww!' cried
Anna-Tara, feeling its pain, but the monkey picked himself up
and made off.

The cat had gone, but another lurked nearby and luckily Rula
had her video to hand. She described the incident in her diary:

*Seriously disappointed at having missed a tiger sighting yet again, Anna
and I atop Chan Chan Kali turned around to make our way back to
the camp. Suddenly Dhan tapped me on the shoulder and, as I turned,
put his finger to his lips and pointed to where the elephant grass descended
down to a stream. I motioned to him that I could see nothing, but he
pointed to the video camera and again made a sign to keep quiet.*

*I strained my eyes through the tightly packed grasses and then saw a
brief movement. There through the grass, about twice the size of a domestic cat, I saw the elegant head of a jungle cat. Chan Chan had by now
come to a standstill and the handsome feline sniffed the air cautiously
and then emerged gracefully from his camouflage to stand in front of
us. He seemed to be completely unaware of our presence. Obviously he
had just seen the elephant's legs and hadn't bothered to look any higher.
Video poised and focused, I zoomed in on him as he stood perfectly at*

*ease for several minutes. Then, carefully picking his way across the little stream, he sauntered back into the elephant grass. Delighted with my little cat captured on film, I turned to Dhan. 'You know Rula, jungle cat is much more rare to see in such proximity than tiger,' he said. Appeased and thrilled with my photographic capture, though still longing for a proper view of that most famous cat of the Asian jungle, we rode back to camp for a well-earned, and as always, delicious brunch.*

The rain caused Pat's team some problems on the Babai as the river was flooded and time and again they had to wade across, the water up to their armpits. Brook found the Karnali was running very high and his crossing was difficult when he went back to the village to talk to the headman and view the damaged houses. At supper he was describing his day when Pradeep came up to me, 'Quick, John, bring the image intensifier, the young bull is here in the camp.'

Putting down our plates, we made quickly for the elephant lines. The boys were standing by the fire, the ladies, chained in their night positions, had stopped eating. In the light of the fire I could just make out the glimmer of tusks. Div Guj, for I am sure it was him, was fifty yards away, sniffing the cows.

'Let him come,' I said. 'Let's see what he does. Put out torches and we'll use the image intensifier.'

Slowly and cautiously the young tusker came forward, his trunk raised, sniffing all around. Watching his every move through the instrument, I saw him approach Sundar Kali. He was so close I could see him clearly by the light of the fire. Reaching forward with his trunk, he felt her hind quarters. She did not move. Then he wrapped his trunk around her tail and gave it a sharp pull. 'Eeekk!' shrieked the little elephant, giving a jump, and her suitor stepped back. After this rebuff, he turned his attention to Honey Blossom and tried again. The matriarch looked round at him rather slowly and then lifted her leg and deliberately hoofed him hard. Abashed, he retreated.

'I think we'd better get him out of here before there's a panic,' hissed Pradeep as the boys lit flaming torches.

'What a shame,' said Wendy, 'I thought we were going to witness a mating.'

\*     \*     \*

We'd been given a supply of Stahly's tinned haggis (with Drambuie) and we planned a Burns' night celebration, albeit somewhat belated, for our last evening in camp. Doc David had rigged up a pretty amazing Highland outfit from local materials and used his stethoscope, plus Brook's Walkman playing 'Amazing Grace', as an improvised bagpipe. With this he ceremoniously played in the haggis. He then recited his own interpretation of Burns' 'Ode to the Haggis', retitled 'Ode to a Haggis in a Tin'. With lashings of rum and a little J&B scotch, the party proceeded.

The Nepalese were a little unsure about the haggis, 'Where did you shoot it, sir?' asked Chandra, Raj Kali's phanit.

Wendy had adapted her frog game of the previous year to racing elephants and our elephant boys entered into the contest with gusto, playing many elimination rounds to determine the champions, who were awarded splendid Chobham Dog Show rosettes and plastic elephants. Rula, tutored by Pradeep, made a sterling speech of thanks in Nepalese, which was much appreciated.

As I settled into my cot for the night, I summed up our activities in my mind: Adrian had his dung samples, the new jumbos had been surveyed, Raja Gaj and Kancha studied and we'd done our bit for Gola. Pat's game counts on the Babai completed the work. There was only one disappointment – that we had not had a really good tiger sighting, and I mentioned this to Pradeep in the morning.

'There is a tigress right here,' he said. 'When the camp was being built, she visited every day, leaving her tracks along the line of tents. Prem saw her only two days ago in daylight, walking in the track leading into the camp. If you have finished the elephant study, why not see if we can find her? We must be careful though, she has cubs.'

So early next morning, our last elephant safari, we mounted up and headed north. Only two hundred yards from the camp was a patch of tall grass, a line of distinct pug marks leading to it from a dry stream bed. 'That's her,' muttered Pradeep. Without a word the ladies deployed and we pressed forward. 'Swish, swish,' went the grass, then suddenly a flash of orange exploded twenty paces in front. Mrs Stripes was on her way.

'There's her kill,' said Dhan, pointing to the remains of a deer.

I'd never seen Sundar Kali move so fast; the little elephant almost galloped as we raced to head off the cat. Forming a crescent, we swept back through the grass. Several times the tigress was glimpsed as we retraced our steps south towards the kill.

Swishing through the long thick grass, the scene was very peaceful and we had almost given up all hopes of another sighting when a blood-curdling roar rose from the grass and made Carol jump, grabbing my arm. There, fifteen feet away and back on her breakfast, was the huge cat. For a moment she stared at us full in the face, her lethal fangs bared. Then with an enormous burst of energy, she turned and tore off through the dense cover. Trumpeting with excitement, our elephants rushed after her, but eventually pulled up at the river's edge, trembling and rumbling to each other, discussing the chase and our disappointment when we had to concede that the tigress had given us the slip.

And so, with huge regret, we packed up camp. Back at the Karnali Lodge, having relished the luxury of a shower and clean clothes, I presented the anti-poaching unit with more equipment including binoculars kindly donated by listeners to Charlie Chester's BBC Radio programme. Ram Din was staying on at the lodge, so we left him a supply of film and later sent out a camera for him to record the situation with the wild elephants. Down at the village we equipped the school with pencil, crayons, drawing books and a plastic globe of the world. The first-aid centre was restocked with simple medical supplies and David sent what was left of our drugs and dressings up to the local hospital.

As I was packing my bag, Sakali came up to my door.

'Sir,' he said quietly, 'the trackers say there is another very big elephant in the forest.'

'So that's that,' I replied. 'Raja Gaj does have a rival. I wonder if this is the elusive Maila that we had heard so much about in the early days of the quest.'

As the sun was setting, I strolled over to say farewell to Honey Blossom, now back in her permanent home. She had a small length of bamboo in her trunk with which she was neatly cleaning between her toes where she has important sweat glands.

'Goodbye, old girl,' I said, slipping her a banana. 'Thank you for looking after us so well.'

She held up the banana in her trunk, eyeing it as if to say 'Haven't had one of these lately,' then popped it whole into her mouth. Burbling her appreciation, she gave me one of her glorious winks as if to say, 'You'll be back.'

## Chapter Eleven

# DNA AND DUNG

THE Avro dipped out of the haze and roared in along the airstrip.

'Good to see a British plane,' remarked the ever-patriotic Brook Hanson, who had been examining some old helicopters that were used to shuttle passengers up into the mountains.

'Even the heads are an improvement; you don't need wellies any more!' exclaimed Pat Troy.

Indeed, Nepalganj airport and the service provided had improved considerably over the years. Progress was sweeping westwards.

Before we set out, Gary Hodges had put his artistic talents to good use and designed a colourful expedition motif. Whilst we were away this had been embroidered on traditional Nepalese tops, so now we had a splendid souvenir of the trip to wear at the farewell party at Rum Doodle's which my old friend Lisa Choegyal had organized. As ever the food was spicy and tasty and the beer plentiful.

Amongst our many friends who came along was one I had not expected to see: Peter Byrne had arrived that day and was on his way to Sukla Phanta. This was especially useful as he came with news of the latest situation west of Bardia, and soon he and Adrian were discussing the possibility of excavating the carcass of Tula Hatti. As the grave is just inside India there could be enormous bureaucratic difficulties, but Peter reckoned he could find the spot where another large tusker, killed earlier by poachers, had been buried just inside the Nepalese border. Whatever DNA results the dung produced, it would still be worth trying to get a sample from a skeleton. One could also examine the skull to see if it had a huge, pronounced dome similar to Raja Gaj and Kancha. Once again we began to plan another phase for the quest.

At Gatwick, a jolly customs officer whom I'd seen on previous occasions recognized me. 'Been on another trip, Colonel?' he smiled. 'Find anything interesting?'

'Just a load of elephant dung,' I said, trying to steer the luggage trolley in a straight line.

'Well, as long as you haven't got the elephant too, that's okay,' laughed the excise man.

'That's quite right,' I replied, 'and I hope you bag anyone trying to bring in ivory.'

Only six years before ivory had reached an all-time high of $114 per pound in the Japanese market, and consequently the decline in the elephant population had accelerated disastrously. Even before this the numbers slaughtered had been rising steadily following the arrival of high-powered hunting rifles. By the early part of this century the demands of the billiard ball and piano key manufacturers had meant that an estimated 100,000 beasts were being killed each year. There was a respite with the invention of plastics that could fill the role more cheaply. However, the white gold was still desired for ornamental purposes and one ridiculous use is the manufacture of chops or personal seals that many Orientals use as their official signature.

As a young officer, I had visited a Chinese ivory carver in Singapore and watched, admiringly, as the old man sat by a dull yellow lamp, working with painstaking care to fashion one intricate sphere within another and another. 'It will take him many years to complete this work of art,' said the salesman, who obviously thought I was someone of enormous wealth. To encourage me, he went on to say that ivory contains a mass of tiny pores holding the waxy substance which gives the beautiful soft lustre to the finished article. Ivory from different regions ages in different ways, he explained, pulling out a small Buddha with a pinkish hue. 'From Sri Lanka,' he smiled, and then produced a silver box inlaid with pale, golden panels and said, 'Siamese.'

Ivory carving dates back to the earliest times and, although tusks from a freshly killed beast are reckoned to be the best, there are plenty of examples of works done using the tusks of long dead mammoths, frozen in the depths of Siberia. It is rather ironic that it is often used for carving crucifixes and to depict religious symbols. Whilst there was an abundance of the great creatures no one worried. As they are now near to extinction, surely man can stop this senseless massacre and develop an alternative material.

To try and discourage poaching in India, parts of the tusks are sawn off the living beasts for perfectly legal sale. Care is taken not to cut the nerve, and if the operation is carried out properly the tusk will grow again.

In fact, a palm nut grown in South America produces a kernel with many of the qualities of ivory. By farming this one could provide a livelihood in a depressed area while saving the elephant at the same time.

Thanks to the activities of conservation organizations and the widespread public condemnation of the slaughter of elephants, the resultant ban on the sale of ivory is having an effect. However, it is more difficult to tackle the problem of habitat. The population in India is increasing at a rate of a million a month and is rising in Nepal too. Both man and elephant need to eat. Crops to feed the ever-growing number of people must be cultivated and this means the reduction of the forest. As the trees are felled, erosion sets in and overgrazing, especially by the all-consuming goats, leads to the destruction of the delicate eco-system.

The increase in the elephant population of Bardia shows how they are running out of space in which to live in India. Without the forests to provide their diet, the largest mammals on earth must turn to stealing from man's pantry, which often leads to a head-on clash. In places like Gola, where the people are Hindu, the elephant is still regarded as the god Ganesh and as such is sacred. Thus rather than use firearms to protect their fields, the farmers send out children to chase off the raiders by banging gongs or throwing fire-crackers. But how long will the power of religious belief save Raja Gaj and his pals?

If the herd continues to grow, culling will become inevitable. There are only 370 square miles in the Bardia reserve and not all of that is forest.

This topic was debated endlessly around our camp fires and in an effort to help we agreed to continue our policy of supporting the Nepalese Wildlife Department's anti-poaching unit whilst trying to do something for the people who live on the edge of the reserve.

Dr John Davies, now the medical adviser to the Scientific Exploration Society, had examined the Tharu village near the Karnali Lodge at Bardia and found the people well cared for by the Tiger Mountain clinic. But, as we were to discover, Gola on the western boundary, being isolated by the river, received less attention. All we could do was to help with drugs and medical supplies, plus some first aid, when we were in the area. We had grown to love Bardia because it was so remote and undisturbed, whereas Chitwan was growing like Blackpool Beach on a bank holiday. However, the lack of visitors to Bardia means less revenue and if one is to maintain this oasis of unspoiled forest and its wildlife there must be more income. The new road and improved air service to Nepalganj will help, but the presence of wild elephants, and in particular the strange giants, does make it a special place. Chitwan has only a handful of wild jumbos to offer. So we have turned our attention to promoting Bardia and its abundant game, whilst continuing the investigation into the origin of the huge tuskers.

Back in Britain, Adrian Lister and his colleagues wasted no time in examining the dung samples we had collected. Putting in long hours at Cambridge University, Dr Mark Thomas and Dr Erika Hagelberg succeeded in extracting genetic material, or DNA as it is commonly known, from the droppings of Raja Gaj and Kancha. This in itself was a great achievement. It was the first time that elephant DNA had been obtained from dung. This breakthrough is an important development in the study of elephant genetics and conservation. It allows such research to be undertaken without the need to bring down a six-ton animal to get a blood sample, with all the attendant problems of having to keep the great beast cool whilst it is unconscious. In the Asian jungle you can't use a water truck as they do on the plains of Africa.

As a result of our five expeditions the genetic code of one particular gene – the so-called cytochrome b – has now been established for the Bardia beasts, as well as for elephants from elsewhere in Asia, from Africa and also for the mammoth. The work has shown that Raja Gaj and Kancha have the same genetic sequence as Asian elephants and thus are members of this species. Comparison of the three species is still in progress, but so far it seems that the Asian elephant (including the Nepalese animals), mammoth, and African elephant are about equally related to each other, having diverged from a common ancestor some 5 million years ago.

Adrian was as pleased as punch when he called me at the end of October 1995 to report his findings:

'Within the Asian elephants we have to compare the Nepalese beasts with populations in India, Sri Lanka, Malaysia and Burma, to see if the Nepalese animals are genetically distinct, maybe forming a grouping with nearby populations from northern India. It would not surprise me to find that the Nepalese population has a low genetic variability, due to a phenomenon we call "bottlenecking", a result of isolation and the small numbers in the area. This might in turn account for the unusual anatomy of the Bardia elephants,' he enthused.

For those of us who had hoped that Adrian's findings might establish a closer link between the Nepalese elephant and the mammoth, the news was somewhat disappointing. 'Mammoths are a separate evolutionary line from the Asian elephant,' said Adrian. 'They were restricted to cold, northern climates. No remains of mammoth have ever been found as far south as Nepal.* And when looked at closely, there are important differences of detail between Raja Gaj and the mammoth. Seen from the front, the head dome of the Nepalese beasts is divided into two peaks, side by side, as in the Asian elephant. In mammoths, there was a single hemispherical dome. And mammoth tusks were more strongly twisted than any of the living elephants'.'

Yet Adrian was far from downcast that our mammoth hunt had found no mammoths, pointing out that the mammoth was merely one of a number of extinct species of elephant which had once roamed the world: 'In the rocks of the Siwalik hills, the very ranges overlooking Bardia, remains of at least three species have been found. These include the stegodon and the species called

---

* No trace of the discovery Clive Coy reported (see p. 127) was found

*Elephas hysudricus*. There is no common name for this species, but it is believed to be the ancestor of the living Asian elephant, *Elephas maximus*. Huge skulls and skeletons have been found in Siwalik rocks around two million years old. I've looked at one of the skulls in the Natural History Museum in London and its appearance is striking: very high forehead and prominent, almost overhanging head domes. Placed alongside a picture of Raja Gaj, the resemblance is almost uncanny.'

So, not a mammoth but a prehistoric throwback nonetheless. Quite why the Nepalese elephants resemble their ancient ancestors is unclear as yet. Most likely, an unusual genetic combination has cropped up, perhaps the result of 'genetic bottlenecking'. The effect is probably accentuated by the very large size of the Nepalese animals, because head domes are generally more prominent the larger the animal. The explanation for the exceptionally large size of the Bardia elephants has yet to be explained, and may be due either to genetics or good feeding, or perhaps a combination of the two. Either way, the original idea that the Nepalese animals had something prehistoric about them was not so far-fetched.

It was clear that the work of our expeditions had helped to mark a new chapter in the understanding of elephant in general and the Nepalese animals in particular. Furthermore it was the first time that such a wide study had been made across the range of Asian elephants in comparison with their African cousins and mammoths.

'Where did you get the mammoth samples from?' I asked.

'Oh, they came from three carcasses discovered frozen in the permafrost of north-east Siberia,' he replied. 'There is still more work to be done, I can't wait to get back into the field.'

'I hope he means Nepal and not Siberia,' muttered Carol, turning up the office heater.

In the meantime our conservation efforts continued, with Brook Hanson organizing a display of photographs from Bardia at the Bar Circa in Berkeley Square. We gathered a great band of supporters at the exhibition and got more promises of help and bequests. Media interest was also strong: I was approached by Frances Berrigan of Cicada Films about the possibility of making a television documentary.

Then, in September 1995 a fax arrived from K. P. Sharma of Tiger Mountain in Kathmandu. It read: 'For your kind information, there are now approximately twenty-three cows, nine bulls and eight baby elephants in Bardia.'

'Oh Lord!' said Rula, when I told her the news. 'That's forty elephants. They'll be tearing the forest apart.'

I called Adrian to tell him the news. Elated by the success of the DNA testing and tempted by Peter Byrne's offer to unearth the skeleton of a large bull for examination, our Scientific Director needed little further encouragement. 'I'm free at the end of January,' he said eagerly, so I started to get a team together.

Sue Hilliard, who had become passionate about elephants on the 1993 expedition, felt she needed another visit to revitalize her work with the fingerprint department of the Merseyside Police. Phyllis Angliss, the Society's Honorary Secretary, had been longing to come on an expedition for years, Garry Savin, the doctor on one of our previous projects in Guyana, offered to come as MO, and another ex-Guyana hand, Londoner Sheila Finch, was eager to study birds and elephants. Brook Hanson, who knew the area, said he would act as deputy leader in case Raja Gaj sat on me, and a couple of adventurous Dutch brothers, Eric and Maurice Smulders, would also join. Another newcomer was a delightful retired lady called Eve Horner, who was an intrepid traveller and spent much of her time on environmental projects.

'You're not going without me this time,' said Judith, my wife, who had heard all the tales of the giants but had never had the chance to see them.

Faxes flashed to and from Nepal. Sadly, Rula had a play on at the time and could not come, but film clips of our lady elephants were used when she was featured on *This is Your Life*.

With a few weeks to go I met the TV crew who would accompany Frances Berrigan. Alistair Kenneil, a rugged, quiet Scot, would handle the sound whilst the film was to be shot and directed by John Bulmer (who had, it later transpired, been a schoolmate of mine at the age of six). Assisting John was a cheery Girl Friday, Catherine Brandish from London, and minutes before we departed I met Des Willie, another cockney who would follow us out there to take photographs for publicizing the programme on Channel Four.

Unlike most of our previous teams, it had not been possible for members to meet beforehand, but I felt confident that we had a pretty compatible bunch and so it turned out.

As usual, Royal Nepal Airlines, who would carry the main party, had problems: one of their planes ran into a truck at Dubai airport, and going out twenty-four hours ahead I got stuck in Delhi, finally arriving in Kathmandu only a few hours before the main party. Despite the delay I was in time to attend a dinner organized by Lisa Choegyal where I was surprised to meet Alexandra Dixon, the zoologist who had been dramatically rescued from a charging elephant by Chris Thouless in 1990. She looked to have recovered from her terrifying experience extraordinarily well.

The problem with the flights eventually delayed our arrival at Ridi on the Kali Gandaki and it was late in the afternoon before our rafts were launched. The stores boat had gone ahead to set up camp at Rani Mahal and knowing we had a two- to three-hour trip ahead I turned to Sundar Thapa, our boat captain, and enquired, 'Ever been white-water rafting by moonlight?'

'This will be my first time,' he grinned, pulling back on the heavy oars.

The sun had already disappeared as we swung into the current and within an hour the gorges were growing dark. The last time I had rafted at night was on the Blue Nile in 1968 when, to escape a life-threatening attack by insurgents, we had to brave some ferocious cataracts. It was an experience I will never forget – and one I had no wish to repeat. However, this holy Nepalese river gave us a gentle ride and, the water being low, the rapids were modest. As the moon rose, our eyes became accustomed to the gloom and we navigated our way easily past rocks and shallows. 'This really is exhilarating,' cried Brook when my torch beam caught him in his bobbing craft. Opposite the ruined palace, a high-pressure lamp lit up our camp on the beach and soon we were ashore, sipping hot tea and kukri rum before tucking into a warming curry.

Next day, after a quick survey of the Rani Mahal, the film crew and Adrian helicoptered off to Sukla Phanta to excavate Peter Byrne's elephant skeleton. The rest of us set out to examine the remains of the road built to the palace for Shumser's big elephants. Although heavily eroded, the steep track was still wide and smooth enough in places for a car to have driven along it. Rock overhangs had been dug out or blasted away to a height of thirty feet. 'Enough for very tall beasts,' remarked Phyllis as we climbed up through the magnificent scenery.

The following day we shot one or two sporting rapids before leaving the river to camp overnight on a mountaintop near Tansen. Then it was on to Bardia and one could sense the general air of excitement and anticipation in the team at the prospect of meeting Raja Gaj and his pals.

Adrian and the film crew rejoined us at Bardia, delighted by their success in digging up several skeletons and taking good DNA samples.

Our base on the Karnali riverbank was splendidly set up. Few safari camps in Africa could have exceeded the excellence of the arrangements. In the lines Honey Blossom greeted me with a deep rumble and reached out with her trunk for the customary apple.

'Do you really think she remembers you?' asked Judith.

'No, she just likes apples,' I smiled.

Within two hours on the first morning we had seen a rhino, met Kancha (now in the company of his own escorting young bull), and discovered Raja Gaj lurking in a shady grove, also with a new young tusker to mind him. Cameras whirred into action and the film crew were elated – until the minder saw them off with a spirited charge.

Rubber-gloved to avoid human contamination, Adrian scooped up dung samples – much to the surprise of my phanit, Dhuki, who was quite happy to pick up the lot in his bare hands. Using the Polaroid camera technique, we made height measurements and took readings of the footprints. Sue drew sketches of iden- tifying ear patterns, others listed birds and mammal sightings.

On the second day we sighted Raja Gaj moving north-east towards the deep forest. Adrian and Brook found him at last light and watched him wrestling in a slow ballet with his escort, trunks entwined. The two pachyderms pushed and shoved each other in a friendly test of strength. Then, as if tiring of the game, the King bulldozed the young tusker backwards for fifty yards to show that he was still the boss. Thereafter they strolled off into the gathering darkness. Alas, it was the last sighting of these elusive creatures for us on this expedition. Once again, like phantoms, they simply disappeared. Later that week we found Raja Gaj's twenty-two-and-a-half-inch print near an army post in the north of the reserve where he had bathed in a shallow pool and fed on a clump of bamboo before vanishing into the depths of the forest.

Pressing on over the foothills to the Babai Valley we saw signs of many wild elephant cows and calves, and found the carcass of a young bull killed by Div Guj, who had moved there to become the dominant male of this distant valley. Div showed himself as we left the area and made it clear he was in command. Now he had his cows and territory he would defend them against any intruder. Perhaps one day his superior position would be challenged by Raja Gaj or Kancha in a fight to the death.

Our final days were enriched by a pair of tiger who set up home half a mile from our camp; in fact, we almost trod on them twice and none of us will forget their blood-curdling roars as they bounded away.

As always, our expedition ended with a visit to the people of Gola to donate school books and other gifts. Phyllis persuaded some of the children, who were bursting with curiosity, to ride on our elephants. Later, whilst we were dispensing spectacles at a nearby farm, a father brought in his daughter with a badly gashed knee. Whilst the poor child howled in pain, Garry stitched up the wound. Hearing the commotion, Honey Blossom and two of our ladies strolled into the yard of the house and looked on with great concern. To my utter amazement the farmer's wife brought out a bowl of her finest grain and the best pumpkins to feed the elephants. As the old girls hoovered up the offerings, little children came forward to touch their trunks and I knew then that we were making progress in the battle to get the people to love and understand these great and gentle creatures.

We too had learned more about our mounts; their moods, their childish tricks, their fears and jealousies, and their courage. Although this was my sixth expedition with them, I felt as if I was just beginning to be able to interpret what was going on in the minds of these remarkable creatures.

Adrian summarized our findings in his report on the 1996

expedition. In addition to recording details of the migrations of the elephants along the Terai (vital to conservation planning), we had compiled a manual for the identification of each of the individual wild elephants by measurement, sketches and photographs. We had also been able to observe at first hand the shifting of allegiances between males:

> For a number of years Kancha has been the almost constant companion of Raja Gaj, but this year Raja Gaj is seen either alone or in the company of Bahadur Guj, while Kancha is accompanied by younger bulls. On one occasion this season Raja Gaj was observed 'tussling' with Bahadur Guj, but the former asserted his dominance by pushing the latter decisively back. It is suggested that these pairs of males may represent animals of similar status in a hierarchy and are assessing and testing each other. In particular the junior one is challenging the senior one for his position. This could explain why the younger bull often appears the more aggressive of the two and appears to 'protect' the older tusker from oncomers. In effect he may be saying, 'If you want to challenge the boss, you have to get past me first.' If this theory is correct, it suggests that there may have been a change of status. Bahadur Guj, who has grown considerably and is now of substantial size, may have taken over from Kancha as second in the hierarchy whilst Raja Gaj clearly remains the dominant male.

The new data we collected (including bone samples from skeletons) will now be analysed by Adrian and compared with other Asian elephants. Head measurements can be compared to the skull of the ancestral fossil *Elephas hysudricus* to which the Nepalese beasts bear some resemblance. Our ladies contributed to the conservation effort by donating specimens of tail hairs to assist in the study, although Luksmi Kali, objecting to having her tail plucked, gave poor John Bulmer a hefty kick!

Our concerns prior to the 1996 visit – that as persecution and population pressure force the elephants of northern India into Bardia, the last refuge before the deforested hills rise up to the icy summits of the Himalayas and the desert wastes of Tibet, the area will be faced with a growing population that it cannot sustain

– are steadily being realized. We have witnessed the natural consequences of the increasing elephant numbers with their dispersal to other feeding grounds, as in the case of Div Guj who has established his new herd and territory. The words of a Cree Indian poem, read by Dr Chandra Gurung at a meeting we had with the King Mahendra Trust in Kathmandu, ring poignantly true in Bardia:

> Only after the last tree has been cut down,
> Only after the last river has been poisoned,
> Only after the last fish has been caught,
> Only then will you find that money cannot be eaten.

# EPILOGUE

SUCH interest in one species of elephant is bound to give rise to concern for them all. Thus those who have grown to admire Raja Gaj and his fellows began to consider whether there was anything that could be done to improve elephants' harmony with man.

Whilst they are still used for logging in parts of Asia, and Jim Edwards had started elephant polo tournaments in Nepal, in Africa little had been done to domesticate them on a wide scale. 'Would Indian elephants survive in Africa?' I wondered. In 1868 General Sir Robert Napier had used them in Ethiopia to carry forward his artillery to the battle of Magdala, so I could see no reason why some might not be worked on this continent. However, at the same time as we were operating in Nepal, an interesting development was taking place in Africa.

Those who can really communicate with animals are rare and wonderful people. I once watched my mother calming an Alsatian driven mad by thirst, having been locked in a caravan for many days during a long hot summer. On another occasion, John Aspinall took me on a visit to his big cats in Kent and, safe behind a wire fence, I saw him comfort a heavily pregnant tigress whilst her mate growled menacingly at him from the corner of the pen. But one of my most extraordinary experiences was in Zimbabwe.

Julian Matthews, my son-in-law, has a legendary uncle and aunt: Norman and Gill Travers who farm 10,000 acres of bush at Imire, some ninety minutes' drive east of Harare. On a visit to

Zimbabwe, Peter Enzer, who had once been my adjutant and was now with the British Army Training Team in the country, drove me out to meet them.

'He has several leopards, a couple of lions and a pair of otters,' said Peter, who shared my interest in wildlife. 'There are buffalo, sable, hippo and rhino. They have really pioneered letting game and cattle run together. It's becoming a pretty popular place for people to visit at weekends,' he explained.

The farm was in an idyllic setting. It had an old-style colonial building with guest accommodation in neat rondavels, and beyond the well-trimmed lawns and flower beds were a line of wired enclosures. As we climbed out of the car a big man in shorts, an old check shirt and a bush hat sauntered over to meet us. He walked with a slow confident stride. Stretching out a deeply tanned arm, he grabbed my hand and pumped it. A warm smile spread across his weather-beaten face. 'Welcome to Imire,' he said, then, turning his attention to Peter's young daughter, Georgina, he asked, 'Would you like to come and feed my young rhinos?' The child's eyes lit up with pleasure as we strolled over to a boma built of eight-inch timber rails beyond which something large was milling round making a strange miaowing sound.

As we reached the fence, seven prehensile snouts jutted between the rails. They were year-old black rhino, lent to farmers who would rear them and protect them from certain death by poachers. If they had been allowed to roam free in the Zambesi Valley they wouldn't have lasted long.

'Aren't they lovely?' said Norman, handing us each a three-gallon plastic container full of milk. A spout and teat made up this giant baby's bottle. 'Take one rhino each and offer them the teat,' he instructed. Mewing and shoving, the young but already powerful beasts pressed forward to suck, emptying the contents in record time.

'After tea we can take a drive and I will show you a few more animals,' he chuckled as he tickled the ears of one greedy baby that was still demanding more milk.

Tea was served on the lawn as if we were in an English vicarage garden, except that thirty feet away a large old lion watched us with interest from within his enclosure. 'He comes in the house sometimes,' said Gill, passing round a plate of wafer-thin sand-wiches, 'but he will keep climbing on the beds.'

The heat of the day had subsided and as the Land Rover bumped over the dirt track, stately sable were making their way towards the waterhole. We had reached the centre of a shallow valley in open country when Norman pointed to a clump of trees on a low hill, about five hundred yards away. 'Do you see those buffalo?' he asked. My binoculars picked up the grey shapes of six cape buffalo in some low bush; the cows were browsing but the bull had his head erect, nostrils twitching. Then I saw some-thing else, indeed all the trees seemed to move and into view came a magnificent elephant, ears flapping gently to cool its great body, the heavy tusks gleaming in the late afternoon sun.

'Stay in the car,' said Norman, getting out and walking forward towards the hill. After twenty yards he stopped and gave a series of calls, 'Nzow, Nzow.' At once all the buffalo started trotting down the slope towards him and behind them came the elephant. 'I presume he knows what he's doing,' I said to myself. By now the buffalo were running, in what I would have said was an aggressive mode, straight at Norman, who stood unarmed and unperturbed, sucking on his pipe, as a farmer might await his cattle in an English field. I shifted in my seat uneasily thinking, 'Well, if anything goes wrong there's damn all I can do except try to drive them off with the Land Rover.'

Twenty yards from my host the buffalo divided and swept past him on both sides kicking up the dust with their hooves, heads tossing, black eyes glistening. Norman waved them on and then through the dust I saw the elephant bearing down on him. I could see now that it was a mature cow. At fifty yards it was a monster, the ears, much larger than the Asian cousins, were for-ward and its trunk was waving as it began to charge. 'Oh my God,' I thought, 'the man's mad . . .' Norman raised his hand and in a firm voice said, 'Stop,' which halted the elephant in its tracks as surely as if it had been hit by a .450 express rifle. Ambling over to the great beast, he greeted her, 'Hello, old girl,' and slapped her trunk.

'You can get out now,' he said, grinning at me, 'she's very tame.'

Back at the house one of the staff brought in a young elephant and Georgina had a ride. A fearless horsewoman, it did not worry her to sit on a docile, slow-moving pachyderm.

'We have never ridden Nzow,' said Norman.

'How did you train them?' I asked, fascinated.

'Just with kindness,' he remarked, as if referring to a Labrador puppy. 'I talk to them a lot, and they seem to understand.'

We discussed the possibilities of more formal training and the use of African elephants for domestic purposes. Norman's experience went back eighteen years when the Rhodesian National Parks were culling and wanted homes for baby elephants.

'I didn't know how to control them,' he said, 'but felt they would be fun for the children, and perhaps we could learn to train them.' So he got his first babies and then read a book by an American, Randall Moore. Apparently Mr Moore had taken trained African circus elephants to Kenya to see if they would mix with wild ones. However, after a few months the Kenyan government ordered him to leave as they discovered his elephants came from South Africa. Nevertheless he continued the process in South Africa and sometimes used them in films. Later he took tourists for rides but, for safety's sake, avoided contact with wild elephants.

So Norman went to see the Indian High Commissioner in Harare and asked if his government would find and fund two mahouts to come to Zimbabwe to train African elephants. The High Commissioner was enthusiastic but said the request must go through the National Parks. Sadly, they wrote: 'We see no need to train elephants,' and it was turned down. Two years later, Norman tried again and once more bureaucracy killed the proposal.

In the meantime I had contacted Jim Edwards, who agreed to help if funds could be found, but the problem was that most Nepalese phanits would want to bring their wives, and possibly children, along. Also young Indian elephants are trained by using an older, domesticated one. The cost of bringing an Asian elephant over was prohibitive and politics prevented the moving of one from South Africa. No one was sure if any of the ex-Belgian logging elephants still existed in Zaire. Norman was starting from scratch.

By 1993 poaching was in full swing and the herding of his

rhinos, now almost fully grown, from their bomas to the feeding grounds, guarding them and bringing them home at night was beginning to trouble Norman. Except for Nzow, his own elephants were still giving rides around the farm. 'What if we could train them to carry an armed African game guard and accompany the rhino?' he thought.

A polo-playing farmer in another part of the country had trained a baby elephant to herd cattle, so Norman took some of his African workers along to watch. Three days later, back at Imire, the boys were riding Norman's elephants. 'As soon as I saw how easy it was, I shopped around,' he said. In no time he had six elephants plus the older Nzow, who was now twenty-two. Each morning they and their well-armed riders would lumber off after the rhino and stay near them all day. As elephant and rhino don't always get on well together, this was even more remarkable.

At this point the publicity began and Norman's experiment became a favourite subject for TV documentaries. It also gave him a useful platform from which to preach the lessons of wildlife conservation.

'Could this be a way of showing Africans the value of elephants?' I wondered. My friends were sceptical, but the Imire beasts had an incredible track record. Occasionally one would mock-charge Norman but he would check with a wave of his hand and a cry of, 'Hey! Stop it!'

Nzow was always tricky. However, on one occasion she had saved the life of Murambiwa, one of the older hands. The big male buffalo on the farm could sometimes be aggressive and one evening when Murambiwa was walking the herd home together with Nzow, the bull got very stroppy. Suddenly it lunged at him, knocking the old man to the ground, cracking two of his ribs. As he struggled to his feet the African saw the menacing head of the buffalo go down. 'He was coming to kill me, I knew it,' he said later. Then with a blast of trumpeting, Nzow rushed at the bull, forcing him back. Murambiwa got up but, quick as a flash, the great black beast was on him again. This time the elephant did a full charge, and, striking the buffalo with her coiled trunk, she bowled it over, then stood beside the injured African and protected him all the way back to the farm. Neither the old man nor Nzow ever forgot that day.

This sort of behaviour is not unheard of amongst elephants, who have been known to defend humans against tiger in India by pulling them between their legs and trumpeting loudly at the attacker. If elephants do have a natural enemy, it can only be the tiger. Indeed zoologist Dr Jane Wilson Howarth and her husband Simon had an extraordinary experience in Bardia.

They were working on an irrigation project in the region and decided to visit the reserve. Riding Chan Chan they set off into the woodlands. Quite casually their phanit muttered, 'There's a tiger there.' Recalling the incident Jane said, 'It was hard to believe him. How did he know? We had neither heard nor seen anything, no tell-tale alarm calls. Peering into the undergrowth we could see nothing.' But as their eyes searched the gloom they suddenly realized that, lying only a few yards away, was a perfectly camouflaged tiger and to their astonishment there were two more nearby. It seemed incredible that such a big, brightly coloured animal could blend in so well with the scrub. Silently the female and a large cub slipped away into the bushes, but the male sat very still, watching them. Occasionally he gave a nervous yawn as Chan Chan pushed forward, knocking down some small trees to give her passengers a closer view. Suddenly the big cat glanced behind him and leaping up, came bounding straight at Jane's elephant. Before they had time to react, they saw the reason. Out of nowhere an enormous, wild and very angry tusker came crashing after the tiger which fled for its life, right past Chan Chan and out of sight.

'We were left face to face with this massive bull,' said Jane, who noticed that it had a broken tusk. 'Although no threat, we were clearly in his way.' The tusker's fury now seemed to be directed at them. Mounted on a tame elephant the couple, perhaps naively, felt safe, but their mount did not share their confidence and with no room to turn went into full speed reverse. Behind them the great bull stood, ears flapping and contemplating another charge to clear his feeding ground of intruders. Luckily for Jane and Simon, he decided that he'd done enough and could return to his lunch. They had met Raja Gaj.

I asked Norman about the problems of musth but it had not caused his elephants any difficulty.

'We just keep them in the boma,' he told me.

Indeed the only problem they had had with Nzow was when Gill brought a little dachshund near her. The elephant went crazy. Just like their Asian cousins, African elephants clearly dislike dogs. For some reason Nzow also disliked buffalo and over the years had killed eight of the bulls. 'Perhaps she feels she is the matriarch of the little herd and is challenged by the males,' remarked Norman.

The relationship of Norman Travers' elephants with other animals continues to grow and, in January 1995, the African handlers found Nyasha, a fourteen-year-old tusker, playing in the river with a huge bull hippo they called Magogle, after a pair of diver's goggles. It seemed he had been chased out of the herd by other males. Now, when the water is warm enough for swimming, these two unlikely playmates frolic together for hours. It is an amazing sight watching tons of flesh colliding, tusks and teeth flashing, the elephant squirting the hippo and Magogle even climbing on Nyasha's back as if to get a ride. Strangely only Nyasha plays with the hippo; although the other elephants swim up alongside, they don't join in.

One has only to observe elephants interacting and socializing to believe that they can experience joy in a way similar to humans. Watching Nyasha and Magogle playing I had no doubt that they were enjoying every minute. Indeed, I have always felt that animals do have emotions. In their fascinating book *When Elephants Weep*,* Jeffrey Masson and Susan McCarthy give many examples. The one I like most is a simple story of a young bird falling into a chimpanzee's cage:

> When a young sparrow crash-landed in the chimpanzee's cage at Basle Zoo, one of the apes instantly snatched it in her hand. Expecting the bird to be gobbled up the keeper was astonished to see the chimpanzee cradle the terrified fledgling in a cupped palm, gazing at it with what seemed like delight. The other chimpanzees gathered and the bird was delicately passed from hand to hand. The last to receive the bird took it to the bars and handed it to the astounded keeper. Was it joy or compassion or a combination of both that the chimpanzee felt?

* Jeffrey Masson and Susan McCarthy, *When Elephants Weep* (Jonathan Cape, 1994)

I still wonder if the extraordinary behaviour at Imire can be used to good effect to help save the African elephants. Could they be used for ploughing? They would certainly have the strength to pull a multi-bladed plough, but although they would do less damage to the ground than a tractor and be ecologically more friendly, the problem is feeding them. A working elephant can eat up to six hundred pounds of vegetation a day. Logging, as in Zaire, could be a better use because of the proximity of a plentiful food supply in the forest.

Norman favours using them for patrolling national parkland where an armed game guard mounted on an elephant would have an excellent field of view and see much further than at ground level. Maybe some imaginative sponsor could be found to provide aid for say up to twenty elephants to be trained in Zimbabwe and used in the country's parks.

Alas, the Scientific Exploration Society's funds don't run to that, but we have been able to help in other ways. My friend Barry Owen, of the property developers Mason Owen of Liverpool, kindly donated an old Range Rover which was completely rebuilt by Conwy Land Rover. Rula accepted it at a ceremony at Llandudno, and Andrew Christensen, with a team of young members of our society, delivered it to Zimbabwe together with some Raleigh bicycles for the use of the Imire Trust. We shall continue to support Norman and his team in the hope that although the African traditionally uses ox and donkeys as beasts of burden a way may be found to harness the greatest of beasts and thus appreciate their value.

Another idea was to move other elephants to safer homes in developed nations, rather as exotic species have been relocated in America, well away from the threat of poaching. Having seen ranches where this is done in Texas, I must confess that, as a last resort, it has an appeal.

It might be all right in America but even trying to get an elephant from one zoo to another in Europe can be a major headache. John Taylor, who owns the Cricket St Thomas Wildlife Park in Somerset where Dhan Bahadur had worked, sent me an account of one particularly difficult operation:

We have kept elephants for the last thirty years; Millie had come from a zoo up north, Toto was rescued from a circus, and Chikki I collected from Holland when she was about four years old. I drove over and put her in the back of a small transit van. The journey across Holland was memorable and eventually we reached the ferry which took us from the Hook to Harwich, and we continued by road on through London. The young elephant's trunk managed to push out the glass between the rear compartment of the van and the driver's cab so that the rest of the journey was spent with the trunk dangling between the driver and the passenger seat, only to be placated by constant stops at greengrocers for bunches of bananas on which to feed her. Her appetite was only arrested by a halt at the BBC scenery department, where we got a piece of plywood and fixed it over the offending window to keep the trunk in the right compartment. That four-year-old, Chikki, has now grown into our oldest elephant – something like twenty-four – and is the matriarch of the herd.

One day I heard through the zoo grapevine that Skansen Zoo in Sweden had two elephants it could no longer house. I got in touch with them to see if I could help and Hans-Ove Larsson, the man in charge of elephants in Sweden, said that they would be prepared to give them to us on condition that the accommodation and facilities were suitable but we would have to provide transport.

A few days later, in the middle of winter, a Swedish delegation arrived to view our elephants' quarters and left, delighted in the knowledge that their two jumbos would soon be roaming the English countryside together with our three.

The next problem was how to move them. Loading elephants can be a time-consuming and difficult problem and, as there is only one lorry in the country that transports elephants, we resolved to use crates. The Swedes already had one and Whipsnade had another which needed major modifications. I flew over to Sweden to inspect the beasts and examine their crate. It appeared that the whole of the Swedish press and television had turned out to report my arrival and I soon discovered that these two elephants were national celebrities. I satisfied myself that it was possible to lift the crates by crane into their compound. The doors at each end would open, providing a short tunnel through which the elephants could move freely, and we arranged for them to have several days in order to acclimatize themselves in the crates before being led in and the doors shut.

The next problem was to ensure that all their papers were in order to bring them into England. Now there would have been no problem in moving them within Europe, but as Sweden had only just applied to join the EC and had not yet been accepted, we had to have CITES documents which proved that the elephants had not been caught in the wild. For one elephant this was no problem, but the other had no paperwork of any sort. By now the passage had been booked, the lorry arranged, the crates had been made and we were running out of time.

The Department of the Environment in Bristol was particularly unhelpful about processing the paperwork with any degree of urgency and in the end I had to telephone to say that within forty-eight hours the animals would be at Harwich. As they had no particular identification marks, the Department's Animal Inspector would not know which elephant had its passport and which had not. I explained that the elephants could not be separated and, if they were turned away, they would be homeless. Thus, unless they were both permitted to enter the country they would have to be put down on the quay-side and this would be the responsibility of the Department of the Environment, with the ensuing publicity. In the light of the elephants' triumphal departure from Stockholm with a large police escort and many sightseers and well-wishers, television and radio crews and newspaper journalists to wave them away, the press would make a meal of it. At the eleventh hour the authorities agreed to waive all formalities and the elephants were granted entry.

On the wider front, the battle to save the elephant goes on. Mark Shand's superb book, *Travels on my Elephant*, and the accompanying publicity, has done much to focus attention on the Asian elephant, and in Britain a number of charities including Elefriends and Tusk Force have also championed the cause.

There are also hopeful signs of a growing interest in conservation in Nepal. But when we had tried to send Barry Owen's twenty-year-old Range Rover out as a gift for the Wildlife Department it was rejected. New laws prohibited the import of vehicles over five-years-old 'for environmental reasons' (which, considering the state of their buses and trucks, was a bit rich). The King Mahendra Trust for Nature Conservation is doing its utmost to promote solar heating and energy-saving programmes to reduce the demand for firewood and thus the destruction of the forests. To protect the environment and assist the communities living along the lovely rivers, Megh Ale, Tej Rana and other rafters have formed the Nepal River Conservation Trust. Their first project has been to help the school at Jamune, a small settlement on the Karnali River where we had stopped several times. The wheelchairs we had brought out for Megh in 1995 had gone to disabled people on the Trisuli. Tiger Mountain is backing the International Fund for Nature Conservation and pursuing other projects. All of which is very encouraging.

As the flaming orange sun sank into the Karnali I watched Raja Gaj emerge from the forest for his evening bathe. In a few months' time I would be back in Africa on the Blue Nile, and so I had been reading Emil Ludwig's book\* on the great river system. His description of an elephant below the Murchison Falls could have been written about the scene that unfolded in front of me:

> The elephant, in the evening, comes to the river. A giant, he still treads an earth whose creatures walk below him. The strongest of all, whom no animal and no tree can withstand, not even the thorn and snake can harm him: like great men, he leaves his ponderous might unused, supreme in the consciousness of a strength which none need fear: neither vainglorious nor predatory, he is the most generous and shrewdest of animals. Gifted with an even temper and a sense of humour, yet terrible in revenge, or in the protection of his young against the attacks of crafty men, possessed of the smallest of eyes in the biggest of faces, the sharpest hearing draped with a huge flap, an organ half nose and half arm, and tusks that can tear anything, he yet seems to carry off only what is strictly neces-

\* Emil Ludwig, *The Nile* (Viking Press, New York, 1937)

sary, seldom alarms and hunts animals, eats none, feeds like a
monster in a fairy-tale, on delicate grasses, barks and juices,
and when he strides the ground with giant legs, he seems to
be taking his colossal body for a gentle walk. Nothing about
this monster is wild or coarse: his gait, his grasp, even his look,
is serene.

Refreshed and shining black as ebony in the last of the dying
sun, the great bull climbed slowly from the water, wet and con-
tent, and ambled back to the cool darkness of the forest. His
massive trunk sniffed at an acacia but decided the bark was not
quite to his taste. At the trees he paused to survey all about him
as if to say, 'This is my territory. I know every inch of it and with
my superior intelligence I rule supreme. This is the land of which
I am King.'
Long may he reign.

# GLOSSARY

| | |
|---|---|
| *ankush* | steel rod used in the control of elephants |
| *chantaara* | stone platforms for travellers to rest on |
| *chara ko masu* | Nepalese dish featuring yak meat |
| *chital* | spotted deer |
| *dhal bat* | staple dish made with lentils and spices |
| *gharial* | fish-eating member of the crocodile family |
| *howdah* | square wooden platform for riding on an elephant |
| *kukri* | traditional Nepalese knife with broad, curved blade |
| *langur* | species of monkey found in Asia |
| *mahout* | elephant driver [Hindi]; attendant to elephant [Nepali] |
| *mahseer* | freshwater game fish |
| *mugger* | large freshwater crocodile, reputedly a maneater |
| *musth* | state of sexual frenzy (usually applies to male elephants) |
| *namaste* | greeting |
| *nilgai* | a species of antelope, also known as the blue bull |
| *phanit* | elephant driver [Nepali]; attendant to elephant [Hindi] |
| *phanta* | an open area, cleared of trees |
| *sahib* | Indian form of address |
| *sal* | deciduous hardwood tree |
| *sambar* | Asian variety of deer |
| *shikari* | hunter/tracker |
| *sirdar* | person in charge of porters on a trek |
| *Terai* | lowland plain running between the Himalayas and India |

# EXPEDITION MEMBERS

All expeditions referred to in this book were led by John Blashford-Snell. Other non-Nepalese team members were as follows:

## 1991 KARNALI QUEST EXPEDITION

Robert Brown
Chris Burke
John Campbell
Cynthia Campsall
Sally Cox
Dr John Davies

Philip Downer
Michael Edwards
John Hunt
Peter Lewis
Chris Mitchinson

Mark O'Shea
Stewart Purton
Libby Smith
Avril Thomas
Adrian Thorogood

## 1992 KARNALI GORGE EXPEDITION

Roderick Barnes
Chris Burke
John Campbell
Janet Charge
John Cochrane

Sally Cox
Sheena Cox
Dr John Davies
John Hunt

Ian Mitchell
Mark O'Shea
Malcolm Procter
David Warren

1993 RAJA GAJ EXPEDITION

Nick Brown
Henning Caesar
Bimbo Coleman
Dr John Cosgrove
Les Dingle

Colin Gutteridge
Sue Hilliard
Denis Jebb
Julian Matthews

Brigid Medlam
Libby Smith
Ruth Stone
Dr Chris Thouless

1994 GIANT ELEPHANT QUEST

Wendy Bentall
Anne Cooke
Sandy Crivello
Graham King
Rula Lenska

Dr Adrian Lister
Ray Lowes
Jack Picone
Robert Rose
Faanya Rose

Wendy Stephens
Major Pat Troy
Paula Urschel
Dr Michael St George
   Wilson

1995 ASIAN ELEPHANT INVESTIGATION

Wendy Bentall
Julian Brown
Geoff Garratt
Brook Hanson
Gary Hodges

Dr David Jenkins
Rula Lenska
Dr Adrian Lister
Anna Lubienska

Dr Ken Reed
David Rowe
Major Pat Troy
Carol Turner

1996 ASIAN ELEPHANT QUEST

Phyllis Angliss
Judith Blashford-Snell
Sheila Finch
Brook Hanson
Sue Hilliard
Eve Horner

Dr Adrian Lister
Dr Garry Savin
Dr Eric Smulders
Maurice Smulders
Des Willie

*Cicada Films crew:*
Frances Berrigan
Catherine Brandish
John Bulmer
Alistair Kennell

# INDEX

The profits from the sale of this book will be used by the Scientific Exploration Society for the protection and preservation of endangered wildlife, and the Asian elephant in particular.

Donations to this cause may be sent to:

> The Hon. Treasurer
> Scientific Exploration Society
> Expedition Base
> Motcombe
> Dorset SP7 9PB, England

*Asian Elephant Conservation Work*

If you have enjoyed reading this book, you may like to know that the work in Nepal continues. If you are interested in joining us, please send your name and address to us at the Expedition Base address above. Alternatively, please telephone Executive Expeditions on 01747 854898.